PENGUIN BOOKS

FENLAND CHRONICLE

Sybil Marshall was born and grew up in East Anglia. A villager all her life, she witnessed the breakdown of the old way of life in a rural community following the sudden growth of mechanized farming and the post-war attitude to sexual morality. Having been a village schoolteacher, at the age of forty-seven she went to Cambridge University to read English. She became a Lecturer in Education at Sheffield University and subsequently Reader in Primary Education at the University of Sussex. In 1965 she devised Granada Television's popular programme *Picture Box*, and continued to act as adviser and to write the teacher's handbook until 1989.

As well as works on education, Sybil Marshall has written a number of non-fiction books recording life in her native fens in their pre-war isolation, including *Fenland Chronicle*, *The Silver New Nothing* and *A Pride of Tigers*. She won the Angel Prize for Literature for *Everyman's Book of English Folk Tales*. She has also written the Swithinford Series of novels, which consists of the bestselling *A Nest of Magpies*, written when she was eighty years old, *Sharp through the Hawthorn*, *Strip the Willow* and, most recently, *A Late Lark Singing*. She has also published a collection of her short stories, entitled *The Chequer-Board*. Most of her books are published in Penguin.

Dr Sybil Marshall lives in Ely, Cambridgeshire, with her husband, Ewart Oakeshott, FSA.

SYBIL MARSHALL

———————

FENLAND CHRONICLE

RECOLLECTIONS OF WILLIAM HENRY
AND KATE MARY EDWARDS
COLLECTED AND EDITED BY THEIR DAUGHTER

WITH DRAWINGS BY EWART OAKESHOTT

PENGUIN BOOKS

PENGUIN BOOKS

Published by the Penguin Group
Penguin Books Ltd, 27 Wrights Lane, London W8 5TZ, England
Penguin Putnam Inc., 375 Hudson Street, New York, New York 10014, USA
Penguin Books Australia Ltd, Ringwood, Victoria, Australia
Penguin Books Canada Ltd, 10 Alcorn Avenue, Toronto, Ontario, Canada M4V 3B2
Penguin Books (NZ) Ltd, 182–190 Wairau Road, Auckland 10, New Zealand

Penguin Books Ltd, Registered Offices: Harmondsworth, Middlesex, England

First published by Cambridge University Press 1967
Published in Penguin Books 1998
1 3 5 7 9 10 8 6 4 2

Set in Berthold Baskerville
Printed in England by Clays Ltd, St Ives plc

AUTHOR'S FOREWORD

THE name that appears as the author's on the cover of this book is my own, but the story the book tells belongs to my father and mother. The work of collecting, collating and recounting has been mine, and has occupied a good deal of my time for the past twenty years, but the words and phrases are those of the old Fen Tiger and his wife who were my parents. They were both magnificent talkers, and fascinated me with their tales of my Huntingdonian forebears from the time when I was wont to be entertained as I rode home on my father's shoulders down a sluddy black fen drove on a cold winter's night, or sat drowsily on the hearthrug with a lap full of kittens before a smouldering, crumbling turf fire and listened as the talk flowed over my head. I have played the part of a recording machine; that is why the books are in autobiographical form, and written in the first person.

It all began exactly as my father recounts in his own preface. He it was who actually began to write the book, and the first four chapters were written by him, very much as they now stand. He wrote in the same way as he talked. He was already seventy-seven when the idea came to him, and by then he was so crippled with gout (of the poor man's variety), that there were many days when he could not hold a pen. He had no plan and no method. He wrote on anything that happened to be lying to his hand—a penny exercise book of pre-first-war issue, a scrap of notepaper, the back of an old letter, even the margin of a newspaper. When I reached home at the end of the day, we sorted it out and put it together. Progress was slow, and there were many months together when he was discouraged by the war situation, or by some minor event; at other times he humbly disparaged his own ability to record a way of life that he realised had slipped already to the edge of oblivion. He died suddenly one night just before his eightieth birthday, and I was left to carry on alone.

It was not a difficult task. To begin with, I had the notes he had left, an odd word here, a sentence there, and sometimes even a whole page or two of his own particular brand of humorous philosophy; then there was his presence, which has never seemed to be any farther away than the next room in all the sixteen years since he died. I had only to sit down, pick up my pen, shut my eyes and deliberately listen, as it were, and I could hear him talking again so well that the sentences formed themselves up, in my mind, but in his words. In this way tales that he had told me years before, with laughter and delight or with grief and pathos, sprang back into my head with every detail clear.

Then there was another tremendous asset—my mother *was* still with me, in the next room, as robust, courageous, sardonically humorous and voluble as ever, in spite of relentless pain, the 'misery in her legs' of the osteo-arthritis which had tied her for many years past to a wheelchair. If a detail did escape me, I had only to ask her, to get all that I needed and a whole lot of new material into the bargain. It was during one of these reinforcement sessions that the idea occurred to me of completing the picture by letting her personal story complement my father's.

I knew her tales, if anything, better than I knew his, for she has repeated them very often during the years since he died. When, a little time ago, she had to be left alone, in spite of her helplessness, while I set out to establish a new home for both of us, she occupied her time, as my father had done, by jotting down her memories. From these, and from her still powerful ability as a *raconteur*, in spite of her eighty-five years, her story also has been built up. A lot has had to be left out, sometimes because a story was too painful to be told, and sometimes because I was afraid of hurting, however gently, an old friend still alive, or any member of the fen community in which my family lived. But with such unlimited wealth of material as there was, I had in any case to pick and choose.

My brother (Gerald) and my sister (Lois) have been of wonderful help to me in reminding me of things I might have forgotten, and even more so because of the laughter (and tears) which we always share whenever a good old fen word or a dialect phrase slips from one of our tongues and sets us off on another session of 'bladging'—that is, of talking for the sake of talk alone.

Finally, there was the question of getting the book illustrated. I longed that my parents' graphic verbal style should be still further enhanced by equally free yet informative drawings, but I realised that my chances of finding an artist who was not only capable, but sympathetic enough to accomplish this task were very slight indeed. Then fate arranged that I should meet Ewart Oakeshott, and my search was over.

He has taken endless trouble to make sure that where his subject is factual, the details are authentic. He has done this by visiting the locality again and again to absorb the peculiar characteristics of the fen landscape, and by visiting folk museums where objects of the past way of life there may still be seen. Portraits and faded photographs have been used to recreate the characters mentioned, and in those cases where no likeness exists, an imaginative portrait has been built up from the text and the combined memories of people still living.

From the moment he met Will 'En in the book, and my mother in the flesh, he loved and appreciated their toughness, their courage, their endurance, warmth and fun as much as if he had known them all his life. The result is that his part in this book, like my own, has been a labour of love.

SYBIL MARSHALL

DAD'S BOOK

PREFACE

IT war' on a Sunday morning, I remember, somewhere about September, 1939, that I heard poor old Neville Chamberlain telling us through the wireless that we were at war again, for the second time in twenty-five year.

Poor old chap, I felt sorrier for him than for any on us, though I realised then that we'd all got plenty to go through afore it were over.

Still, it were nearly another twelve months after that afore 'itler bothered us much, wheer we lived. It were a bit of an anxious time for me, though, 'cos it just happened that my youngest daughter were about to present me with another grandchild. We'd bin warned that we ought to be a-getting some sort of a shelter ready, though nobody round our way had bothered about it. Still, I thought I ought to be doing something about it, in case anything happened just when the baby happened as well. So I started a-sandbagging, and a-barricading our front room window up; and while I war' at it, one o' my neighbours come by. He were allus a bit of a cure, and would allus have something sarcastic to say. So he sez 'Bill,' he sez, ''Ay you 'ad a letter from Hitler, or something, to let you know when 'e's a-coming?'

So I sez, 'Well, not eggsactly, Al, on'y I should like to remind you o' Noah, old friend. I'll bet all 'is neighbours laughed at 'im when he war' a-getting the Ark ready; but when the flood come, they all wanted to git inside it with 'im.'

Well, it war'n't above a week or ten days after that afore Hitler did give us our first baptism o' bombs. It happened at midnight, and about sixteen bombs come a-bundling down within a mile of our house. We all tore downstairs and got into our barricaded room as fast as we could, but afore we'd bin there a minute, in they come from all directions, till there war'n't hardly room to breathe. I had to laugh to see 'em come to take refuge in the Ark, and I'm sure Noah's animals looked as good a selection. The

3

ladies all 'ad their 'air down their backs, an' it war'n't very difficult to pick out them as had false teeth. Some o' the men were in their pyjamas, but them as di'n't wear such new-fangled things had managed to get their trousers on, though in one or two cases, not very well. Anyway, I knowed that night what poor old Noah felt like, though I war' glad to be able to give some o' my dear old neighbours a bit o' shelter and comfort.

But that were on'y the beginning, an' we've had a lot on it to go through since then. For one thing, I never thought about writing such a thing as this 'ere, on'y as it come to me in the middle o' the night, once.

I often lay awake a goodish bit in the night, an' I used to a lot more during the war; 'cos sometimes I used to be woke up by the house a-rocking, an' the bed a-jumping about the floor. Sometimes it were Wailing Winnie as woke me,—not a very melodious tune, I used to think, to anybody like me, as ha'n't got no ear for music. Then I used to lay there, nearly frit to death, till the 'All Clear' went, and then I used to wonder whatever I had been so frit about. But even in them days there were some occasions when I woke up for no special reason, as I remember doing early one morning.

As soon as I roused, I cocked my ear up, but for once everything were still and quiet. While I were a-listening, old 'Grandfather', in the hall downstairs, struck two o'clock. It di'n't seem as if I could get off to sleep again, and there warn't anything else to do on'y think, so my mind went a-wandering back to my old home in the Fens, and all the people and the places I used to know there.

The place as I know best is a little bit of Huntingdonshire, in the Ramsey district, especially a tiny bit called the Lotting Fen. That's weer I were born, eighty year ago, now. An' that's weer I lived for the first forty-seven year o' my life. When I did leave Lotting Fen, it were on'y to cross the road into New Fen. And there I should have been now, no doubt, if it ha'n't a-bin for Hitler; but I ain't the on'y one as he moved, not by a long chalk.

Now I know every field, and every dyke in the Lotting Fen; and as for the mill, about the on'y landmark worth noticing, I know enough to write a book about it, if I could on'y think on it.

4

Well, as I laid in bed that morning, that's what I made up my mind to do, an' here it is.

Mind you, I don't expect as it'll ever be finished, 'cos for one thing I'm such an old man, an' for another, I ain't no scholar. But I'm a-going to write it to please meself, and to 'elp me to git over the long winter evenings. At any rate, my children, and my grandchildren, an' perhaps even a few o' my old fen friends, if there's any on 'em left, 'ull like to read it. So 'ere's a start, as Jack Taylor said when he hit Gozzy Langley on the snout.

1

THE Lotting Fen covers approximately five hundred and four acres, including the dykes. I reckon there's about twenty-three mile o' dyke, and ninety-two fields. So if the Lotting Fen were all in one farm, it woul'n't be a very big one, and the farmer what farmed it all would have a corner of a field to dig every weekday and every Sunday, and two on Good Friday and Christmas Day.

When the mill were first built, a firm from Bury, (a little place near Ramsey), got the building contract. It were a pumping mill, and had three pumps, all of different sized bore, which could be applied according to the strength of the wind. All three pumps could be used in a gale.

Of course the Commissioners wanted a man to take charge o' the mill and my father were lucky enough to be the one they picked on. The first time as ever I remember this mill, I went there with my mother, when I were four year old. While I were there, my father went to ile the pumps down under the floor, and war'n't I terrified until his head poked up again from underneath the boards.

This mill were doomed to disaster, though. For one thing, the tower tapered too much, and it must a-bin finished off something like a castle nut, as my father told me that it had pillars and spaces. The curb wheel laid on top, and the weight o' the sails broke through the castings so as she coul'n't luff herself, that is, so as she coul'n't turn herself to face the wind. Then one day, about March 1874, a south-west wind got up behind her, and off came her head. It bundled down into the mill drain, and some of it lays there still. Two men were working in her head when it happened, but they managed to jump down to the next floor, so nobody got hurt.

Apparently the firm as built her di'n't properly understand how to build mills, and as they ha'n't handed her over to the

6

Lotting Fen Commissioners when she fell, they had to bear the loss, and it ruined 'em.

After that, the firm of Smithdale & Sons, of St Anne's Iron Works, Norwich, undertook to rebuild her.

The new mill was to have a 16 h.p. engine inside the mill tower. The contractors took out the pumps, and put in a water wheel, twenty-eight feet in diameter, instead. This could be worked either by steam or the wind. The vertical boiler was placed on one side o' the wind gearing, and the vertical engine on the other side, next to the water wheel. The millwrights took ten feet from the tapering top of the tower, and built it up again so that the top ten feet was perpendicular; then the curb wheel laid flat on the top. They undertook to do all this, and to run the mill for six months, for the sum of £1,000.

They done it, and everybody was satisfied.

The next time that I remember going to the mill were with my father, one evening after he had finished his work at the brick-yard. The builders had just finished excavating, ready to put the water wheel in. At this time I should hardly be six year old, as I know the date on the sluice door in front o' the water wheel were 1876.

Then in 1880, there came a flood. My father were a-running the mill engine night and day, as there's never much wind to depend on after heavy rains.

We lived on the opposite side of the Catchwater Drain to the mill, a quarter of a mile further down. One night, about nine o'clock, my mother had to take my father's supper to the mill. It were as dark as pitch, and we had to cross the Catchwater in a little boat called a gunning boat, built to carry three or four people.

My mother, being a Upwood woman, di'n't know much about navigation, and things went for us like they used to for Mrs Gummidge, 'contrariwise'. We war'n't half scared, both on us. I remember how thankful we were to get there.

My father were a-firing up, down in the stoke hole, when we arrived; his face were black and his eyes glittered for want of sleep. He had to work twenty-four hours a day in flood time, and

7

all the help he ever had were a man to fire the boilers at night. None o' these men were ever a lot o' good to him, as they were mostly farm clodhoppers as hardly knowed how to break a lump o' coal. They'd allus bin to work all day afore they went to help him, and they'd soon be off to sleep, so it left him with the responsibility, all the same. The man as were a-helping father on the night I'm talking about ferried me and mother home again, so we got back better than we got there.

My father got eleven shillings a week for this job for the winter half of the year, and three shillings a day for every day in the summer that he had to do any pumping. But he had to keep the mill in order, and the luffing gear 'iled, and so on, for love, as the saying is. It were Hobson's choice for him, take it or leave it; and he coul'n't afford to leave it. In them days there were 'no eye to pity, and no arm to save'.

At this time the Upwood farm labourers were on'y having eight shillings a week, and father were getting eleven shillings all through the worst half of the year, standing wages. Then he often got the chance of a fortnight's work at the brickyard at twelve shillings a week as well, so we thought ourselves well away.

I know as I ain't much of a scholard, but I'm often noticed how the newspapers manage to suggest the difference atween the great and the humble folk they talk about just by the words they use. Take the question of a man's family, for instance, especially them as are gone before him; if it war a member o' the peerage they 'appened to be a-talking about, they'd say 'Lord Sludge, whose ancestors have lived at Bilge Castle since the twelfth century,' or somink like that: but about old Bill Smith, they'd say 'William Smith comes of a long line of country forebears.'

Well, accordin'ly to that, I don't claim to 'av no ancestors, but I did 'ave some forebears, on'y they were really tigers—fen tigers. I don't know why old fenmen were allus called tigers, unless it were because they used to act so wild and shy, not being used to seeing many folks, or whether the strangers thought they looked a bit fierce. There's a saying you can use about any man who's got a good crop o' hair, (specially if it's on his chest,) and a good

8

set o' teeth. You can say ''E's all 'air and teeth like a Ramsey man.' Anyway, I reckon there's a lot to be said for tigers, fen or otherwise, an' it ain't never bothered me much as I on'y 'ad forebears instead of ancestors.

My name's Edwards: at least, that's how it's spelt, but when I were an old boy nobody in the fen ever said it like that. They said Etherds. My poor old Dad used to get 'isself into a mess if anybody ever asked hime his name, 'cos my mother had schooled him not to say Etherds, and he coul'n't bring hisself to be stuck up enough to say Edwards, so he used to make a mark somewheer atween the tew and mumble 'Eddards' through his whiskers. The old fen's full o' Etherdses, though it ain't one o' the real old fen names, not by a long chalk. They don't claim no relation now, but I reckon they're all forty-second cousins 'cos they're all descended from the same man.

He were a shoeing-smith as were born on the borders o' Wales, so I'm 'eard tell. His job were to shoe cattle as they set out to walk to market. Somewhere round about the year 1750, he set out from Wales with a herd o' cattle as were a-going to London, but before they got there, he were took bad, and the cattle 'ad to go on without him. That happened in Ramsey, though why the herd come to be in Ramsey in the fust place, I don't suppose we shall ever know now. Perhaps they went from fair to fair to sell beast on the way. Anyways, the blacksmith stopped in the 'um of a real old fen tiger whose forebears 'ad bin there since the days when they 'ad spotted bellies and web feet, and o' course it 'appened that there war a nice lookin' gal on hand to nuss 'im back to 'ealth, so he war'n't in very much of a sweat to catch up the herd again. When he were better, he married the gal, and set up in business as a shoeing-smith in Ramsey. I wish I could tell yer, like the story books dew, that they lived 'appy ever arterwards; but it woul'n't be the truth if I did.

He were such a strong man, like a great stun'oss, as could throw a bullock single 'anded as easy as winking. And he di'n't care how long, n' yit how hard he wukked. He'd be a-shoeing cattle all day long of a Sunday, ready for 'em to start off to Smithfield a-Monday morning, and I dare say he made a tidy bit o' money. But he took to drinking, and one day when he were on'y about forty, he were picked up in his smithy. He'd bin picked up there dead-drunk, a-many a time afore, but this time he were just dead, so that were the end on him.

Now when folks talk about Ramsey, they usually mean a place in the Isle o' Man, wheer people go for their holidays; but of course when I talk about Ramsey, I shan't mean that one. There's another place called Ramsey, in Huntingdonshire; not a very big place now, though at one time it were about the most important place in all the country except London, and I ain't very sure as it di'n't beat that.

You see, Ramsey were an island as stuck out above the waters of the fen all round; and eleven hundred year ago some old monk as wanted to get away from everybody else took and built a monastery there. Then the monks kept on getting hold of a bit of land here, and another bit there, till it war'n't long afore the Abbott of Ramsey were the richest man in all England.

But there war'n't much money in Ramsey a hundred and fifty year ago, when my grandfather were born. He were born in 1805, and Ramsey were a poor sort o' place to be born in then. The scheme for draining the fens had been put into operation a long while afore, but there were still a goodish bit o' land all round Ramsey as ha'n't got well enough drained to be cultivated. The land as were cultivated were on'y used for growing corn, and it war'n't until farmers begun to grow 'taters that there were enough work in Ramsey to keep the farm labourers a-going.

When grandfather were about thirty year old, Ramsey had a terrible experience. A dreadful epidemic of cholera broke out in the district all round, and Ramsey suffered terrible. I heard that grandad had just started a-courting that year. The fair at Ramsey were the high day of all the year, and the young folks used to look forrard to takin' their gals. The fair were held on the Church green, next to the Church. But there war'n't much fun and jollity the year when grandad took his gal. The first day that the fair started, the church bell tolled all day long, and when grandad took his lady round the fair that night, it were such a miserable do that the fair people coul'n't stand it, and they all packed up their traps and away they went.

10

Things went from bad to wuss, and soon there were such a few folks left in Ramsey that the grass growed green over the High Bridge. My mother, as come from Upwood, used to tell me a tale as she'd heard about the cholera there. It seems there were a bit o' barley as wanted mowing in Upwood that summer, and one after another thirteen men went to mow it; but it never got cut, for one after another all thirteen on 'em died o' the cholera. My mother's grandfather were the thirteenth man.

The effect the cholera had on Grandfather were to drive him out o' Ramsey. He got married, and went to seek his fortune in the fen, about four mile away. He bought a bit o' land, roughly four acre. The land war'n't workable then, so it war'n't very expensive. You could buy a four acre field in them days for five shillings and a gallon o' beer, reed, peat, sedge and all. Grandad paid for his field with seven sacks o' taters.

His wife were the daughter of one o' Ramsey's thackers (thatchers). Thackers were very often builders as well. They would build a barn and then thack it. So Grandad's father-in-law come and built him a house on his bit o' land, and a jolly good sort of a house it was, too, compared with the general run of houses in that quarter.

Grandad had a boat, and for a good many year he got his living by cutting reed and sedge and by boating it to wheerever it happened to be wanted. The reed were used for thacking, and the sedge were twisted into cords about as thick as a man's finger, and used for binding the reed down. In case as there is anybody as don't know what sedge is, I'd better tell you afore I go any further. It is a sort of tree edged grass as grows in marshy ground. It grows quite long, as much as five feet long in some places, and when it gets wilted it is as tough as whit-leather.

In the summer time it were possible to cut turf as well, and grandad used to do a good trade a-boating that. I shall have a nice lot to say about turf digging later on, so I shan't stop to explain that now.

Up to this time the Lotting Fen, wheer grandad had gone to live, ha'n't been drained at all. Then, in 1863 the Drainage Commissioners had about five feet took out of all their rivers. This

drained all the fens and meres, and left Lotting Fen high and dry.
Then Grandad and all his colleagues as 'ad earned their living
with boats got upset again. They lost their livelihood, and their
boats laid and rotted down, except in a few cases wheer they were
took to form the foundations o' new houses.

Grandfather got another field or tew, as close to the one his
house were on as he could. He owned another four acre field as
were on'y separated from his fust one by a third four acre lot as
belonged to one o' his neighbours. Both Grandfather's fields
had a way of access to a drove, so as he could get his produce out
whichever way he liked, but the neighbour in the middle had to
bring his stuff through one or other o' grandad's fields to get it
out at all.

Then one year these two silly old men fell out with each other;
I don't know as I'm ever been told what it were about as they got
off hooks with each other, but they did. The quarrel growed till
they war'n't on speaking terms, and then one day grandad locked
and chained up his gates when he knowed the other chap wanted
to cart some stuff outa his field.

Ah, war'n't there a lot o' ompolodge about it, then! Every
night grandad chained up his gates, and every morning his
neighbour broke the chains and got through somehow, until
one morning when he lifted the gate clean off its hinges and
kelped it in the dyke. That done it. Nothing would satisfy 'em
but they must go to law. None on 'em ha'n't got a penny to
throw away, but a fenman's allus got 'is pride when everything
else is gone.

Well, you know how it is once you git into the lawyer's claws.
They both had to 'ev a counsel to speak for 'em, and when the
day o' the hearing come, they walked the twelve mile or so to
Huninkton in their best Sunday clo'es, one about a 'undred yards
in front o' th' other, both on 'em frit to death in case they should
ev to open their mouths in public in the court when they got
there.

Then these 'ere two counsels raved and roared at each other
like mad bulls, and kep' on calling each other sich names as the
two old fen tigers had never 'eard on. Grandad's man said that
the neighbour must be a born fool to buy a field without making

sure as there war a right-o'-way tew it; the neighbour's counsel said that grandad were a plain thief as had robbed his good neighbour of his right-o'-way by ploughing it up, and so on. Well they kep' this cross-warmpling up till the court rose for lunch. Grandfather had took a thumb-bit with him, lapped up in a red handkercher, so he went out and set on the wall of All Saint's Church, just acrost the market square from the court, to eat it. His neighbour done the same, so there they were, setting a little away from each other, and glaring at each other

like a couple o' strange tom-cats. Then, suddenly, out from the court come their tew counsels together, a-bowing and a-scraping and a-smiling at each other as friendly as could be; and then, lo-and-behold-yer, if they di'n't take 'old of each other's arms and go off together into the dining room at the Falcon Hotel.

Grandad and his neighbour set there a-watching wi' their mouths open and their eyes a-sticking out like chapel hat-pegs. When the two lawyers were out o' sight, grandad bolted the bit he were a-chewing and poddled up to his neighbour. 'Neighbour,' he said 'did you see that there?'

'Ah. That ah did,' said the old fenman.

'Neighbour,' says grandfather again, 'fum what I can see o'

13

things, we're got ourselves in wi' a pack o' tidy rogues. They'll 'ev your jacket, and my weskit, ah, and both on us's britches afore this ere case is uvver.'

'Ah, tha'ss what I reckon, anall,' said his adversary.

So they sat down again, cluss together this time, while they finished their dockeys.

Then when their two counsel come back, ready to start their playacting all uvver agin, grandad and his mate met 'em at the door to tell 'em there war'n't going to be no more case for 'em to try. They'd settled it out o' court, they said. Ah, they 'ad, an' all —they'd simply agreed to swap fields.

So they walked back um together, the best o' friends, both on 'em perfectly satisfied, and they lived side by side for a-many a year, good neighbours to the last.

The district laying next to Lotting Fen were a mere,—Ugg Mere it were called. This were drained when the rivers were done out, and to keep it dry, the lord o' the manor, so to speak, who owned it, had a pumping mill erected. This mill drained Lotting Fen as well as the Ugg Mere, and for a little while the folks there thought they had seen the last o' the water laying on the top o' their land.

But they were soon to find out as they were thinking wrong. You see, the fen were all peat, and as soon as it got properly drained, it began to shrink. And it went on a-shrinking until the level o' the Fen were below that o' the Mere. Then the Ugg Mere mill war'n't no more good to the Fen, and the folks as lived there had to start a-thinking about getting a mill o' their own.

The Lotting Fen di'n't belong to the lord o' the manor, nor to any big estate, and by this time it had all been parcelled out into small lots. So a few o' the biggest o' the landowners down there formed themselves into a sort o' drainage board. Anybody who owned eight acre o' land could be a drainage commissioner. They hired some money, and soon the plans for the first Lotting Fen mill were in progress. It were built the same year as I were born, 1870. And I know as there ain't nobody as knows more about it than I do, for my family had been tazzled up with its history from that time until the time it were demolished in 1934.

14

The poor old mill were sold and took down. If I'd a-bin a rich man, I shoul'n't a-let that a-happened. But I ain't, and she'll soon be forgot, now, except by a few old codgers like me.

2

AFORE we go any further with this narrative, or whatever you may call it, I sh'd think I'd better tell you a bit about meself, an' what it were like to be a child in the Fens eighty year ago.

As I said afore, I were born on June the second, 1870, in an old converted brick kiln in Ramsey Heights, on the borders of Lotting Fen. We left this old house for another afore I were eleven year old, but I'm got so many memories of living there that I must recall some of them.

I had one sister ten year older than me; I know as there were two more little brothers atween her and me, both called Samuel but they both died in infancy, and my very first memory is of another sister being born when I were four.

When I were nearly five I started going to school, to a place three mile away. This were a terrible long drag for us little 'uns to walk, especially in winter. We had to take our dockey and were gone all day long; sometimes in the winter it 'ould be pitch dark afore we got home.

Every Monday morning we used to hev a clean white calico dockey bag, and we set off to school carrying this every day. In it 'ould be whatever fare our mothers had scraped together for us for our lunch, or 'dockey' as we allus called it. Sometimes there 'ud be bread and cheese, sometimes sandwiches, and usually a bit o' cake o' some sort. O' course, we were like all other old boys, and afore we had gone very far we used to start and hammer each other round the head with our bags. When we come to eat our

grub it 'ud all be mammygagged together into a solid lump. Often we had ate it afore we ever got to school at all, and then there'd be a long old day in front of us with nothing else at all to eat. There were a railway station close to the school, and we soon learnt the dodge of baiting the worms with carrots stole from the trucks in the station.

The school had children from two villages which were divided by a bridge over the river, a tributary of the Nene. The school stood next to the bridge, and atween the youngsters from the two villages a bitter feud raged. There 'ud mostly be a fight atween the rivals when we were let out o' school at four o'clock, and the victorious party allus 'run the others 'um'. Attendance at the school warn't compulsory and all the summer months the older boys from our side o' the bridge had to stop at home and go a-weeding or some such work in the fields; they were bad days for us little 'uns, and the boys from The Herne could run us home every day. But the boot were on the other foot in the winter when the grut old boys from our end started school again. Then we had the pleasure o' running them home, and many's the time I'm bin a mile or more the wrong side o' the bridge in pursuit of the other gang afore turning back to walk home.

The school was kept going by the generosity of the Fellowes family, (afterwards the de Ramseys), but a penny a week was charged for each scholar. We di'n't very often get a penny to spend, but if we did we could spend it on a penn'orth of treacle toffee made and sold as a sideline by the school master's wife. Sometimes it 'ould be very nice; sometimes it turned to sugar and then you got more, a bigger penn'orth; and sometimes it was the stickiest toffee you ever see, like 'lastic, as you could stretch as long as you liked, but it all went down the same way.

When I were seven or eight year old, I got my first taste o' bad

company, on'y I thought then as it were the best company I could have. A big boy who had attended the local grammar school for some time, left and started to come to our school. His father were one of the few 'rich' men in the fen, and as most of my other friends had started work, my mother paid this big boy threepence a week to take me to school. Now 'Jumper' as I shall call 'im, war'n't really a bad boy, but just at that time 'is father, who had begun to get old and absent minded, went very strange in the head. As there were nobody much to exercise any sort of control over Jumper, he done just as he liked, and soon he were into mischief, and me with him. When his poor old father were asleep, Jumper used to creep into his room and take money out of his trousers pockets. He took me into partnership, and we used to spend the money on sweets and tobacco on our way to school. There were a little shop on the side o' the road, built on the end of the house. It had a little oblong board over the door, saying 'Storror, Grocer, Dealer in Tobacco.'

That old board was read thousands o' times by the children, going to and from school, but allus in the same way, something like this:

> STORR-A
> GROCE-A
> DEAL-A
> INT-A
> BACC-A.

To return to the money business; when Jumper got more than we could spend, we used to bank it. We had a bank of our own, as nobody else knowed about. We cut a little sad (I sh'd think you'd call it a sod) by the side o' the steam'us in Jumper's yard, and hood our money underneath it. Then when we wanted some we just lifted the sad out by the grass. At one time we got as much as thirty shillings there.

There come a time when Jumper's luck were out for a long while, and the bank got very low. So he said to me 'If you see any money laying about at your home, old man, you want to collar it.' There never were any money laying about at our house, but one day fate played into my hands. My father collected the seat-rent for the chapel, then eightpence a quarter, and overnight somebody had called to pay their seat-rent. The next morning the seat-rent shilling lay on the shelf, and as I went out to school I nipped it up and pocketed it.

When I met Jumper I said proudly 'I'm got a bob the smorning, Jumper.' I thought I had done something so clever, and expected a bit of praise from my hero. But all he said was, 'That's all right, you young devil. Get hold of some more when you get a

chance. We shan't need to go to the bank this morning'—and pocketed the shilling.

When I got home from school, the loss of the shilling had been discovered, and I was questioned thoroughly. Of course I denied any knowledge of it, and they believed me. So all the mats had to come up again, and I well remember being down on my hands and knees a-helping to look for the coin. I were so diligent in my search that I looked in the same place twenty times over. The time I spent looking for that shilling were as bad a punishment to me as anything could ever a-bin; and as I hunted under the old knitted rug for the third or fourth time I told myself that if ever I got out of that mess I'd never steal nothing no more. Of course my father had to make good the loss, and a shilling meant half a long day's work for poor old Dad, then.

The bank di'n't last long after that, and no doubt it were a good job for me as it di'n't. But I often think when I read the accounts of the cases in the juvenile courts, that if I were a magistrate I should deal very leniently with the boys who come before me; for I should always remember the bank, and the shilling, and the tobacco we smoked, and the toffee we ate with the proceeds of our theft. What caps me is that until the incident o' the shilling I di'n't realise as what we were doing were wrong, though I'd been told often enough about what happened to other boys as were liars and thieves.

One more tale about Jumper. One Sunday morning we set on the window sill of the chapel waiting for Sunday school to start. Jumper were still a-looking after me, and as we set playing I put my feet on the railings that ran close by the wall, and pushed. I pushed too hard, and the glass behind me gave way, and fell with a crash into the chapel. We thought that nobody else was there, and Jumper said 'Now then, you stick to it that we never done it.' There were another old boy there, but he di'n't actually see it happen. Naturally he told the old men in authority that we done it, but we swore we di'n't. Of course they all thought it had been done with a stone, and once again I found myself down on my knees looking for something I knowed war'n't there. Jumper and me were the most diligent of all the searchers for that stone inside the chapel. When we got outside I threshed the old boy who said I'd done it, and I had the ordeal of being questioned again at home, this time over Sunday tea, and in the presence of visitors. But I stuck it out that I di'n't know anything about it. The glass in the chapel windows was opaque, and when at last the window was repaired, it cou'n't be matched in colour. So there, to this day, among the blue-green of the original panes, there's one of bright orange-yellow; a memorial to me while I still live, and a reminder of my wickedness that pricked my conscience a-many and a-many a Sunday after everybody else had forgot the incident.

I were terribly frightened o' being found out when I had done anything wrong, because my mother were a very strict woman. She allus kept a penny cane, and after any misdemeanour on my part she would say 'Now then, Willie, come here and be flogged' —and I had to walk up and take it. Sometimes I think she were a little too strict, but looking back on my childhood, I have no doubt that I deserved all the canings I got. As I said afore, nobody who lived more than two mile away from the school were compelled to attend, and this applied to a good many children in our district. But I had to go, though I very often wished that my father were a bit more like other boy's fathers, as a good many o' my associates never looked inside the school. Arter I were about nine year old, I got real ashamed o' going to school when other folks went to work. One morning some men were working in a field as I passed on my way to school, and I 'eard one on 'em say 'Look at that bloody grut ol' bor still a-gooing to school. Oughta be getting 'is own living.' After that I used to get into the dykes and slink along out o' sight in case anybody should see me and laugh at me. Still, I remember learning one day that a quadruped is a four-footed animal, and at any rate that's one thing as I'm never forgot.

One morning as I poddled along to school by myself, I had a find. It were a little bodkin case, made o' brass. No children of our sort ever had any sort o' toys, as you can imagine, and anything a little bit out o' the ordinary were a treasure to us. So you can realise what sort of a state I were in that morning, and as soon as school had started, I were caught by the teacher playing with my toy under the desk. The teacher called out, in her 'teacherish' voice, 'What have you got there, boy?'

I were scared, but I said 'I found it th'smorning, coming to school,' and showed her the needle case.

She were very interested in it, and said 'Will you let me have it for my little brother, Fred?'

Of course I war'n't very willing to part with it, but I darn't say 'No,' so I di'n't answer. She added 'If you'll let me have it, I will let you be the teacher for this morning.' Now this was a honour reserved for them whose fathers were well off, and in any case I ha'n't got the pluck to tell her that I wanted it myself, so I reluctantly give in.

21

We gathered round the reading sheet on the wall, and the lesson began, with me in charge. The usual practice was for each boy to read one word, in turn. All went fine, till somebody come to the word 'USE'. He knowed very well what the word was, but he knowed as I di'n't know it, an' all. So he stopped, and 'e 'oul'n't go on, and more 'oul'n't anybody else. The boys begun to grin, and to nudge each other, and at last in desperation, I said 'USSY.' That finished the lesson, and I lost the bodkin case and gained a nickname, for from that morning on I was known as 'Ussy'. Later on, I were allowed to forget my blunder and my nickname was changed to 'Chick'. Later still, when I had left school, I got the one as I have had all the rest o' my life, a corruption of my Christian names, William Henry. All the Fen knowed me as Will 'En. Still, a nickname were quite a useful asset to me, as the Fen is full o' Edwards's and at one time there were eleven William Edwards's, including me. So everybody had to have a nickname so as they di'n't get mixed up. There was Banker, and Rouncer, and Old Uncle, and Young Uncle, and so on, and very often new folks into the village were a long while afore they found out the real names o' these people.

The other memory I have of my school days ain't such a very pleasant one, but I shall have to tell it.

I got into disgrace one day, (though I can't remember now what about,) and the punishment I received was that I had to 'stay in' when the other child'en had gone home. This were a dreadful punishment for me, because I had so far to go, and it happened to be winter time, and the last part of the journey would have to be done in the dark. When there were a lot on us together, it di'n't matter, but the thought of all that long way home by myself in the dark were more than I could face. So when the others had all gone home, there I sat in the classroom, too scared to go home, and too frit to stop where I was. Teacher went out and left the door open. Temptation were too strong for me, and out I bolted. I were never very lucky, and as I went out, full pelt, I met the teacher in the doorway. She made a grab at me, and caught me. But by this time I were desperate, and I kicked and pummelled her till I got away from her, and away

I scuttled. Then I tore along as fast as my legs 'ould carry me till I caught the rest o' my gang up.

Next morning, as soon as I got to school, I was put over the headmaster's knee. He were a man of very violent temper at the best o' times, and on this occasion he lost control of himself altogether. He slashed out at me wheerever he could 'it me, mostly round my head, so that when I got home that night my hair were matted to my head with the blood from several long cuts.

Mother went to school with me the next day. She got no satisfaction from the headmaster, so she took me across to the vicar. He went back with us to the school, but from what I remember we di'n't get much help from him either. The master told him that I was self-willed, and obstinate, and vindictive, and a lot more things as I di'n't know the meaning of then, and as I'm forgot since. The vicar said that such children must be controlled, and that were that.

I need hardly say that the character the master give me were far from being deserved. A more inoffensive and a meeker child never lived, for I never had enough pluck to stick up for myself, and any old boy could 'run me 'um'.

The old schoolmasters lad a lot o' power over the poor un-eddicated fen tigers in them days. If there were anybody we hated it were our school teacher; they thought the on'y way to manage child'en were to frighten 'em to death. I often think how different it is now. I live in a school house, next to the school, and I see a lot o' what goes on there. There ain't a child but what loves to come to school, and it's all as happy as the teacher can possibly make it. I spend a tidy lot o' my time mending broken playthings and making new ones, and I'm 'Grandad' to all the child'en as come to 'our' school, and to some as are too young to start yet, as well. I do like to see their little old faces happy, and if I don't altogether agree with all the new fangled ideas in education, I can't help but think it's a good thing to make the school a bright and happy place for them to remember when they draw their old age pensions.

This 'ere bit about my young days seems to be a-getting out of hand, but there is one more tale to tell before I finish it. When

23

I were about eleven year old, there were a very high flood. One evening the Lotting Fen bank busted. Now my father hired two acre o' land from his father, at five pound a year rent, which were a very high price. It were part o' the bargain that when my grand-parents died, my father were to have the land. So you see it were a sort of hire-purchase deal, though nobody knowed nothing about hire-purchase then. But my grandmother were a tough old gal, and she hung on to be an old 'un, so Dad paid pretty dear for his land in the end.

Now the year o' the flood, it happened to be planted with wheat and 'taters, about an acre of each. The night when the bank busted, the wheat had bin harvested and threshed, but the 'taters ha'n't bin dug. I shall never forget that night. I had gone to bed when the bank blowed, but I could hear such a cabal a-going on downstairs that I knowed something out o' the way had happened. My brother-in-law, John Oliver, come running up, and I heard him telling my mother. Then mother hollered me up.

John, he went and fetched one o' Greenwood's horses, and fetched our corn out o' the neighbour's barn, so that were saved.

Oh dear, what a puggatary we were in. All the men were a-tearing about like ants when you dig up a ant 'ill—moving corn, driving cattle, shifting furniture; everybody were doing something to help.

It were such a beautiful night; there were a full moon, and it seemed nearly as light as day, so clear and still it was. Ah, how well I can remember hearing the people hollering about the fen that night. They were driving cattle, leading horses, rounding up pigs. 'Oooy, Oooy, Oooh. 'Old 'im up there, don't let 'im goo down. Gee-up! Keep 'im outa that there field, else we shay'n't see 'im no more.' It were so still that every word come a-floating across the fen as clear as a bell.

My mother, my sisters and me, and as many o' our women neighbours as could, went out and started clawing up as many of our 'taters as we could get by the light o' the moon. We were desperate to get some on 'em out to last us through the winter. We worked till it were nearly midnight, but by that time the water

24

had reached the top o' the rows, and we coul'n't do no more. We went poddling sorrowfully home.

I were in a terrible state, 'cos that year my father had give me two rows o' 'taters o' my own. They were about ten chain long, so there 'ud a-bin nearly a quarter of a mile if they had all a-bin in one row. I'd planted 'em myself, and looked after 'em all the way along, and when they were sold I were a-going to have the money. But they were left in the water, like a lot of other folks's, so my first business venture war'n't much of a success. I think it must a-bin a bad omen, or 'o'em' as I should a-said afore I got educated. All sorts o' things were reckoned to be 'bad o'ems' by the women in my young day. I shall 'ave to remember to say more about that later on.

There were a few folks as warn't forced to leave their houses, and them as were lucky enough to have a second floor went to live upstairs. But a lot had to flit, for the time being, at any rate. Some went to Upwood, some to Ramsey, and some wheerever they could find a hole to get into. They were the first evacuees as I ever remember, but I'm seen too many since.

It were the Catchwater bank that had busted, about three or four chain from where it joined the Raveley Drain. Now, when I come to look back on this event, the strangest thing, and the one that surprises me most, is that one of the fields close to the breach floated on the top of the water. This field was as low as any in the fen, but while all the other fields round it were under the water, me and the other old boys could run about anywheer on this one. Hund'eds of old iron hurdles, and a boat or two, and a lot of other material as 'ad bin brought up in a vain attempt to prevent the breach, were all washed underneath this field. As the water went down, the field settled again, on top of it all, and most likely it's still there now. I sometimes wonder what sort of a tale will be hatched up to account for them being there, if at any time in the future they are found. But anyway, them as reads this 'ull know the truth.

I did quite a trade, plying about the Fen with our gunning boat that I mentioned afore. I was big enough, by this time, to manage her myself, and I done good business taking people over the water to their houses to fetch out any things they wanted. I got sixpence a trip, mostly, and when I opened my money box in the spring time, I found twenty-five shillings in it.

The Chapel

3

I WENT to school till I were twelve, and then I left. Sometimes I worked, and sometimes I di'n't, and somehow the time soon rolled away to my seventeenth birthday. Then I struck out for myself, a-doing a bit o' turf digging. By turf digging, I mean, of course, digging up the peat in blocks to burn for fuel. We called each block o' peat a 'cess', though I can't find that word in no dictionary.

I hired half an acre o' land, and I expected to get a hund'ed thousand turf from it, near enough.

Now turf digging were a very difficult job for a new beginner, but one o' the old hands come and put me right occasionally, and I got on fairly well. By the time it were night I had dug about seven hundred. For an old experienced hand it were reckoned a good day's work to dig two thousand turf.

When I got home that night, my married sister, Harriet, happened to be there. I were tolerably well pleased with myself over my day's work, and I told them I had dug seven hundred turf.

Harriet had a lodger, a real old digger from Ramsey, who stopped at her house all the week, and on'y went home at weekends. When Harriet went home, my brother-in-law, John, said to her, 'How's Bill got on, today, a-turf digging?' Harriet, who di'n't understand the job, replied, 'Oh, alright I think. He's dug seven thousand.' The old lodger, whose name were John Caton, looked up and said 'Ah. Well, he ain't done so bad at it, seein' as it's on'y 'is fust day a-digging.'

John Caton were a grut, raw-boned old fellow between six and seven feet tall, and looked like something that had got left behind from the stone age. He never took any drink to work with him, but he allus carried a two-gallon jug, which he used to fill with 'frog-skin wine' from the b'ut dyke. When he felt thirsty, he would throw back his head, and holding the jug about two inches or more from his face, he'd open the sluice gates, and guggle, guggle, guggle, down the tunnel went the water. When he had had enough, he'd shut the sluice doors, and away to work again.

These old turf diggers from Ramsey used to work as hard as they could, early and late, for the first five days of the week. Then a-Saturday morning they'd get up, ateen two and three o'clock in the morning, in the pitch dark, walk a mile and a half to their

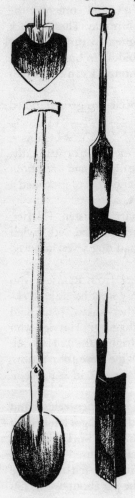

work, and be finished their hag, and off home, by the time other men were going to work. Then they'd go 'ommocksing off the Ramsey, wheer they'd sit in a pub for the rest part o' the day. After they had had a few pints, they'd soon be a-digging three or four thousand turf a day; which were easy enough to do, come to that, when they could sit in a pub and do it. Silly old fools, to work like distraction all the week, and to walk all the way that they did, and then to leave their money in a pub afore they ever so much as got it home at all!

It has just come to my mind that as turf digging is a thing o' the past, there'll be a lot o' folks as don't know what I'm a-talking about at all, no more than a cat knows about Holy Communion. So I'd better start and make some sort of a do a-explaining it.

A turf digger's tools consisted of:

    a hodding, or paring spade, as sharp
        as a carpenter's chisel;
    a shovel, equally sharp;
    a turf digging spade, sharper still;
    a measuring stick with notches in it,
        to mark the width of the 'pit' to be
        dug, according to the number of
        turf, seven or eight, at a time;

28

a line, twenty or thirty yards long;

a gauge, made of wood, two and a half feet long, and two inches wide, with a lip to press against the 'slaughter head', or face of the work, and three pegs in it, eight and three quarter inches apart.

The land to be dug was first cleared of all growth, sallow bushes mostly. The land was then stumped out into acre or half acre lots, as the case might be. Then it was 'beatoned out', that is, the line was used to square each piece. The old diggers always said 'beatoned', but I have an idea that the word must have been 'beaconed'; however, there's a lot of words in a fen-dweller's vocabulary as you won't find in no dictionary, and they come so naturally to me that I'm bound to use them now and then as I go along. So you'll have to take my word for it, and make what you can on't.

After the 'beatoning out', come the paring: that is, taking off the top layer of earth to allow the digger to get at the peat. The 'pare' were cut into squares, that is 'pricked out' with the sharp edge of the paring spade, and then lifted off with the shovel. The layer took off varied in depth from six to ten inches.

The peat had to be cleaned and made as level as a billiard table, and the piece of land on to which the cut blocks were going to be laid had to be levelled as well. This piece of prepared land was called 'the staddle'. When this had been done, the digger cut a hole, thirteen inches deep, to start in. Then he laid his line down, and marked out the width of his pit with his spade. Next he laid his line down again, to show him where to set the cut blocks down, and drawed his gauge across the slaughter head, or face of the peat, to mark his first three slaughters.

Then he rolled his trousers up, took off his top shirt, pulled off his cap and substituted for it a sweating cap—(a sweating cap was a cap of cloth, usually made out of a piece of old shirting,) blew his nose, counted his money, performed any other operations he thought necessary, and 'set in'.

The size of each block, or cess, was $6\frac{1}{2}'' \times 4\frac{1}{2}'' \times 8\frac{3}{4}''$. Two courses were dug at a time, so the pit was thirteen inches deep and eight turf wide. When one row had been dug, sixteen blocks had been cut, and this was called a slaughter. When three slaughters had been dug, the gauge was used to mark out the next three, and so on.

The cesses were set off the spade in rows on the staddle, each block being placed half an inch from the next one. If the pit were eight turf wide, it was necessary to dig fifteen slaughters to get two 'hundred', and you dug eleven 'hundred' to the 'thousand'. That is, to make a sum of it:

$$\frac{16 \times 15 \times 11}{2} = 1320.$$

If a seven turf pit was being dug, you took nine slaughters for one 'hundred', and ten 'hundred' to the 'thousand'; that is,

$$14 \times 9 \times 10 = 1260.$$

In any case the digger cut approximately thirteen hundred to every 'thousand' turf.

For buying and selling, a 'thousand' consisted of twelve 'hundred' blocks of turf, but for digging it consisted of thirteen 'hundred'. It was a bit like the saying I used to hear quoted, though I don't think it was always acted upon,

> Five score to the hundred of men, money and pins,
> Six score to the hundred of all other things.

There wasn't one man out of every hundred who went turf digging as were scholar enough to count up the number of cesses he were digging, but they knowed how many slaughters they had to dig to get a 'thousand', and that's the way they worked it. The price for digging was 1/10d. to 2/- per thousand turf.

As he dug the turf, the digger set them off his spade on to the staddle, in rows three blocks wide and two high. These bottom rows were called 'the walls'. On top of these were two more rows placed: these were called 'the eccles'. If the digger were digging an eight wide pit, one of the eccles, the one nearest the digger, would be three blocks high, to account for the extra turf.

Men took a lot of pride in the setting of their turf and when a pit was finished, the rows of cut turf standing on the staddle presented a clever bit of craftmanship. A bullet from a gun coul'n't go straighter than were the rows of turf, and though the rows were usually about ten chain long, each block was set with such precision that you could see from one end to the other through the eccles, if you put your eye to a gap atween the turf.

As each thousand was completed, a tassle, made from bents of grass, was stuck in the row. By these tassles, you could tell at a glance the number of turf you had dug. It took a good man about four hours to dig a thousand. But of course, the peat varied a bit here and there, and sometimes the digger would be slowed up in his work by tow. This was peat in which there were great hassocks, coarse clumps of grass that had died when the land had been submerged, and over which the peat had subsequently grown.

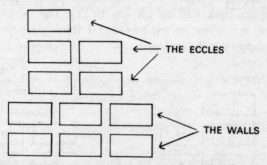

The old men would use some strong language about this ''nation 'ol' tow', partly because it slowed down their speed, but mostly because owing to the fact that it was so tough and would not cut clean, it spoiled the look of their work.

The turf-digging season started round about the first week in April. It had to wait until the frosty nights and mornings were over, because a cess that had once been frez was no good for fuel. A frozen turf would swell to twice its normal size, and when placed on a fire, would never flare, but would simply smoulder away to ashes.

For the first few weeks of the season the diggers would suffer agony with their hands. The bottom hand, that is, the hand nearer the blade of the tool, got blisters from the constant friction, often as far round as a halfpenny. We used to deal with these by threading a needle with wool, and drawing it through the blister, cutting the ends off, and leaving the wool to drain the blister dry.

The other trouble the digger had was, that in the first few weeks of the season, the bottom hand would be constantly in the water as lay in the bottom of the pit, and this would result in the most terrible cracks in the skin. The pain from these gaping cracks were terrible, and the remedy was to seal them up with hot shoemaker's wax, melted over a candle.

When they got too old for the strenuous work of digging, there was the dressing and drying for the old hands to do. There were several operations in this dressing. The first operation was called 'edging', just turning the top course over; the rate of pay for this was $\frac{1}{2}d$. from one thousand mark to the next. The next job was called 'raising', turning the dry blocks down on two walls, and putting the back wall on the top to dry. This is such a complicated movement to explain that I think perhaps a sketch would help to make it clearer.

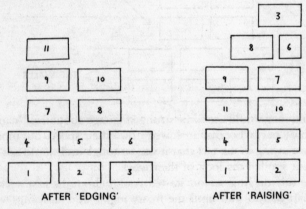

AFTER 'EDGING'   AFTER 'RAISING'

The next process was called 'turning', another complicated movement that resulted in the dry ones being put to the bottom, and the bottom two rows on to the top to dry.

The blocks would by this time, nearly all be fairly dry, except those that had started by being right at the bottom, and which, after turning, had arrived at the top. These would have a tendency to go sour, and a further process, called 'raffling', was performed to change the position of the top six only.

The final process was ricking; the turf were taken to a staddle by the side of the nearest boat dyke, and there stacked in ricks twenty-five blocks high. The ricking had to be done as carefully as every other process, with draught holes left right through the rick, as the cesses were not yet dry enough for fuel. They were carried from the pit where it 'ad been dug and dried, to the staddle by the boat dyke in a special sort of wheel-barrow called a turf-barrow. The blocks were piled on to the barrow in a special, exact formation, so that the barrow was perfectly

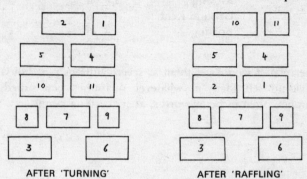

AFTER 'TURNING'   AFTER 'RAFFLING'

balanced, and the turf 'bound' by each other so that they did not roll off in transit. Each barrowload consisted of a digger's hundred of turf, one hundred and twenty cesses. The old men got so accustomed to running with their turf-barrows that they could go better with one than without one; and one old chap from Ramsey, named Goakes, always wheeled his empty barrow the four miles each way to and from his home. With his barrow he used to run, at his usual ricking dog-trot, and without it 'e 'ad to walk!

The processes of drying the turf from digging to ricking took about three months. The men who carried out the various processes were paid at the following rates; if they were just labouring for somebody else, for edging, $\frac{1}{2}d$. from one thousand mark to the next: for raising, $2\frac{1}{2}d$. per thousand: for turning, $4d$. per thousand: for raffling, $1\frac{1}{2}d$. per thousand; and for ricking, 1/- per thousand.

The rent a digger working for hisself paid for his land worked out at 1/- for every thousand, and the charge made by the boatman for transporting them by water was 2/6d. per thousand.

The total cost, per thousand, was, therefore:

	s. : d.
Digging	1 − 10
Edging	½
Raising	2½
Turning	4
Raffling	1½
Ricking	1 − 0
Ground Rent	1 − 0
Boating	2 − 6
	7 : 0½

The retailer would get them at seven shillings per thousand, and would sell them in whatever quantities best suited his customers, often in pennyworths, at six cesses a penny.

4

NOT all the characters in the Fen worked in the turf, of course. The Lotting Fen had another real flourishing industry. I believe I have mentioned that I were born in a house converted from a brick kiln, and brick making was still in full swing in the district when I was young. The brick industry must have been going on in those parts for many years, as there were, in evidence, the ruins of many old kilns, besides the ones still flourishing.

In my young days, there were three main brickyards, on the south side of Lotting Fen, belonging respectively to Mr Bridgefoot, Mr Summers and Mr Greenwood.

My father worked in Mr Greenwood's yard, making tiles for roofing; corrugated tiles, pan tiles, hip tiles, valley tiles and ridge tiles. There were several machines for making tiles in the yard, and each man had his own machine. A man was told off to grind the clay, one day for each machine. The grinding machine was called a 'pug-mill', and was in the middle of the 'millus'. It was turned by a horse. There were a beam, about thirty feet long, across the top of the mill, so that two horses could be used if necessary, though usually one was enough. The poor old horse walked round and round and round his endless path all day.

When I were very small, my mother worked in the brickyards. I had a little swing fixed up for me on the beam opposite the horse, and round and round I used to go all day. If the horse dropped any dung, it had to be cleared away immediately, to keep the path from becoming greasy and in bad condition. So as I travelled round, I kept a diligent watch for this, and was delighted when I could call out, 'Tom, old Jack's messing agin,' thinking I had done an all-important job.

The tile-maker was a nice, compact little affair, turned by a crank. It were filled with clay, which had been previously ground,

and it squeezed this through a die on to a long, narrow table made up of little rollers. A wire cutter came over it, and cut the tiles the required length. Then they were took off the table and put on to a tray called a horse, though I don't know what the old tilemakers would have said if anybody had referred to it as anything but a 'oss'. The corners of the tiles were cut off, and the knob pressed on with the thumb.

The tiles were then turned off the horse on to a gadget like a three-pronged fork, made of wood, and carried on that to the blockings. The blockings were tiers of laths, laid about three or four inches apart, and stretching for twenty feet or more in length. The tiles were laid on the laths, and blocks of wood put in between them at intervals; the next layer of laths then rested on the blocks. In this way the blockings were built up to a height of ten to twelve feet, so as you 'ad to use a pair of steps to lay the top courses. In the blockings the tile dried, to be ready for the kiln.

My mother were a very good hand at making tiles, and has made hundreds of thousands, especially corrugated tiles. Whenever I see a roof covered with corrugated tiles, I always wonder if they should happen to be some that my mother made. The pay rate for tile making was 3/6d. per thousand.

There were brickmakers in the yards, as well, of course.

Old Saunders Bedford used to 'set the kiln', as it was called.

Other men wheeled, or barrowed, the brick and tile to him. When he had filled the kiln, he used to burn it.

The kilns were built of brick, about twenty feet square and twenty feet high. There were a doorway, about four feet wide, in one side of the kiln, called the wicket, though we always called it the 'wickerway.' A small building called the 'hopper' joined on to the kiln, and the fuel for burning were stored there. The floor of the kiln were dug out, so that three trenches for the fires ran across the kiln from the hopper to the opposite side. It warn't just anybody as could 'crowd' the kiln. The first thing to do were to build arches with the green brick, over the trenches. When these arches met, the first course was completed, and the level brick was flush with the bottom of the wicket. At this stage planks were laid over the brick, so that the men could move about over 'em without damaging 'em, while the second course were laid. In the second course the bricks were laid in a different pattern, like herring-bone, and both sides of the kiln were built up first, leaving a gangway down the middle from the wicket to the other side of the kiln, at right angles to the trenches.

The first course in the kiln had to be brick, but as tile was a lot better paying proposition, they put in as much tile as they could in the second and third courses. In the latter days of the brick-yards, brick was made only to burn the tile with. When the kiln was full of brick only, its capacity was approximately 40,000 brick.

The job of fitting in all the different types of tile was very skilled, and the man setting the kiln would have three other men a-waiting on him, running back'ards and for'ards with wheel-barrows to fetch him the exact sort of tile he needed for any particular spot, while he bellowed orders at them that nobody on'y brickmakers 'ould ever understand, like 'Cowhold' or 'Currug-gaters' or 'Pipes'. When the top course were reached he moved about over the top in a pair of slippers like a cat on hot bricks, while his helpers handed the brick and tile up to him as he needed it, as he was now well above their heads. Drain pipes were always placed upright, on one end, for the firing, and the practice was to 'thread', or place, the smaller pipes inside the larger ones, to save valuable space.

37

When the kiln was full to capacity, the wicket was bricked up with old brick, as close to the tile as possible, and the space between was filled up with 'wickerdust', brick dust saved from one burning to another. Next came the 'splatting', that is, covering the whole top surface of the kiln with old brick.

The men setting the kiln had twelve shillings each for their work, which wer'n't extra ordinary good pay, because it took them four full days of the heaviest, hardest work of any in the brickyard.

Then come the tanning. A little fire were made in each trench, on the same side as the hopper, and this were gradually increased until the lane of fire reached right across the kiln to the opposite side. The tanning process continued until all the moisture had been druv out of the goods in the kiln, and the experienced judgement of the kilnman told him he could start a-burning. The tanning process took nine days, on an average, and for the last three or four days the kilnman would have to be on hand to tend his fires at four-hourly intervals, day and night. Turf was used for heating the kilns in some cases, while in others coal was the fuel. The coal burning kilns were not very popular on account of the tremendous volume of black smoke that swept across the fens when a kiln was being fired, but the peat burners made a very little blue-grey smoke. The peat burners di'n't lose so much in wastage, either, as the heat was not fierce enough to melt the brick in the lower courses down; in a coal-burning kiln this very often happened.

At two o'clock on the morning of the first day of burning, the kilnman and his helper started to brick up the furnaces, and to put in the iron furnace doors. Then they hotted up their fires as much as ever they could. The old experienced hands could stand at the hopper end and send a peat block to any particular place they wanted in the lane of fire in front of them, barrowload after barrowload.

About the third day of the burning, a red patch would appear at the top of the kiln, where the fire had burned through. The kilnman, who would be on the watch for this, would rush to the place with a load of wet clay, which he emptied on to the place and treaded down. The fire, driven in at one place, would break out in a few minutes in another, and so the process went on, time after time, until the whole of the top of the kiln had been heated. During this time, when putting the ballast on to the kiln, the kilnman would run about the scorching top with his mouth open, gasping for breath at the side of the kiln, for the heat and the fumes were a'most overpowering. It di'n't last very long, however, and was the last process. Windy weather sometimes lengthened the burning time by half a day, as special boards had to be fixed to keep off the wind from the kiln.

People who worked in the tile and brickmaking sheds had the privilege of making their own pig troughs, etc. and they were burned in the kiln. Us kids in the fen liked to put in our own little bits and pieces, an' all and this 'ere clay modelling, what you 'ear so much about nowadays warn't at all new to us eighty year ago.

Old Saunders Bedford used to make nine inch paving, fire brick and floor brick, work that needed more skill than the making of ordinary brick and tile. He was a man as coul'n't a-bear children, and if by any chance a strange boy went to see what he were doing, he would say 'Fetch me a pound o' seam (lard), and I'll swaller 'im.' Then he would seize the boy's jacket collar with his teeth, and lift him bodily off the ground, and shake the poor child till he screamed with fright, and then let him fall. As soon as he was free the old boy would scamper off as fast as his legs would carry him, and Bedford would never be troubled with that particular child again.

Clay for making brick did not have to be ground; it were dug in the winter, turned twice in the spring, and made up into bricks in the summer. It was made with stocks and moulds, and set in hacks to dry. I remember one day, another old boy whose father worked in Bridgefoot's brickyard said that Mr Bridgefoot had a lot more money than Mr Greenwood, my father's master. I said he hadn't, and the other boy said he 'knowed' he had. So I said that at any rate Mr Greenwood had two kilns in his yard, and none of the others had. That done it. Into battle we went. I don't know now which one on us won, though I should think the other must a' done, for I were never much good at fighting.

One reason for there being so many brickyards in Ramsey

Heights was undoubtedly the fact that the brick and tile could be took by water across the fen, across Ugg Mere, and into the river at Hitson's Bridge, now called St Mary's Bridge. Each brickyard had its own gang of barges, or lighters, as they were called, and some men were employed entirely as watermen, to take the brick and tile up to the towns by water, and to bring back coal on the return journey.

One o' my uncles sometimes acted as a waterman for Summers's yard. One day him and another old fellow set out on one o' these trips. They delivered their stuff alright, and on their way 'um again, they called, like they allus used to, at the pub aside o' the river. The pub were called 'The Exhibition', though that don't matter to the story. It were about five mile, by the river, from 'ome. They stopped there an hour or two, and by that time they'd had enough to loosen up their tongues a bit.

While they were there, a 'oss dealer come in with another man, and a good deal o' bargaining were a-going on, after which the 'oss dealer managed to buy a 'oss from the other man for seven pound. Old Uncle Billy—'e were my grut uncle, really, but everybody called him 'Uncle' and I doubt if he would have answered to any other name—loved a bit o' dealing, and were very interested in the transaction. He were still more interested when the dealer, feeling as 'e had had a good deal, stood a pint o' beer each all round the house.

While they were a-drinking this pint, old Joe Smith, Uncle's mate, suddenly said 'Uncle, the mairster said as we could sell our old pony, if we could git seven pound forrim.'

'*Did* 'e?' said Uncle, surprised.

'Yis,' said Joe, ' 'e said as we could sell 'im fer seven pound.'

The pony in question were the one they 'ad got with 'em, a cob that used to haul the boat. Uncle coul'n't resist the temptation to 'ev a deal so 'e turned to the dealer and said 'I—I—I say, Guv'ner, my mate 'ere says that the mairster said as we can sell th'ole porny we're got 'ere.'

'Oh?' said the dealer. 'How much do yer want for 'im?'

'Well,' said Uncle, 'My mate 'ere says as we can sell 'im fer seven pound.'

'I never see such a thing in me life,' said the dealer. 'They're all seven pounders today. Fill the mugs up, landlord, and then we'll go outside and 'ev a look at this other seven pounder.'

So the mugs were filled and emptied, and they went out to sell the pony. They trotted 'im up and down a bit to show its paces, and after a bit of 'umming and ah-ing, the old pony changed owners, for seven pound. Uncle had enough sense to put one condition in the bargain, though, and that was that if 'the

mairster' war'n't satisfied, they could 'ev the old pony back again, upon the payment of expenses.

When the pony 'ad gone, the two old boat men had to set theirselves to work, and haul the boats 'ome 'by shoulder,' as they called it. They plodded along, and suddenly Joe said 'Uncle, what shall yer dew wi' the money, when yer git 'um?'

'What shall a-dew?' said Uncle. 'Whoi, chuck it on the table, to be sure.' 'But,' said Uncle, telling the tale long afterwards, 'as soon as 'e said that there, I knowed as 'e'd begun to see fear o' what we'd done.'

It took the rest of the day for them to haul the boats 'ome, and they reached the brickyard just such time as the other men were a-getting ready to leave off for the day. I can't tell the rest of the story half so well as Uncle used to tell it hisself, afterwards, so I'm going to use his words from now on.

'When we got 'um,' he would say, 'the mairster war about ten or twelve foot down in a golt pit, a-digging golt wi' the other men. So I went and stood aside the pit. None on 'em di'n't take no notice on me, so I said "I—I—I say, mairster, we're sold th'ole porny." Nobody took no notice, not even to look up. No, there warn't a sentence, not a bloody sentence. All I could 'ear were the click, click, click, o' their fut-irons aginst their spades. So I said agin, "I say, mairster, we're sold the ole porny." But 'e never looked up, even then, on'y said, quicklike, like 'e allus did. "I don't understand your langwidge."

Aah,—I understood his'n well enough. But 'e still went on wukkin', and never looked up. So arter a little while I said "Well, mairster, we ain't done nothink as we cayn't roightle."

"Yew'd better goo an' roightle it then," the mairster said. So I went off to find Joe, and when I 'ad found 'im, I said, "Joe, bor, we're got tew goo an' git th'ole porny agin."

"What's 'e say," arst Joe. So I says, "Yew'd better goo an' see 'im fer yerself if yew want to know" I says. "Now then, Joe bor, yew better git orf 'um an' git a bit o' grub, and then we'll be a-'ommuxing orf towards Sawtry." (Sawtry was the village where the dealer lived, about seven miles away by the very shortest route they could take across the fields).

So we went 'um and got ourselves a bit o' grub, and got ready ter goo, but fust we thought we'd call for a pint at the mairster's 'ouse.

(I ought to explain here that 'the Mairster' also kept a pub, at which, during the evening, his men spent a good deal of the wages they had earned in his brickyard during the day.)

The mairster's woife cum t' serve us, so I said "Bring us a point o' beer a-piece, Missus."

She fetched the beer, an' when she set it down, she stairted. "They tell me as you're sold the mairster's pony. Idea o' the thing. I-*dea* o' the thing. Never 'eard such a thing in me life. I-*deea* o' the thing. Sell the mairster's pony. Idea o' the thing. I-*dea* o' the thing"—on'y *ten thowsand* toimes faster than I can say it. If she'd a-bin my woife I should a-give 'er a punch or tew o' the skull. But there, *she* woul'n't a-done it, she woul'n't.'

'So I told the Missus stroight, a-did. I said, "Well, missus, we ain't murdered nubuddy, an' we ain't done nothink as we cayn't roightle." I knowed as I were orlroight, 'cos I 'ad twenty foive-penny bills in me pocket all the while.'

(He meant five pound notes, of course, but I very much doubt whether he ever see so much money in all his life, let alone owned it.)

So we drunk our beer, an' away we went. When we got outside the noight were dark, an' I says to Joe, "Well bor, this is a tidy kettle o' fish", but I knowed as we'd got ter goo, an' it warn't no use a-thinking as we a'nt. It took us a tidy while, ter git roight acrorss t' Sawtry in the pitch dairk. When we did git there we went an' found the man what we selled the porny tew. We telled 'im what we'd come fer. 'E di'n't take a lot tew it, neither. "You're the rummest lot o' dealers I ever see in me loife," 'e said.

Anyway, we did git th'ole porny back, on'y we 'ad t' pay 'im fifteen shillin's. I reckon as 'e could see as we 'ad got wrong wi' the mairster.

We led the porny 'um, but coming along the road, I see a gate afront on us, and I said "Joe, bor, we're wrong 'ere. I never see a gate anend the high road afore. We may goo back." So we 'ad to turn round an' goo back a goodish way to find the roight road agin, but we did git'um at larst, somewheer atween tew and three o'clock in the morning. An' when we 'ad stabled the porny, we went 'um to bed.'

The pub in the brickyard brings to my mind another incident that happened there. This story concerned another old boatman whose nickname was Fiddy. One day Fiddy called at the pub, as usual, and ordered his pint. 'The Missus' had a cat what used to set in the taproom, purring on the hearth.

Fiddy said, 'That's a noice ole cat you're got there, Missus.'

'So 'e ought to be,' replied the Missus, 'So he ought to be.

43

He lives on the best of everything, and has all the new milk he can drink.'

'New milk?' said Fiddy. 'That's no good. Why don't yer feed 'im on mustard?'

'Mustard? Never heard o' such a thing! Feed a cat on mustard. Th' idea o' the thing.'

'Ah, Well,' said Fiddy. 'I'll bet yer airf a gallon o' beer as I can make that ole cat leave off drinking new milk to eat mustard.'

'Never heard o' such a thing. But I'll *gi'* you half a gallon o' beer, my man, if you can get *my* old cat to leave off drinking milk to eat mustard.'

'Orl right,' said Fiddy. 'Fetch the milk, and the mustard.' So Missus fetched a saucer o' milk and a pot o' made mustard. The milk she set afore Pussy, and the mustard she handed to Fiddy.

Puss got up and begun to lap the milk. Fiddy watched his chance, and then dabbed the mustard spoon, covered with made mustard, right on to the spot what lays just under the cat's tail.

For a moment or two nothing happened, and Puss went on, unconcernedly, enjoying the milk. Then, suddenly, he left off lapping, turned himself upside down, and began to lick furiously at the mustard.

Fiddy were a queer chap in many ways. He would not work, if he could help it, at anything except the boating which he was used to. Once when there was no work for the boats, Fiddy's master told him that he'd have to go hoeing wheat.

'How am I got to dew it, mairster? B'the day, or b'the grut (piece)?'

'By the piece,' said the master, 'Two shillings an acre, same as anybody else 'ould get.'

Fiddy pointed down at the ground, and all round him. 'D'yer see these 'ere little blades o' grass all round 'ere, Mairster?' he said. 'Well, afore I shall goo a-scratching the face o' th'earth for two bob an acre, I's'all eat every one on 'em.'

Fiddy was as good as his word, too. Instead o' goin' a-hoeing, he took hisself off to the nearest workhouse. Unfortunately for him, the Mairster, who di'n't reckon much to sich conduct, happened to be one of the Board of Guardians, and Fiddy soon found his presence warn't welcome there.

44

Occasionally he got 'on the road'. Even there he resorted to a trick or two. One cold day he went up to a house with a little pat o' dried 'oss muck in 'is hand, that he had picked from the road a minute or two afore. When the good lady of the house opened the door to him, he held it out to her and said 'Ayer got a little bit o' salt yer could let me 'ev Missus? I cayn't eat this without a little bit o' som'ink tew it.'

The lady looked, and saw what it was. 'My poor man,' she said, 'Throw it away, do. I'll find you a bit o' something to eat.' Of course, Fiddy knowed exactly what any woman 'ould do.

But Fiddy warn't allus hard up. He once had a little bit o' money left him. He had quite a bother, to decide what he should do with it, and coul'n't make up his mind whether to lay it out in land or houses. But eventually he laid it out in houses—public houses.

There were no road to the brickyards until 1884, when the Heights Drove was gravelled. This was done by public subscription, and them as 'ad no money give a week's work. My father worked a week, for his share. They had a set of carts, carrying ballast, and I were one of the boys who were employed to lead the horses.

The brickyards are all gone, now, and will soon be forgotten, no doubt, like all the old characters who spent their lives at work there are already forgotten. The only traces left now of this formerly busy spot are the many water-filled gault pits, a few old brick hovels, and the ruins of one or two of the kilns.

5

BACK to work again. I di'n't stop turf-digging very long; for one thing I di'n't see much future in it, and for another, it ha'n't got enough variety in it to suit me. I got the feeling then, and I'm never lost it since, that what I should like better than anything were to have an interest o' some sort in the fenland rivers. I felt a longing for them, and now, after sixty year, I still think it 'ould be nice to go and live the rest o' my days, and die and be buried, by the side o' one of 'em. So I went into business as a waterman.

There were a family o' boys as I'd allus been friendly with—I liked the whole issue on 'em, though some a lot better than others. One on 'em become my brother-in-law when I were on'y ten in 1880. I'm mentioned him before. I remember his wedding day well enough. He come for Harriet when it were time to start for the wedding, and accompanied by most o' their respective families, they set off to walk to church. It were a matter o' three mile or so, up the drove and along the highway to St Mary's. It were February, fill-dyke, either black or white, and that year it were white and no mistake. The fen were just one level sheet o' frozen snow, like a cake as is just been iced. There were no telling the dykes from the land, for they were all level full with snow.

Still, both John and Harriet had just turned twenty, and a six mile walk in their wedding clothes di'n't worry them.

It had been decided as I shou'n't go to the wedding, 'cos somebody had got to stop behind to mind the wedding feast. So one o' John's brothers, named Charlie, stopped behind as well, to help me. As soon as the wedding party were out o' sight, we forgot we were in our Sunday clothes, and away we went, out into the snow. We tore about the fields a-chasing and a-pelting each other, and as we coul'n't see wheer the dykes were, every few minutes we would both blunder into one and be covered in snow four or five feet deep. We wer'n't in no danger o' being

46

drownded, because the water in the dykes had frez solid before the snow fell. But when the party returned from church, we wer'n't exactly presentable as wedding guests. I don't remember getting into much of a row about it, though—partly because, as I learned years afterwards, the bride and groom, coming home a little in front o' the others and not having their minds on the road had also took a dyke for the path and had stumbled in together.

Besides John and Charlie, there were four more brothers, the other favourite o' mine being another Bill. When I were fed up with turf-digging, this same Charlie and me decided to go into partnership. We ha'n't got much to start a business on, now I come to think about it; in fact we were as bare o' money as a pig is o' side pockets, as my old grandad used to say. I had one single gold sovereign, and Charlie ha'n't nothing at all. Still we war'n't put off by that. I went to see Mr Greenwood, and offered him my one sovereign as a deposit on one of his lighters, (barges), and he let us have it. Then we hired another boat to go with it. By that time it were nearly harvest time, so we both went to work like fury in the fields while the harvest work lasted to get a bit more capital. The night we drawed all our harvest money, we went straight off to Upwood to buy a donkey to haul the barges along.

We went early in the evening, but by the time we had done the deal and had a drink on it, the dusk had begun to fall, and by the time we were ready to leave Upwood it were pitch dark. We had to come down the main street of the village, and the light from the cottage windows streamed out and made light patches across the road. We found out straight away what an awk'ard customer we'd took on, for that obstropolous old donkey would not go across the light patches. We had to get behind him and above him over every single one!

He proved to be a desperate kicker who would sometimes kick for two hours at a time, just for the fun on it. He were as quick as lightning and kicked me many and many a time, for he never lost a chance of giving me or Charlie a sly one. Charlie were a very quick tempered chap, an' it used to aggravate him a lot more than it did me. He allus used to leave his jack-knife aboard

47

the boat when it were his turn to be out on the tow-path with the donkey: he used to say 'If I'm got it wi' me, I know as I shall stick the bo-enk if he kicks me.'

All riverside public houses had a stable for the convenience of watermen. One night we laid at Puddock Toll, and we put the old donkey into the stable, which were on'y a lean-to place joined on to the side o' the house. In the middle of the night, when me and Charlie were asleep in our boat-house on the river, the moon worked its way round till it shone through the slatted window o'

the stable where our donkey was. He could see his own shadow a-moving on the wall, and he began to kick.

When he really cou'n't stand it no longer, the landlord o' the pub got up and went to see what the matter was, but our bo-enk had really got hisself worked up properly by then, and his kicking was so fast and furious that the landlord dares'n't go into the stable. So he had to go back to bed and put up with it as well as he could, but there war'n't much more sleep for anybody in the house that night.

It war'n't the donkey kicking that used to keep me awake, though, it were Charlie's snoring. He were the king of all snorers that I ever met. I di'n't care so much as long as he kept at it reg'lar; it were when he got set as I cou'n't bear it. H'd give a snort, and then 'old his breath until you'd think all the powers of the earth and heaven coul'n't never start him breathing again—and then when you'd give up all hope and were sure that he really were a done-er this time, he'd let out such an old sowser of a snore that the timbers of the boat house 'ould shiver all over with it.

We di'n't keep the donkey very long after the incident at Puddock Toll. We swapped him for a pony one night at the Ram Inn, and a good bargain we got. Our business prospered, and we soon had three more lighters, two on 'em with houses to sleep in. We boated hundreds of thousands of turf to Ramsey, Chatteris, March, Whittlesay, Peterborough, Benwick and other places, too many to mention; we worked for one o' the brick-yards as well, boating brick and tile up to Chatteris docks; we fetched 'silt' (fine sand) from Three Hole Bridge for use in the brickyards, and we carted produce from the fen by water to Holme railway station. So we were kept pretty busy.

We never had no argueing atween ourselves as to who should go here or there, or as to which of us should do this thing or that. We allus tossed up a penny—heads Charlie went, tails I went. We made this bargain and we stuck to it, though it di'n't prevent us from having a 'set to' occasionally in our private lives. One day we got as far as peeling our clothes off to have a go at each other, and no doubt we should ha' done if it ha'n't just hap-pened that we'd got Charlie's brother Bill with us. When we started to strip, Bill got up an' said "Ere! I'll stop that game. I'll 'ammer both on yer.' So he give Charlie one then and there to get on with, and then turned to me and said 'Now I'll serve you the same'—and did. 'If you want to fight, I'll take both on yer on at once' he said; and he would a-done, an' all, I believe, but were I glad to be done with the affair, for I were never much of a fighter.

Ah! I liked old Bill, as well as anybody I ever knowed. He were a curious chap though, and could allus make me laugh. He were one of a tidy big family and they all lived with their father and mother in one o' the tiny cottages in the fen. Such houses meant home to the people who lived in 'em, but they cou'n't really be called much more than huts. It war'n't nobody's fault; to start with, you coul'n't get no sort of a foundation for a proper house in the peat of the fen. You had to start by making some sort o' foundation other than the peat. Sometimes you dug all the peat right out and put loads of gault into the hole you'd made; sometimes wood 'ould be used, and when the first lot of old fenmen lost their livelihood with their boats when the fens were drained better, a good many o' their old boats went to make foundations for houses. Later on, railway sleepers proved to be very useful.

Lotting Fen, being close to the edge o' the high lands, were surrounded by brickyards, so the houses here could be made o' stuff as were fairly durable. The brickyards made all sorts o' tiles, and the corrugated variety were very popular for roofing. When my father built a house for himself in 1881, my mother made every single tile as were on it herself, in the brickyard. She made hundreds of thousands of tile beside them, and I never pass a house with tile on it but I wonder if she perhaps made every one on 'em.

While the peat were still in its half-drained, spongy condition, no house could have a second storey; most on 'em were like that

George's Cottage

wall as the man is supposed to have built, six feet high and nine feet wide, so if the wind did happen to blow it over it 'ould be higher than it were to start with. The floors o' the houses were laid wi' floor brick or nine inch paving, just laid down side by side on the earth, and not bound down nor together in any way at all. After a year or so the floor 'ould be so unlevel it would have to come up and be re-laid, and it made the job easier if they were just loose on the earth. Besides, when there were a flood, as there were most years, the spaces atween the tiles made it a lot easier for the water to drain away. Most winters the water 'ould come up high enough to stand all over them. It 'ould bring a lot of black, soft earth in with it, and when it drained away again the floor 'ould be covered with the silt it had dropped. Then the housewife 'ould take a pail or two o' clean water and swish it acrost her floor and sweep vigourously with a besom brush till she'd pushed water and dirt firmly down atween the cracks. Unless the flood were really very bad, folks di'n't make a lot o' fuss about it, but just went on living as best they could. They'd keep a set o' wooden blocks handy, and when the water begun to rise, they'd put the four legs o' the bed on the blocks; then they'd 'ave a plank o' wood ready, and at bedtime the family 'ould walk the plank to get in bed, with water standing all round them.

I'm 'eard a tale about a chap as I knowed what used to get a fair amount o' beer down 'im whenever 'e 'ad a chance. One night when the water were just a-coming up 'e'd bin out and 'ad a goodish allowance, and after 'e'd got in bed nice and comfortable he found as 'e'd got to get out again to get rid o' some o' the beer. But by that time the water had ris' so that it stood about nine inches all over the floor all round the bed, so 'e just rolled over to the side o' the bed and done what 'e wanted. The noise on it roused his wife, and she set up in bed, very indignant, and said 'You mucky beast, you. Whativer d'y'think you're a-doin' on?'

'Don't worrit, missus, don't worrit' replied her husband, 'Wha's a little drop more matter? It'll all goo out wi' the rest.'

What with the floods in the wintertime and the damp constantly rising up the walls, these little old houses were never really dry. They allus smelt o' damp and peat smoke, and because they were so damp, every household 'ould be pestered with enormous crickets what used to live in the walls. As soon as it begun to get dark, out they'd come and start making such a row that you could 'ardly 'ear yourself speak for 'em, and they'd go zoomin' across the room an' slap into your face, or land in your tea or the gravy on your plate. O' course, many a house ha'n't no other light on'y a rushlight as the woman had made herself, or at the best a candle, and every now and then a cricket 'ould flip across the flame and put the light out as neat as could be. There warn't no way o' exterminatin' 'em, so you 'ad to put up with 'em. Some households used to keep a hedgehog as a pet, a-purpose to keep the crickets down a bit. They'd get one from a nest when it were a baby, and nice pets they make, an' all, especially when they earn their own keep by eating the crickets. My wife remembers going to stop a night with her grandmother as lived in one o' these little houses. She slept with her grandmam in a little lean-to place, and when they were in bed, the door atween this and the houseplace begun to tap in the draught, so her grandmother told her to get out o' bed and shut it. She nipped out with 'er bare feet and set 'er foot right on the family 'edge'og what were about on 'is nightly cricket-'unting prowl. So she remembers the hedgehog pets as well as anybody, I should think.

The fire-places were all of the open hearth type, so as to be able to burn peat, and most of the houses had their own brick oven. It took thirteen cesses (turf) to heat the oven for baking. The cesses would be stood in a ring round the edge of the oven, with one or two broken up in the centre of the ring. When they were all burnt to ashes, the woman would rake them out, and in would go her bread. Pastry 'ould come out a beautiful brown all over. I know that all this electricity and other modern gadgets are all very well in their way, but in my opinion there never has been, and never will be, anything to beat food cooked in a brick oven.

Most of the fire-places 'ould smoke (I should a-said 'smook' if I'd a-bin a-talking) fit to stifle anybody, so a door or a window had always to be open to let the 'smook' out.

This brings me back to Bill again. Early one morning, afore it were light, a neighbour called Fred went to see Bill. He rattled on the door, and he heard Bill's voice say 'Come in,' so he opened the door and stepped inside. Bill were having his break-fast by the light o' a candle at the other side o' the room, but the room were so full o' smook that all Fred could see were the tiny glimmer of the candle through the murk.

'Who is it?' called Bill. 'I can't see through this 'ere smook. Is it yew, Fred? If it is, come in and shut the door.'

'Why, man, you'll be choked,' said Fred, still a-holding the door in his hand.

'Come in, and *shut the door,* I tell yer,' yelled Bill, 'Don't let any o' this smook git outa the door. The chimbley's the place for it to get out and I'll make the b—— go up it. So come in, and shut the door.'

Bill had a tendency towards the quinsey; nearly every year he'd have such an attack as you'd think he must be choked with 'em. But it were a good five mile to the nearest doctor, so unless anybody were really a-dying they had to grin and bear it. Bill did go to the doctor one year when he felt his annual attack of quinsey 'hanging about'. He walked the five mile to see the doctor, who give 'im a bottle o' medicine; it said on the label that he was to take one tablespoonful every four hours. When Bill got on his way home, he felt so queer that he decided to take a dose. On'y he were in a bit o' difficulty, 'cos he had never learned to read or write, an' he coul'n't remember what the doctor had told 'im. So he said to hisself that if a little 'ould do good, a lot 'ould do a sight more good, and he took out the cork and bolted the lot at one go. Then he swacked the bottle into the dyke and hummoxed off home. I can't remember whether he had the quinseys as bad that year as usual, but at any rate 'e never suffered no ill-effects from the overdose of whatever the doctor had give him. He never did learn to read, though when he became a small-holder he learned to write his name. He told me once as he used to have to make two straight strokes and turn the tops over till they met to make the big O that began his surname.

All my pals could take a tidy drop o' drink, when they'd a mind to, and Bill were no exception. There warn't on'y one exception, and that were me. I allus thought I were on'y half a man, for I could never drink more than a couple o' pints without feeling quimmy; and then I should come over so lither and lawless that I thought I'd never 'ev another drop to drink as long as I lived. Beer were on'y tuppence a pint, though, and you could make it last as long as you liked, so like a lot more folks, I used to go to the pubs for the company and not for the drink. The landlords kept other things besides drink, like nuts and dates. By the time closing time arrived the floor o' the tap-room 'ould be ankle deep in nutshells. We 'ould call for a pint o' 'Barceloneys' and when the landlord brought 'em, 'e'd emp'y 'em out on the middle o' the tap-room table. Then we'd play 'Nabnut' with 'em; each would draw one nut in turn from the heap, and whoever drawed the last nut had to pay for the lot.

The pubs di'n't close while 11 p.m. There were one pub in particular that were kept be a very strange, queer old couple. I shall have to remember to say some more about them later on. The old fellow must somehow a-got a bit more eddication than the rest of us young tigers, and he talked a bit different and 'ikey' as we thought. The nuts and dates were kept down the cellar, and when the clock showed five minutes to eleven, the first of our gang 'ould call for 'Hairf-a-pint o' monkey nuts,' or 'Hairf o' dates.' No sooner than the old chap got back up the cellar steps with one order, the next of us 'ould give his. And there we kept him poddling up and down the cellar steps till the clock said five or ten past eleven. Then he'd come up grumbling under his breath and say 'You must get your dates before eleven'—which of course, was just what we intended, and that 'ould finish our day up properly for us.

I keep on a-leaving poor old Bill a long way a-hint me, though it were thinking about 'im as made me start remembering evenings in the pubs. We'd been to the fair at Ramsey one July, and we'd called for a drink or two at the Jolly Sailor. Bill 'ad 'ad just about as much as 'e could carry, though I'd 'ad to be careful, as usual. We walked 'ome across the Biggin Fields, and then started down the drove. Suddenly Bill stopped and turned towards me. The moon shone on his face, and he were so white he looked about like Jonah must a-done after three days in the whale's belly. We allus used to say that if anybody looked very weak and pale, they looked as if they'd bin 'ate and spewed up again'. No doubt this was a reference to Jonah, but I'm on'y just connected the two. Anyway, that's how Bill looked. He sort o' swayed on his legs, and looked as if he coul'n't quite understand what were the matter.

'Bill,' he said to me (remember my name's Bill, an' all). 'Should yer be sick, if yew were me?'

I could see there warn't no help for it, so I said 'Ah. I reckon I should.'

He moved in a sort o' deliberate way towards the side o' the dyke, and made a real ceremony o' getting down on his knees. He turned his green face sideways to me again and said, 'I say, though, Bill, should yer really?'

I were a-gitting a bit tired o' these preliminaries, so I encouraged him to get on with it, and he did. Poor old Bill, 'e were bad for a few minutes. While 'e were still at it, a dog appeared from somewhere and begun to gobble up the vomit. Bill di'n't take no notice, but in another minute there were two dogs. They begun to set their 'ickles up at one another, and showed their teeth, and growled. That roused Bill, even in his misery. 'You nee'n't quarrel,' he said between spasms, 'there'll be enough for both on yer.'

He were a cheerful friend and neighbour to the last. In after years we both became small-holders and had holdings next to each other, and lived next door. He died a terrible, lingering death with a cancer in his stomach, and during that time I liked to find time every day to see him, for as long as he could be bothered with anybody at all.

'How ayer to-day, old pal?' I'd say, and no matter how near death he was, and whatever pain he'd had, he'd allus answer, 'Oh, I'm a bit better to-day, I'm sure, Bill. I shall wuk it, yet.'

After I'd moved away from the fen, another one o' my old friends passed away. I just happened to be making a business trip down there when I heard about it, so I visited the house. He ha'n't been buried then, and I had to go and look at the dear old chap in his coffin. His wife stood over him and said, 'Ah, wou'n't 'e a-bin pleased if 'e could on'y a-known it were you a-standing 'ere a-looking at 'im, Will 'En.' That made my eyes sting, I can tell you; as I said afore I were never above half a man, and I were allus as tender hearted as a chicken.

6

THIS boating, now; I liked it as well as any occupation I ever 'ad. I never found it monotonous, an' if ever I asked the time, I allus found as it were an hour or two later than I'd expected it to be, which is one sure way o' knowing that you are enj'ying yourself. We 'ad to work 'ard loading and unloading, specially unloading, because all fenland rivers run atween high banks, and we 'ad to barrow whatever goods we were transportin' up the steep side to the top. But we got plenty o' rest when we were travelling, which we did mainly in the evening and through the nights.

We took turns being out on the towpath with the ol' pony, though 'e di'n't take a lot o' tending. There were a tidy few stiles along the towpath that 'ad to be negotiated, but the ol' pony soon got to know which on 'em 'e could jump, and which 'e coul'n't. He'd take the easy ones without being told, and 'e soon learnt 'ow to navigate the others as well. When we come to one as were too 'igh for 'im to jump over, we pulled the boats in close to the shore and took 'im aboard till 'e could scramble ashore again on the other side o' the obstacle. Pulling the boats were really very light work for a horse, but he warn't no more fond on it than most human bein's are, and 'e made the most o' these little breathing spaces in his job. He were such a knowing old animal that he got a bit too expert at jumping aboard, and if we got the boats a bit close in to the side 'e'd notice it and come aboard without an invitation. Then his visit 'ould take us a bit too much by surprise, and 'e'd get a welcome in words that were warm enough to suit anybody. Many a time I'm bin a-leaning over the side, looking the other way, when 'e's come a-lumber-

ing aboard without warning an' tippled me 'ead-over'eels into the river.

We di'n't stop much at pubs, except the one at St Mary's, which we never could get by without wasting two or three hours. We used to tell folks as we'd got stuck on one o' the stumps o' the old bridge. We'd yoke up and get away towards the evening, and make up for lost time by travelling at night. I loved to lay aboard on a rough night when the wind laid straight down the river, sending the big waves flop-flop-flopping against the prow all night. I used to lay there, snug and warm in the boathouse, listening to the rain a-pattering on the roof, and think that I were the luckiest young fellow that ever lived, and wonder what even a millionaire 'ad to make 'im any happier or more content with 'is lot than I was. Some people 'oul'n't have liked the loneliness, perhaps, and certainly there were times when it were a bit eerie to be so far away from civilisation. I were never much of a believer in ghosts and spirits, though a lot o' folks in the fen were. My mother and all my sisters 'ould tell you tales as 'ould make the hair on your neck rise up in spite of all your common-sense, and they believed wholeheartedly in signs and portents (or 'o'ems' as they'd a-said), and the meaning o' dreams. Still they were on'y women, and you 'ad to make excuses for 'em because they 'ad such lonely lives they imagined things, and besides, it give 'em something to talk about. But some o' my brawny rough-an'-ready mates at work 'ould tell you the same sort o' tale about sperrits an' apparitions as they'd seen, specially one family called Allpress, as 'ad the gift o' seeing. It were a gift as I were on'y too well pleased to do without, and I allus used to laugh and make fun o' my mates what told such tales; it really did cap me to think that folk like them, as I'd knowed all their lives, could really believe what they were a-telling you. However, during this time I were a-boating, I 'ad one experience myself that give me cause for a lot o' thought, even if it never succeeded quite in making me change my tune about such things.

We 'ad left St Mary's Bridge about six o'clock one evening, and at ten o'clock we 'ad reached a point atween Bodsey Bridge and Ingle's Bridge where we dicided to stop for the night. It were a beautiful evening in summer, with the air sort of soft and yet clear, no wind at all, and the sun had gone down on'y a little while afore an' left everywhere a sort o' rosy pink. The banks were standing up each side of us, so we coul'n't see the flat black fields, and we were trapped in a sort o' world of our own, with on'y the pink sky up above us, and the other pink sky reflected in the water all round and underneath us. Everything were so quiet and still that I remember thinking that it felt as if it war'n't real at all, but on'y in a picture as I were a-standing looking at. The boats were rubbing gently along the side o' the bank, and Joe, Charlie's youngest brother, who had come out with us for the trip, just for the pleasure on it, were on the towpath, leading the pony. Charlie sat on top o' the boathouse, dozing, with his legs dangling inside. I called to Joe, who were about fourteen year old, to stop. He stopped the old pony and stood on the towpath, holding the horse's head. I were just about to make fast, when along the bank come a man on horseback. I watched him come nearer, because he were the only thing visible besides our own little party in the world; besides, he were interesting in any case on account of his queer old-fashioned clothes, especi- ally his high silk hat. He passed Joe no more'n about two yards from him where he stood on the towpath with the pony, and not more than three feet from Charlie where he sat on top o' the boathouse. But neither one nor the other as much as turned their heads or glanced towards him. I thought they must both be more 'n half asleep already, so I called out to Joe, a bit sharp, 'Wake up, bor—di'n't yew see that there man on that 'oss?'

'No' said Joe; but he were allus a bit of a yawnucks, and I di'n't take much notice of him. So I turned to Charlie. 'Well, di'n't yew see 'im?' I asked.

'What 'oss?' Charlie said, staring at me as if I'd took leave o' my senses. 'I never see no 'oss, n'yit no man neither.'

By this time Joe had begun to realise there were something queer about the whull affair, an' 'e di'n't reckon much to being out on the towpath by hisself while we were in the boat. His eyes were nearly bolting out of 'is 'ead when I looked at 'im again, and he said 'I know what that wa'. That were somink what BANISHES away' and he let go o' the 'oss's 'ead and come blundering 'ead over 'eels into the boat. Nothing me or Charlie could say or do could get him out o' the boathouse no more that night.

Well, as I said afore, I ain't in no way superstitious, but after fifty year this still appears a bit mysterious to me. You see, I 'ad

'eard many a time as there were supposed to be a ghost along this very stretch o' bank. It were said it were the spirit of a farmer what had once lived at Bodsey House, and what's more, he were supposed to ride along the bank on a horse. I have tried and tried to remember if I could 'ear the noise of the horse's hoofs coming towards me, but I can never be quite certain. Sometimes I think it were the utter, dead silence of his approach that made me so interested in him afore he got to us, but then I reason that if that had been so I must have remarked on it there and then. So I shall never know whether I really did see a ghost there or not, but whichever way I should think both 'oss and rider are wore out by now.

There were another spot, along the high road to St Mary's that had a haunt. At one particular place, a white cat 'ould come out from the dyke on one side o' the road, and cross it, a bit squywannick, right in front o' the feet of any late travellers, and go down into the dyke on the other side. The finny thing was that it di'n't matter how long you looked for 'er once she'd gone down over the dykeside, you could never find her. Scores o' people 'ave seen 'er, but whether she were just a ordinary flesh and blood cat wi' very reg'lar habits, or a feline ghost, is never been proved as I know on. Once, when I were young, I were coming down the road with a gang of other young fellows. Me and Bill (same old Bill as I'm mentioned afore) were very scornful about it, and Bill said 'If the b——— shows itself to-night I'll prove as it ain't no sperrit: I'll kelp it into the drain on the toe o' my boot.' So on we went, and at the very identical spot, out come pussy, across the road no mor'n a foot in front of our feet. I don't know how the others felt, but my hair rose up and very near pushed my cap off. I see Bill lift 'is foot up, and it seemed to me as if the ol' cat lingered about deliberately, right in front on 'im; then she turned 'er 'ead, and looked straight at 'im, an' 'is foot wavered about a bit, and then 'e put it down again. Puss slunk off across the road, an' over the side o' the dyke she went, just like she allus did.

Soon as sh'd gone out o' sight, I felt better, and tried to pretend I ha'n't bin frit at all. 'Well,' I said to Bill, 'Why di'n't you give it one?'

'Bill,' 'e answered, 'Bill, I daresn't. I were afraid as me fut 'ould goo right through it.'

So for all I know it might still a-bin a ordinary quadruped, though if it were it must 'ave had a sight more than the nine lives a cat is supposed to have; for that tale were an old 'un when I were a boy, sixty-odd year ago, and my three children all reckon they've seen it at the very same place within the last twenty year when they 'ave been coming home late after parties or dances. If I believed in ghosts at all, I'd as lief believe in a animal ghost as any other. The Allpress family 'ould tell you of a great big black dog what allus come out o' the fen and appeared to any o' their family to warn 'em of some coming trouble or tragedy, and my sister Harriet had a special dream as used to warn her of a death in the family. That were, if she ever dreampt she were lousy, or combing a child's hair and getting lice out of it, or any other dream concerning lice. Then when she woke up in the morning she'd be that upset, and more often than not afore the specified period o' three days were up, she'd 'ear of a death of a blood relation. On'y you did really 'ave to keep some sort o' common sense about Harriet's dream, for she di'n't dream it no oftener'n she could 'elp, an' on the rare occasions when she did, somebody or other in the fens round about 'ould nearly allus be sure to die; and as nearly everybody in the fen were blood relation to nearly everybody else, her interpretation of it stood a very good chance o' being the right one. After all, a blood relation could be a forty-second cousin you knowed nothing about on'y 'is name, and we were pretty well blessed with them we did know on. My mother had eight sisters and two brothers, as all 'ad big families, and my father had three brothers and a sister, and one o' the brothers 'ad thirteen children and another one nine. I reckoned up as I 'ad seventy-nine first cousins—so 'blood relation' di'n't 'ave to mean one of your own nearest and dearest. Still, it used to please Harriet to think she had a dream she could rely on to warn her.

We earned a nice lot o' money with the boats, but we spent a tidy lot as well. Wherever we went, everybody seemed to know us, and they all wanted treating. My mate were a pretty good hand at this, but it all had to come out of the accounts. If we di'n't go out at night, we played nap in the boathouse, but as the winner put all his winnings back into the housekeeping, the loser allus got half his losses back again in kind. We knowed a good few girls in those days too, very pretty, some of 'em, especially at Chatteris; but I'll bet if I could see 'em now they are some wrinkled old crones. (I nearly said 'haybags', 'cos that's what we allus called an ugly or a nasty old woman; but I don't know what it means, and I fear it may have some meaning as I don't know about; like the word my poor old dad allus used—if 'e were aggravated with anything 'e'd call it a 'horsebud'. It was a very common word among men who prided themselves that they di'n't swear. I never knowed what it meant until I was more than

middle aged, and met it in *Tess of the d'Urbervilles,* spelt, correctly I don't doubt, as 'whore'sbird'. Well, my dad 'ould never have used such an indelicate expression if 'e had knowed what he was saying. My mother wou'n't have allowed it.)

One evening at the Black Horse, a man were a-reading out loud from a paper that there were ten shilling offered as a reward to the finder of a spaniel dog, answering to the name of Nelly, and belonging to a Mr W. Ellis. We said 'Well, we're a-going down to Chatteris, and we shall be back in about ten days. If we see her, we'll bring her, alive or dead, and get the ten shillings.' And sure enough, as we went we see a dog lying on the bank. 'If she's there when we come back, we'll take her,' I said.

She was still there when we returned, but she di'n't answer to the name of Nelly, for we found her, like 'poor Eddard' in *Dombey and Son,* 'drownded and dead'.

I jumped out with a piece of thin chain, which I snickled round her neck, and pulled her aboard. I set her up against the stern sheets, and she bent her head forward and down until she tippled over. I called 'Nell, Nell, Nell' and when she bent her head I said 'Look, she's answering her name.'

Charlie said 'Chuck the thing out, do. I never see anybody as soft as you are.'

Anyway, we got to St Mary's Bridge about five o'clock, and the landlord of the Black Horse was there, standing on the bridge. He offered to go and tell Mr Ellis that his dog had been found. When he came, he said 'Yes, that's her. Poor old Nell.' We told him we would bury her, which we did, and we got our ten shillings; we should have been home fairly early that night, if it hadn't been for that dog, but as it was we found a good company at the pub, so we stopped till we'd spent the ten shillings. Then we had to haul home the next morning, which muddled half another day away, so we were worse off than if we'd never heard about poor Nell. I really don't know why I've bothered to remember that story, 'cos there ain't much point in it and no moral at all; but I set out to write this just as it came into my head, and that's one of the things that's come.

I was twenty-four now—a lovely age to be. I thought nobody could be better off than I was, and neither past nor future troubled me much. About this time we did a lot of boating for the owner of one of the brickyards, but we di'n't get our money, and the bill kept a-creeping up until he owed us a little over £60. In the end he had to confess that the brick trade was very bad, and he was in rather a poor way financially; so after some discussion we agreed to take sixty thousand brick at 17/6d. per thousand, a very low rate, in settlement. Then we remembered that we'd got nowhere to stack them, so we went off and bought a field from another man for £160. We halved it, and then out came the penny to see which was to have which half. Then we each carted our bricks on to our own land, and we both had a house built. I don't know how much Charlie's house cost, but I have got all the details of mine. The bricklayer's contract was for £24–10–0d., and I found all the materials, such as lime, cement and slate. The carpenter's contract was for £54, and he found all his own materials, wood, glass and so on. Altogether, for land, labour, dyke-cutting, hedge-planting and all complete, my house cost £220. I di'n't really want a house just then, for I ha'n't thought about such a thing as getting married, but it did come in useful about nine year afterwards, and in the end, after living in it for fifteen years, I sold it for £500. It looks like a new house to-day, but it is down one of the droves, and in a few years from now nobody will want to live down there.

I don't know how it was, but soon after the houses were built, Charlie and me seemed to suddenly get tired of each other, or of the job, or at any rate of doing the job together. So one day we sat down and valued all the goods we owned. I can't remember what the sum was that we arrived at, but the next day I said to Charlie 'I'll take the lot at the price we said, or if you want them you can have them at the same price.'

He said 'Do you really want 'em?' I said 'I don't care a mossel. Do *you* want 'em?'

He replied 'I don't care one way or th' other.' so of course, out came the penny, the settler of all arguments. If it fell a woman, I was to have them, if a man then they were to be Charlie's. A man it fell, so he took the gang, and that parted me from my mate, though not from the boating life. The boats had paid us well, and Charlie could have prospered, too; in fact for a little while he did, but soon after he left me he started to drink like distraction, and died when he was forty.

I bought another 8-ton boat, but sold it again straight away, because another man who owned a gang o' lighters was in need of someone to take charge of them. So I hired his lighters from him, on condition that I would cart his stuff at an agreed rate. As he was a brickyard owner, he kept me and the boats very busy. I took a trip for him to Isleham, and then I stopped there, boating clunch (white stuff, very like chalk, but a bit harder.) I took it from Isleham, down the Ten Mile river. These Isleham trips were very good, as there was less work on long trips. Here is the route I took from the brickyards in Ramsey Heights to Isleham. We went first to Ponder's Bridge, and through Bevels Leam to Angle Bridge, Whittlesea; from there to the Twenty-foot river till we neared March, and through the Priory Sluice to Upwell and Outwell; then through Well Creek via Northdelph to Salter's Lode, through the sluice and over the river to Denver Sluice; through the sluice, into the Ten mile river, and soon to Little-port. Then on the River Lark, and up it to Prickwillow, and so on to Isleham, through Isleham Sluice, and on to Judes Ferry, where we unloaded.

After a summer boating round about Isleham, I came home and did a few more little trips close to. But I had a disagreement with the brickyard owner who didn't keep his part of the bargain and treated me very shabbily, so I packed up the boats, I suppose for ever.

7

TURF digging and boating done, and I were twenty-seven, but still with no permanent situation in hand. However, as soon as one door shuts, another opens, and like Micawber, I kept expecting as something 'ould soon turn up. It did.

Just at that time, Mr John Evison, of Upwood House, who owned and farmed atween three and four hundred acres in the New Fen, decided to cut up his farm into small holdings and let it. He built several new houses making the holdings little or bigger accord'n-ly to what tenant he had in mind. Of course, these holdings were very much sought after. Mr Evison was a staunch Weslyan, and so was my father, and I reckon there's no doubt that that had a good deal to do with him being one of the chosen. He was offered, and accepted a holding of about fifty acres, including one of the new houses, and we moved from Lotting Fen to New Fen.

Fifty acres ain't much compared with the farms of to-day, but of course it was intensive, fenland farming, and it was quite an undertaking for my old dad. So he felt he should 'ave to give notice to the Lotting Fen Commissioners that he would have to resign his post at the mill. They offered the job to me at the same rate of pay that my father had; that was eleven shillings a week for the winter half of the year, and three shillings a day for every day he had to work in the summer. This looks very poor pay, on the surface, but he had only to work when it was necessary, in good winters hardly at all. I warn't willing to take the job on these terms, and I turned it down, but anyone with any knowledge of machinery was at a premium in those parts, and I was eventually given the job at £26 p.a., flat rate,—and so I became a miller.

I still lived at home with my parents, and all the time I did not have to be at the mill, I filled in doing any job that came handy on the farm. So the time slipped by till I was thirty-two. My friends had all got married, one by one, but I'd been clever enough to escape up till then. I used to remind myself of a man I knew of at Upwood, a small farmer who only had one man to work for him, a man called Jack. One day, Jack said to him, 'Mairster, I warnt a day orf, a-Thursday; I'm a-goin' ter git married.'

'Well, bor, I don't know as I blame yer,' said the mairster. 'Yew'll be at the end o' your troubles, then.' So Jack got married, and after about twelve months Jack had to approach the mairster again.

'Can I have a sub. on this week's wages, mairster? We've got a new baby the smorning, and we h'aint got a penny in th'ouse.'

The mairster were an understanding sort o' chap, so he said 'Yes Jack, o' course you can—and I'll tell you what, you can work it out in overtime so as you're still got a full week's wages to come a-Friday!'

'Thank yer,' said Jack. Then he said, 'You told me as I should be at the end o' my troubles when I got married.'

'Ah, so I did,' said the mairster, 'but I di'n't say which end. I meant the fust end.'

My youngest sister had been married nearly four year and she used to say, 'You think you're clever, but one o' these days you'll marry some young gal and be a fool for her all your life.' Well, her words came true—but then the country is full o' fools, so I ain't the on'y one. Look at all the sayings there is about fools: 'fools for luck' they say; 'fools and their money are soon parted'; 'if there were no fools there'd be no fun'; 'kill all the fools and the wise would soon starve'; 'everybody is a fool sometimes, but nobody always'. Anyway, on December 24th, 1902, I went to church and waited to see if one o' the young girls my sister had mentioned 'ould turn up. She did—and before we had got outside the church, bells began 'Silly fool is come to church! Silly fool is come to church!'—and I wondered if I was at the end o' my troubles. I don't think so—I'd plenty before that day and I'm had plenty since—but never more than my share.

We went to live in the house I'd had built, which wasn't above a quarter of a mile from the mill. After twelve months of married life my wife had our first baby—a boy.

The morning after he were born one of our neighbours called

out to me and said, 'How's your missus and the little old bor a-getting on, Bill?'

I replied, 'Oh, they're all right—on'y the boy ain't got all his fingers on one hand.'

My neighbour was so sorry—said what a disadvantage it 'ould be to him all his life etc. When he'd finished I said 'Well, I think it's all right George—he's got five on one hand, and five on the other.' He were took back, but he had his answer ready 'Ah! Well if he's as cunning as his father, he'll be cunning enough for these parts,' he said.

Now that's brought to my mind a lot of other bits about babies —like when Fred Tatt's wife had another one. Fred went to work so pleased. He said to his mates 'We're got a new baby this morning.' 'What is it?' asked one.

'Guess,' said Fred.

'A boy,' said his friend.

'No,' said Fred, squirming with glee, 'guess again.'

'A girl,' said the obliging friend.

'Ah,' said Fred, disappointedly, 'somebody's bin a-telling yer.'

Another time a young man recently married was late for work. His mates—a gang of brothers as uncouth as you'd find 'em, asked him why. 'We're got a baby,' he said. The others began to ask questions. 'Why—you call in to-night and see it,' said the proud father. The other old boys had never seen a woman in bed afore, and they were very impressed. 'There she lay' said one of 'em 'all done up in a night-gown wi' pig's fry round the neck and all down the front!'

My next door neighbour said he allus nussed (nursed) his son backside uppards 'cos he were the prettiest that way—and my brother-in-law John, used to tell us how his mother used to fetch his baby brothers a slap across the behind and say 'I'll knock your brains out,'—which led John (as a small child) to regards that area of his own anatomy as his brain box. 'Still,' he used to say, 'I'm got as many brains as anybody else; I were born with the same amount and I'm never used none.'

To the mill, again, though. She was a big mill with a tower 50 ft high and sails with a 30 ft whip—which means that the part of the sails which had shutters or vanes in, was 30 ft long.

She had patent sails and would regulate herself with a striking-rod running through the wind-shaft and geared to a spur-wheel, round which a chain ran, which hung nearly down to the ground and was weighted. When a shuft of wind came, the vanes—(or shutters) opened and up went the weights, closed the shutters again, and so regulated the speed of the mill. She had a fan-tail, so that she could luff herself—that is—keep the sails always facing the wind. If the direction of the wind changed, it would catch the fan-tail and spin it round like a hoop, and the sails would soon face the wind again. The gearing in the mill ran smoother than any gear I ever saw or heard anywhere else—all running wood cogs to iron. I had a 16 h.p. steam engine on the floor of the mill'us, so that I could connect it to the water wheel if the wind failed.

It was necessary to pump when the water reached a certain level in the drain, so as to empty the dykes which drained about 1400 acres. In the winter I was supposed always to run the mill if there was a wind, night or day, so as to save coal. I never cared if the wind rose before bedtime, but it would not be true to say I always got up and went, once I was tucked up in bed, in spite of the old saying that a good miller can't sleep when the wind blows.

I had a good many nights there by myself, though. Not that I minded; there was very little to do, and a good fire to sit or lay down by. If I wanted to sleep, I could, and if I di'n't, well tobacco was on'y threepence an ounce.

I had to walk round with my oil can every four or five hours. Sometimes the tail-brass at the bottom of the wind-shaft would scream out in a dreadful, eerie way because of the wind pressing into the sails, and oil alone was no cure for that. I had a special thick oil called lard-oil, which I mixed with brimstone or gunpowder, and this would soon quieten her. There were five flights of stairs to go up to get right to the top of the mill.

Sometimes I used to leave her running on her own, while I went home to have my supper, returning to the mill about midnight.

I were going back one night about twelve o'clock, with a flagon basket on my back. It had some grub in it, and a bottle of cold tea to hot up if I wanted any liquid refreshment in the early hours. The basket hung over my shoulder by its strap, and I walked along with my head poked for'ard, deep in thought. The moon lit up the world as bright as day, and I were the on'y living thing in it, or so it seemed.

Suddenly, my basket was lifted clean away from my shoulder, and then flapped down again, as if somebody had crept up behind me and deliberately raised it. 'Oh, orlright' says I, 'I know yer little game'—thinking that it were one o' my pals as were out late and had seen the chance o' playing a trick on me. Then I turned round, but the path behind me was bare, not a soul for miles. My hair stood up on end, till it nearly pushed my cap off. I sweated in terror as I turned round to investigate, but I knowed that for my own peace of mind in the early hours, I dare not leave it unexplained. I soon found out what had happened. The constant chafing of the bottle 'ad wore the last threads of the plaited straw away, and the bottle had slipped gently through the hole. It ha'n't made no noise as it fell on the soft, long grass by the dyke side, but the sudden easing of the strain on the strap had lifted the lightened basket away from my shoulder. I picked up my bottle and was soon on my way again; but I don't think I have ever been more scared than I was at the moment when I turned round and see the path empty behind me.

The water wheel, or scoop-wheel, was 28 ft in diameter, and had 52 ladles, or scoops, on its circumference. It revolved at the rate of $3\frac{1}{2}$ times a minute, when the sails were passing at 85 points. I should think that for the benefit of them as don't understand, I had better explain that. In the days of the old cloth-sailed mills, the mill had to be stopped when necessary and the sails furled to a point on the arm, at the end farthest away from the mill head. When the arm of the sail was vertical this point came near enough to the ground to kill a dog passing underneath. The speed of the sails was calculated according to the number of points passing the lowest place in their orbit, in one minute.

I was a miller for twenty years, and during that time I had a good few floods to contend with, besides many memorable storms. I think the year 1912 brought the wettest summer and the worst flood of any I can recall.

On Monday, August 26th, 1912, the water were running over the river banks. It started to rain again, that day, and kept on, all day and all night. When dawn came on August 27th, you couldn't see where the banks were at all, and whichever way you looked, the fen lay blea. Soon the whole fen was under two feet of water. Potatoes and other root crops were completely ruined, and corn stooks stood in water up to the bands. The harvest had to be fetched in by boat, a sight I never see afore or since.

The Drainage Commissioners met to see whether I should keep pumping or not, and they agreed that I'd better keep the pump a-going to save the houses as much as possible. It happened lucky that, the previous year, a new pump had been fixed to the engine, so that I could now pump by wind and steam at the same time. It usually took about three weeks of constant pumping to clear the water after a flood, but in 1912 nothing went according to plan. In Woodwalton Fen, one of the banks busted, and the whull fen were filled with water. Of course it warn't no good pumping into a drain with a hole in the bank, so the Woodwalton commissioners had to shut down their engine and wait for the water to drain away naturally. The Mill at Monk's Lode had been built the same year as mine, and was its twin in nearly every respect. The miller at Monk's Lode was John William Lines, so of course, everybody called his mill 'Johnny Billy's Mill', and mine 'Bill 'Arry's Mill' and there must be a good many folks about as would remember them under those names if they failed to recognise them as Monk's Lode and Lotting Fen Mills.

When Johnny Billy had to shut down in 1912, he come across in a boat to see how things were with me. I was in desperate need of help, so he stopped with me, and for eight weeks we kept vigil, night and day. We cleared the water out at last, and after fourty-four nights at a stretch I was able to go home to bed again.

Time at the mill used to hang heavy in long spells like that. I could never bear to sit, just doing nothing; and if, for any reason, I was forced to do so, I worked harder in my mind than I ever did with my hands. I had one advantage over a good many millers, for there's nothing I like better than a book, a thing as proved very strange to the various odd helpers I used to get in emergencies, for the biggest part of my generation couldn't read at all, and those who could di'n't see no sense in it. But I could never settle to read much at the mill. I fixed myself a work bench up, and I had a good selection of tools, so I were always concocting something, either for myself or my children. As each of my children were born, I took a diamond and engraved their names on a window pane somewhere in the mill, with the date of their birth, etc. The windows had all been broken by the time the mill was demolished, or I should have asked for them for souvenirs. One winter, I took it into my head to make a set of miniature roundabouts for the children. The whole affair was made out of waste material—a potato riddle that had seen its best days, the handle and ribs of an umbrella, a lot of old empty cocoa tins and mustard tins, and so on. I made and painted all the animals, and the little human figures to ride them. There was even a man to take the money, and, finest touch of all, I was able to put in the working part of a little musical box, so that as the roundabouts turned, the music box tinkled out its little tune. The roundabout was such a success that I went on to make a model of the 'Flip-flap'; and last of all I made a model of the mill herself.

Years afterwards, when I had been farming in the New Fen for many year, these models were resurrected. The new hospital at Peterborough, which was to be used by all the Ramsey area, was being built. It had been planned as a memorial hospital, and each district it was to serve, was asked to raise a certain amount of money. Ramsey has never been left behind on such occasions, and set with a will about the task of raising its quota. Our postman was a Ramsey man, though I should think nobody knew our old fens better than he did, for he walked from Ramsey and delivered letters all over the fen every day for over forty years. Of course, there was none of this modern rush and tear about Tom. He took his time and had a chat with anybody he came across, and it would take one of these new fangled counting machines to calculate all the cups of tea he had on his round. Still, he had his regular stopping places, and as he used to reach our house at such time as my wife was having her breakfast, that was one of them.

One day, while he was having his usual cup of tea, the subject of these models was raised, and of course he remembered them from seeing them years afore. He was quite excited when he knew that they were still intact, and immediately had the idea of using them to make some money for the hospital. A Grand Carnival was being arranged, to take place in Ramsey on August Bank Holiday that year, and Tom suggested that we should make a sort o' peep-show of them. I was inclined to hold back, not because I di'n't want them to be used, but because I was afraid that folks 'ould laugh. However, I was no match for Tom's enthusiasm, and afore we knew where we were, we'd got them out and cleaned them, and repaired them a bit here and there. Then a young electrician fixed them up with a tiny electric motor, so that all we had to do was to press a button and away they went. The horses swung round and round, the music played, and the flip-flap gave its little celluloid passengers ride after thrilling ride, and the sails of the mill turned in their stately fashion while the water well scooped up imaginary water.

The day of the carnival came, and Tom and I found ourselves in a tent waiting for our first customers at 2d. a time. I was never so flabbergasted in my life. We couldn't deal with the folks, and soon had a long queue waiting to get in. All day we switched on and off, and answered questions. Folk went in one door of the tent and out the other, and a good many went straight out and joined the end of the queue again, for another turn. At the end of the day we had collected about £20 as near as I remember. So my time a-building them wasn't altogether wasted, apart from the pleasure my children and their friends had out of them.

Ah! Milling is a lovely job, when the wind is strong, and regular; but storms are the miller's worst enemy. March 28th, 1916, is a date I sha'n't forget in a hurry, for it brought the worst storm as ever I remember. The wind lay in the north, very strong, and with shufts reaching gale force every few minutes all day long. It snowed on and off, too, and the temperature was well below freezing point. At five o'clock in the evening, a real blizzard developed. The snow froze thick on the shutters of the mill sails, making each sail a solid block. The striking tackle refused to work, and I just coul'n't check the power. Round and round she went, for half an hour or more, like a child's penny paper windmill. I expected something terrible to happen every minute, though I coul'n't quite make up my mind what to expect. The least catastrophe I expected was that she 'ould throw a sail, or smash the gearing to smithereens. I kept putting the brake on for a few seconds at a time, but I knowed it 'ouldn't do to keep it on any longer, for she 'ould soon have been on fire from the friction.

I was as alarmed on that occasion as I ever was in all my days a-milling. I tore about jerking chains and frantically trying to release the striking gear. In the end it was the wind itself that came to my rescue; it blowed an extra hard gust on the sails and moved some of the snow. The shutters began to open, and she soon slowed down.

At the end of that day, there was hardly a telegraph pole in the whole area left standing. Three chaps as I knowed on went a-dressing 'taters for market that morning in a field near Ponder's Bridge. When the snow started a-putherin' down so 'ard that they coul'n't see no longer, and it were evident that the weather war'n't going to get a lot better, they left off work and 'ommuxed off as fast as they could to the Green Man. They stopped there all day, so as to be near if the weather did improve at all, and by the time it were turning out time they were just about drunk. It were pitch dark, and there were the telegraph poles all a-laying flat, and the wires all over the road. As the two chaps stumbled along, one on 'em said to the other, 'Well, I'm bin drunk a goodish few times in my life afore, 'an I'm bin in some queer perdicaments; but I'm niver got up among the telegrarf wires afore!'

The day ha'n't finished playing its tricks with me, either. When the wind had calmed down a little, about eight o'clock in the evening, I left the mill running on her own and battled through the snow towards home for a wash, a warm-up, and a meal afore going back to the mill for the night. When I got home, I found a snow drift frozen solid against the big sliding door that led into the outer shed, through which I had to go to reach the back door of the house. All my efforts failed to budge it an inch, so I decided to go round to the front door. That was locked, of course, so I called to be let in. The wind howled, and the windows rattled, and my wife had got a visitor, and the children were still playing noisily on the floor. I yelled, and roared, and banged, and rattled, but none of them heard a sound above the clatter of the elements. So after about half an hour of vain effort to get in, I turned round and went back to the mill again, and ''nation glad I was to get there' as my old Dad would a-said.

Soon after this, my career as a miller came to an abrupt end. It were in the middle of the 1914–1918 war. My mother was still farming, though Dad was no longer there. He had died many a year afore, in 1906, from a heart attack as a result of a shock. They were having such a struggle to keep the farm going, and were always worried about where next week's money was coming from. They had two beautiful horses, and one morning when Dad went to feed them he found the barn door open and all signs that the horses had been in and helped themselves to the wheat. Of course, everybody knows that a pint of wheat will kill a horse, and the chance of doing anything about it depends upon whether the horse has had any water after his unwise meal. If he's had a good drink, there ain't much that can be done to save him. On this occasion the water trough stood in the yard, and the chances were that Dad would lose both his horses. He was distracted with worry, for it would have meant the end of farming for him.

But as it turned out, he had disturbed the horses afore they had had enough wheat to do them any harm; they both survived, but poor old Dad had a heart attack, and died about a week later.

(A few years later, we had a similar occurrence. I had bought a condemned army horse, named Short. He had been somebody's pet, I'll bet, for a more loveable and intelligent animal of his kind I never come across. He was a good worker, too, and when he got so that he couldn't do much work, I hadn't the heart to sell him. So I pensioned him, and a nice life he had, just browsing about the yard and the farm. But he was the craftiest old animal I ever knew. The barn door led straight out into the horse yard, so of course we had to be very careful to fasten the door with a latch that coul'n't easily be undone. But whatever we did with it, Short could find a way to undo it, and he done it once too often. He helped himself to the scrapings in the bottom of a corn bin, and then went straight out and had a good drink. Poor old fellow, he wandered in pain round to the stack-yard, and there he laid when I found him. He gave me such an agonised look as I bent over him, and then, just as if he understood that I coul'n't do anything for him, he rolled over away from me and died.)

When father died, my mother struggled on to keep the farm going on her own, with me to be her general foreman and horse-keeper. Then the war came, and she soon began to make some money. Naturally, I carried a good deal more responsibility than an ordinary workman, but mother only paid me 18/- a week, the same as everyone else. Soon wages began to rise, and before long men were having nearly one-and-a-half times as much as they had had before the war, but mother refused to increase my wages by a penny. She said she coul'n't understand these high wages! (She was always a bit 'near' with money, and I sometimes thought she di'n't try very hard to understand.)

Prices kept rising, though, and I had a wife and family to keep. I di'n't want to make a family row, so I thought I'd better try to get my other source of income increased.

The Drainage Commissioners always met on the second Thursday in October. I asked if I might be allowed to attend their meeting, and state my case. They agreed to my request, but they soon told me that they could not see their way clear to raising my salary. So I resigned, there and then, agreeing to stop on and serve a month's notice to give them time to find a competent man to take my place. The chairman thanked me for this, but neither he nor any other commissioner had the grace or decency to thank me for the forty-five years of faithful service my father and I had given them. I noticed this omission, and I also noticed that they di'n't seem very upset at the thought of losing me. I soon found out the reason for that, though. One of my so-called friends had got wind of my intention to ask for a rise, and had gone behind my back to the chairman of the Commissioners (a chemist from Ramsey, a man who I never had any reason to like, for he thought his little mo'sel of education had made him a different sort of man from the rest of us), and had offered to do the miller's job at the old rate of pay. Within two days of the Commissioners' meeting, this other chap came to see me, and asked if I would take him and instruct him in all the intricacies of milling, during the month's notice I was to serve. I wasn't very pleased with him, I can tell you. I refused to have anything to do with him; I told him that when my month was up I should deliver the key of the mill up to the chairman of the Commissioners, and nobody else, and I indicated that when they gave him the key, they could give him his instructions about running the mill, as well. As I let him know, plainly, I di'n't care about him having the job, but I di'n't like the way he had got it.

When he took over, he remarked to his mate 'Ah! The water's got to come out now, different from what it has done in Bill 'Arry's time.' His prophecy came true, though not in the way he meant it, exactly. The Commissioners soon had cause to regret their underhand dealing with me, and their hasty choice of my successor. His knowledge of machinery was gained mostly from travelling with a traction engine and a threshing tackle, and as it turned out, he was not a very skilled mechanic. The windmill was never set in motion again after I left, for nobody knowed how to start her going, so there war'n't any worry about how to stop her, and as a windmill she became derelict. The pumping had all to be done with the pump, but that soon came to grief as well. The feed pipe to the boiler stopped working, but the miller di'n't notice, so of course the boiler was soon red hot. The lagging (of wood, cased in with sheet iron) was all burnt away, and a nice mess the poor old girl looked. It was only the mercy of Providence that prevented a serious explosion, and it cost the Commissioners £70 to have the boiler lagged again. I heard long afterwards that the Chairman had accused me of neglect before I left the job, and even of tampering with her, out of spite.

So that was the end of my milling days, though I loved the old mill till the day she fell under the breaker's axe. It is more than thirty years now since I handed in the key, but I still seem to be milling sometimes in my dreams. Often it is a restful, longing sort o' dream, and I wake up wishing I was young again, and just climbing up to the head with my oil can. But sometimes I get into difficulties with the mill now, just as I used to then. Sometimes I am clinging on to the sails and riding round on them, (as I have

77

seen a friend of mine do many a time, though I was always too scared to do it myself, for I hated the thought of hanging upside down as the sail went over the top) or I have seen her, in my dreams, running across the fen on the tops of her sails, about a hundred miles an hour; and up in the air, with her sails going round horizontally, like a helicopter, or flying round so fast that you coul'n't see the sails at all, but only the pin, wobbling about and just on the point of falling out.

I had failed on one job to better myself, so I was now bound to try the other. Mother said she couldn't, and wouldn't, pay more wages, so I was forced to tell her that in that case I should have to leave her and go where I could better myself. I think that was a shock for her, for she said 'In that case, I sh'd think you had better come and take the farm over.' Farming was paying very well, just then, and mother's offer di'n't suit my sisters at all. I went to see the landlord, to see how he felt about it, and met him by accident in St Ives market. I told him the tale as simply as I could, and he replied, 'Very well, Edwards, very well'—so there and then I became a tenant farmer, and some three years afterwards, I bought the farm from the landlord.

We moved from the Lotting Fen to the New Fen in October, and the second night we were there, the Germans came and tried to oust us out again. A Zeppelin came over and dropped a bomb in one of my fields. It was only an incendiary bomb, and a very crude one at that, but it scared everybody nearly out of their wits. A funny thing, I think, that we began, and ended our time at the farm with the sound of a German bomb.

As I was now a farmer with the required acreage of land, I was eligible for election as a Drainage Commissioner, and before long that honour fell to me. So I was sworn in, but within the next few minutes the district's Drainage Officer resigned his post, and before I had had time to realise what was happening, I had been given his job. It was against the rules for a Commissioner to hold office under the board, so I had no choice but to resign my new honour. My career as a Commissioner had lasted approximately ten minutes! My career as a Drainage Officer, however, lasted over twenty-five years, and in the end I had the other job as well. For, many years afterwards, the whole of the drainage system was reviewed, and all our little districts were amalgamated into 'The Ramsey, Upwood and Great Ravely Drainage District,' with a new boards of commissioners. I stood for election, and to my surprise, was head of the poll. My job as a drainage officer had been discontinued, but much to my amusement, I was compensated for the loss of it, by a pension,—of four pounds, twelve shillings, per annum, to be paid on the first of March for the rest of my life.

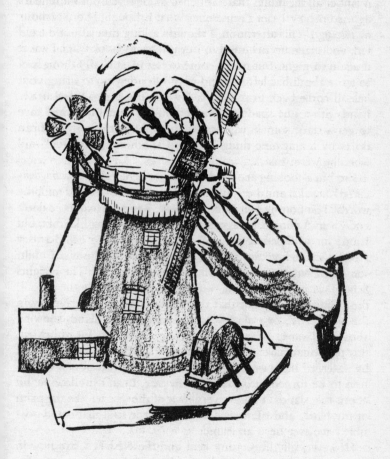

8

I'VE said before that I'm an old man. When you get old, your memory plays you all sorts of tricks, and though I can remember all the things that happened to me seventy or more years ago, somehow I can't remember what I thought about an hour or two ago. This afternoon, I thought a long time about the old fen, and made up my mind to put it into my book when I got at it again to-night. But now I come to 'set in' at it, all I thought of to write about has left me, and what I decided not to write about has all come back to me, now. I were allus a good deal better hand with a turf spade than a pen, in any case, but I shall have to get a start, somehow, because the only sort of writing I can do is by letting one thing bring up another, as the sailor said when he were seasick.

I'm bin a-looking at a book as I'm got here, called *Huntingdonshire Windmills,* and I see, under a photograph of my old mill, the words 'The Lotting Fen Pumping Mill, Ramsey Heights.' I don't know why I should be aggravated by a little thing like that, but I am; for why people will call this part of Lotting Fen 'Ramsey Heights', I do not know. The 'Heights Council Houses' are built, some in Lotting Fen, and some in New Fen, and 'The Heights School' is in Lotting Fen, without a doubt. Inside the school, the children are taught that the word 'Heights' is derived from the word 'aits', or even 'eyots', meaning small islands showing above the water. I can't and won't agree to that; for one thing, this particular part of the fen coul'n't have been entirely covered by water, or there woul'n't have been such a profusion of vegetation to be turned into peat. In any case, I can't swallow the bit about the islands. I know every inch of the district like the palm of my hand, and I fail to identify even one spot that could possibly have ever been an island.

However, all the Lotting Fen, and the New Fen, are now in 'The Heights.' The Post Office authorities have made it so, for the convenience of the postman. It reminds me of one of these conkers that my little granddaughter, Prudence, has to play with. It is a horse chestnut; turn it halfway round, and you would have a chestnut horse. Put four matchsticks in for legs, and you could call him a thoroughbred, but it wouldn't alter the fact that it was still be a conker. So it is with Lotting Fen; it will probably be called 'The Alps' when it gets another new name. When I were a boy, Lotting Fen were Lotting Fen, New Fen were New Fen, and the Heights were the name o' the part where the brickyards were, where the land begins to rise towards the high lands. But it ain't a bit o' good me getting agitated about it, now, 'cos I can't alter it, so I'd better turn my attention to something else.

As I said afore, I went turf digging till the year I were seventeen. That were the year of old Queen Vicky's Diamond Jubilee. It were a very dry summer, that year, and the water all dried up in the but-dykes, and in most o' the rivers as well. We had all the eels we wanted to eat, that time. Poor things—they all gathered together in the last few pools o' water when the dykes and rivers begun to dry up. Then as these little pools evaporated, the eels were left, in their hundreds, with about two inches o' their heads sticking out o' the mud. We could pick 'em out as hard as we liked with a pair o' eel-scissors, but nobody relished 'em a lot when we'd got 'em, for their heads were all one white mass o' fly-blows. That were the year my grandfather died. I liked my old granddad, and I reckon he liked me. He used to chew tobacco. If he were a-doing anything a bit out o' the ordinary, he'd say 'Bor, this 'ere needs a bit more baccy,' and he'd pull his tin out o' his pocket, and roll about a sixth part of an ounce o' 'bacca into a ball, and stow it away in his mouth. I used to have to keep a wary eye on him, 'cos he'd play a mucky trick on me if he could. When 'e 'ad chewed all the nicotine out o' his quid, he'd take it out o' his mouth and watch his chance to snatch my cap off. Then he'd rub the horrible mess o' chewed bacca into my hair, saying 'Ah, bor, you'll be a man when I'm dead and gone.'

I di'n't like my grandmother half so well. She were a masterful old woman, especially to my poor old granddad. He were bent nearly double with hard work, and I should think he must have suffered from the palsy, for his poor old hands shook so he coul'n't hold a cup o' tea without spilling it. 'Tottering ol' fool' were the on'y sympathy he ever got from my grandmother, though.

There's one thing, it weren't the good living he had as kep' 'im alive so long, for e'd lived through some o' the 'ardest times the fen ever 'ad. Try as they might the poor fellows coul'n't wring a living out o' their soggy little bits o' land. They were glad to go to work for somebody as 'ad got a big farm in another fen as were better drained, or in a brickyard, or with a gang o' lighters. This often meant anything up to a six mile walk to and from work, six days a week. They worked like distraction when there were any work to be done, because there warn't no work in wet time and in the depth o' winter very often, but there were no help coming from anywhere else, either. No eye to pity, and no arm to save, as my poor old granddad used to say.

In a long hard winter, many a mother 'as 'ad to tell her hungry child'en that ol' Jack Frost 'ad bin and frez the cupboard doors up so as she coul'n't get 'em open, 'cos there were nothing in the cupboard to give 'em to stop their crying with hunger anyway. I suppose there is some folks about as would say that were a very poetical way o' speaking about it, but there warn't much poetry in it for either the mother of the child'en, nor for their father who coul'n't do anything to help hisself nor them.

When he had any work to do, it di'n't bring 'is family a very luxurious living. Wages fell as low as eight shillings a week, and in the middle o' the century wheat ris in price till it were five pound a quarter. A family o' four or five working men and boys 'ould eat a eighteen stone sack o' flour in a month. There warn't much money left over to buy anything else with. A hunk o' bread and 'a hungin' (an onion) made a-many a working man's meal, and meat were a luxury nearly unheard on. Lucky families, where the father had reg'lar work, 'ould be well enough off to keep a pig, so they could have a bit o' pickled pork in the pot. Other families as coul'n't afford a pig o' their own to kill, used to buy about a pound o' pickled pork for Sundays. The mother o' the family 'ould cut it up into as many bits as there were workers in the house, and the little 'uns 'ould on'y get a drop o' fat or gravy with their 'taters or dumpling. When everybody 'ad got his share, 'e could do as 'e liked with it, though 'e knowed there woul'n't be no more till next Sunday. The bit they got would only be about as big as eight postage stamps put together, and about an inch to an inch and a half thick. If he were very hungry, 'e could eat it all at one go, and feel satisfied for once, even if it meant he woul'n't taste meat no more till next week. Some women took the law into their own hands and decided for their families. They'd cut the ration up into seven bits, and make a pork dumpling for every day o' the week. To do this they just mixed flour and water to a dough (with a bit o' seam if they had such a thing—I sh'd think you'd call it lard) and then make a ball o' dough. Then they'd push their thumb or finger down into the ball to make a hole, and put the little cube o' pork in the middle, and seal it up again and boil it. In this way the tiny bit o' meat flavoured the whole dumpling and made it more appetising. Sometimes it 'ould be made into a 'tater pudden', especially if all the family were coming home at the same time and could eat it hot. Then the pork 'ould be cut up into very small bits, and mixed with sliced up 'taters and onions in a basin, with a thick flour and water dough lining and lid.

A good many o' the families 'ad seen better times, and some on 'em were a bit troubled with a sort o' pride, as well as with hunger and hardship. I'm 'eard my old dad say that his family hated for their workmates to see as they were so hard up as they coul'n't afford a bit o' meat for their dockey; so they'd cut their week's ration in half, and eat half on it a-Sunday. Then they'd take the other bit to work with 'em a-Monday and get it out o' their flagon-basket at dockey time so as it could be seen. Then they'd manage to put it back again and substitute a 'hungin' or a cold 'tater to eat with their 'thumb-bit'; and so the same bit o' meat 'ould go to work with 'em on Monday, Tuesday, Wednesday, Thursday, and on'y be ate a-Friday, when the next week's meat were in sight again.

Some o' the men spent their lives attending to the wants o' the bullocks in the yard o' some big farmer, and they'd take such pride in their beasts' fatness as you'd think they owned 'em themselves; but their families never tasted beef from one year's end to the next, not even at Christmastime, when a joint o' beef and a

83

Dockey time

shilling's worth of oranges were what the better-off families marked the joyful season with. One old fellow as were stockman for a farmer five mile away said he thought he should have the taste o' beef one Christmas Day. He had to get up afore five o'clock and walk five mile to feed 'is bullocks, so 'e said 'e should take a slice o' bread and wipe it round the bullock's behinds. He were on'y 'eving a joke, o' course, but there were a good deal o' feeling behind such bits o' wit. There were another family I knowed myself, as belonged to an old chap what 'ad spent all his life tending sheep, though 'is family di'n't know the taste o' mutton, 'ardly. I say 'hardly' because now and agin, when things got very bad a sheep 'ould get drownded, accidently-for-the-purpose. I knowed old George, the father, myself, and I know as he were an honest, and God-fearing chap, and I can imagine what straights he must a-bin in to 'ave took anything as belonged to 'the mairster', for 'is own conscience's sake; but when you think o' the risk 'e run, into the bargain, you can see 'ow desperate 'e must a-bin.

Dockey fare out in the field consisted mainly o' a hunk o' bread and cheese, or a cold 'tater or a 'hungin'; the cheese had bin kept in the pantry a goodish while afore it were packed up, for the purpose, to make it hard so as the men woul'n't be able to eat so much. The ploughboys used to make a joke on it, and say they never 'ad no need to worrit about their plough wedges a-breaking, 'cos they could allus make do with their dockey cheese as a substitute.

The dockey 'ould be a long way down by the time the next meal were due at three o'clock in the afternoon, when the 'osses were unyoked, so the men used to encourage their 'osses at every turn by chanting:

> Right up and in again
> The pot's on and the pudden's in.

This meal at three o'clock were the main meal o' the day, and the 'pudden' were ate first at it, to take the edge off the men's appetite. Not that it were very appetising as a rule, at any rate by our standards, though as the old proverb says, 'hunger is a good sauce.' The flour the mother had made the pudden with warn't of a very special quality, to start with. Very often it 'ad been gleaned by the mother and the little children, and would 'ave a lot o' barley with it. In a wet 'arvest, it 'ad very often growed in the ear afore they gleaned it. Then it went to the village miller, who coul'n't, and di'n't, grind it very fine. So it would be coarse, and dark, and perhaps a bit fusty. To make the pudden all the woman could do mostly were to mix the flour with some water to a dough, and wrap it up in a bag and boil it in a long oval iron pot hung over a turf fire. When the pudden were done, it 'ould come out o' the pot about as far round as a dinner plate, a flat disc about four inches thick, dark grey in colour, and covered all over with a thick slimy skin as you could take 'old of and peel off like orange peel. It 'ould be as 'ard and tough as leather, but it were helped down with a mixture o' vinegar and brown sugar.

My old grandmother made one o' these 'water-wallopers', as they were called, one day, as wou'n't be forgot in a hurry. I ought to explain that by the time this happened, my family had

recovered financially a bit, partly through the little they got
extra from the milling job, partly because they had more land
than a good many others so that when the fen did get a bit better
drained, they could make use on it, and no doubt partly because
there were four healthy strapping sons to do a good deal o' the
work without much recompense. So at this time there were not
quite the same need for 'em to live as 'ard as they 'ad to do once,
and as many a family still 'ad to from sheer necessity. But as I'm
said afore, my grandmother were a mean old gal, and it di'n't
worry her that her family lived 'ard, if she could scrape a shilling
or two together to save. What were good enough for other folk
were good enough for them, were 'er motto, so she fed 'em on
water-wallopers to the last. Well, this day she made one as were
specially 'ard. When she dished it up, she set it in front o'
grandad. He picked up 'is knife and fork to cut 'isself a slice—you
'ad to 'ave a knife to get it to bits, but in any case most folks ate
everything with their knife. The knives had usually bin wore
down till they were on'y about three inches long in the blade, and
the forks had three little short tines as sharp as needles, and the
same little black bone 'andles as the knives. Well, grandfather
pulled the pudden towards him and went to stab the fork in to
'old it firm while 'e cut 'isself a slice; but the pudden were so
'ard, 'is fork bounced right off. So 'e took the fork into 'is right
'and, so as to have more power over it, and stabbed again, with
all his might. This time the prongs o' the fork went in, but the
pudden never broke. So 'e picked the whull pudden up by the
fork, till it rested a-top o' his fist, and then 'e slewed it—with all
his might across the kitchen. It travelled beautiful across the
table, and hit the opposite wall with a loud plop, *but still never
broke*. 'B—— sich pudden as that' said he.

But by this time, two other things 'ad 'appened. One were that
the four sons, who 'ad been sittin' at the table waiting for their
share o' the pudden, 'ad seen the funny side on it. I know there's
folks as think fen tigers are very nearly like animals, without
much sense and with 'ardly any feeling. But that ain't the truth,
by a long chalk. A real fenman's usually got a real good sense of
'umour, and it usually comes out when things are getting a bit
awkward, especially if he can turn the joke against 'isself. I'm

read somewhere that some old Greek said that laughter was a sort o' declaration o' freedom, and a refusal to give in to your troubles. I reckon that's about it. Anyway, my father and 'is three brothers jumped up from the table and picked up the pudden, and away they went with it outside. One on 'em fetched a spike o' the sort they used for thatching, and another one o' the great heavy beetle-'ammers they used to split black oak with. Then they started solemnly to nail the pudden on the gatepost.

Now I shall 'ev to explain the gatepost. It were a log o' wood set upright, like other gateposts, and when it 'ad first been put in, the gate 'ung in its proper place. But years of draining 'ad lowered the peat all round it till the gate 'ung up in the air by this time. There's many a gate in the fens that it's a lot easier to go underneath than to go through. Anyway, this 'ere gatepost were fairly tall, and the ol' boys 'ad to climb up on something to nail the pudden on top. While they were busy at it, an old neighbour come by. When 'e got to them, 'e stopped and watched, but cou'n't make out what they were doing, an' they never told 'im. When 'e cou'n't bear it no longer, 'e said 'What the 'nation dew yew young davils think you're a-dewin' on?' and the one as

87

were at the top o' the gatepost looked down in as 'aughty a way as 'e could, and replied 'Well, Mr Jackson, we're a-gooin' to 'ev a knob on our gatepost same as other gentlemen.'

Inside the house, the incident warn't over, neither. My ol' grandmother were a deep 'un, an' no mistake. She use to 'ev fits —well that is, she *could* 'ev a fit when she liked, and she very often took to this method as a way out when things got a bit difficult for 'er. It appears as she really could make 'erself go off, and I'm 'eard that wherever she were touched when she was in one o' these fits, she bruised all over as if she'd bin threshed with a stick. When she saw that poor ol' grandad 'ad really got 'isself worked up about the pudden, she promptly 'ad a fit and fell down on the 'earthrug. The poor ol' chap, who were really as mild as a sucking duck and coul'n't bear to upset anybody, were in a state then. When the boys come back in, they found their poor ole father down on 'is knees pushing the door key atween their mother's teeth and promising 'er if she'd on'y come round quick, 'e'd never throw the pudden away again, 'owever 'ard it were.

It may be funny for us to look back on, but I reckon it warn't so funny to any o' the family then. Grandmother really were a queer old woman though, and di'n't merit a lot o' sympathy except in the same way as any woman as 'ad to endure such conditions did. She were such a 'ard old woman, and 'ould do even 'er own child'en down to save a 'apenny. Poor old grandad 'ad the palsy, and 'is 'ands used to shake. He coul'n't pick up a cup o' drink without slopping some of it over on the tablecloth, and this used to make 'er savage. 'Totterin' ol' fool' were all the sympathy 'e ever got.

There were one daughter in this family, and she took after 'er mother. When she got married, she looked for a man who 'ad a bit o' money, as well as a desire to get more if 'e could. They spent their lives pinching and scraping, and as they never had chick nor child to care for, they soon 'ad a tidy bit in the bank. When grandad were dead, and grandmother got old, she went to live with this couple. One Sunday morning my dad got up and announced to my mother that 'e felt it were about time 'e paid 'is mother a visit. The village where she lived were several miles away, and there were on'y one way o' getting there, and that were to walk, so 'e knowed as 'e'd be a goodish while gone. My mother, who were on the mean side herself, ha'n't got no illusions about her sister-in-law's hospitality, so she packed 'im a thumb-bit up in a red 'andkercher and away 'e went. He got there well afore Sunday dinner time, and as soon as 'e got in the house, his nose told 'im that they were gooin' to 'ave a fowl for dinner. (Telling my mother about it afterwards, he said 'I dessay it were one as 'ad got drownded.') He were very surprised, when dinner time come, to be offered a bit of it, but he accepted and they set down to it. Whether it was that he on'y had a little bit, or that after 'is long walk 'e were extra-specially 'ungry, I don't know, but 'is plate were cleaned up first. His sister, in an un-wonted flash of liberality, said 'John, will you 'ev a bit more?' but before 'e could answer, 'er 'usband looked up from the bone 'e were a-gnawing and thumped the table with 'is 'and. 'Don't *'awk* it, missus' he said, '*it'll git ate.*'

I never could understand why folks as 'ad lived so 'ard cared about spending a bit to make theirselves comfortable when they could a-done, but I dare say it were fear o' the workhouse in their old age. When this old couple died, they were worth a goodish bit o' money, but it all went to the other side o' the family, and I reckon the way it were spent then must a-made them turn in their graves. But I dessay they warn't resting any too comfortable, anyway. After 'is wife were dead, the ol' man robbed the corpse of 'er wedding ring and ear rings, 'cos he cou'n't abide the thought of a bit o' gold being buried with 'er.

Folks who lived on pickled pork and water-wallopers for most o' the year looked for'ard to the one good meal they got at the 'arvest supper. Corn 'arvest ended in September, as a rule, and most o' the farmers had a horkey then. The men who went to it 'ould make the most o' their chance while it lasted. There were one ol' fellow who had a-many a good point to recommend 'im, particularly for work, but 'e were a glutton when there were any-thing 'e could get at. One year, at the 'arvest supper, 'e were given a real good 'elping o' roast beef and baked pudden. He started to shovel it down 'im as 'ard as ever 'e could, keeping 'is bright little eyes fixed on the serving woman while 'e ate. When she got near enough to 'im, 'e turned to 'er and said, 'Cut me a bit more o' that there pudden, afore it's all gone; I could eat a nacre o' that.' So she done what 'e asked, and give 'im another big helping; but 'is eyes were bigger than 'is belly, and when the second course arrived, 'e were took aback, 'cos 'e found 'e really coul'n't eat all 'e'd got on 'is plate and leave room for some sweet course an' all. He were in real distress, and tried to slide some o' the baked pudden off 'is plate an' on to 'is neighbour, but the neighbour weren't willing to 'elp 'im, an 'e 'ad to give in.

This same chap used to kill pigs for people. Soon after I got married, we 'eard tell of imported foreign meat for the first time. There were a chap as used to sell it on Ramsey Market Hill a-Saturdays, and as 'is name 'appened to be 'Hugo', the meat 'e sold were called 'Ugo' arter 'im. There were a lot o' argument about it at first, and there were a lot o' folks as said 'they coul'n't touch a mossel on't even if they were a-starvin''. We thought we should like to give it a trial, so one night my wife and her best friend set out to fetch us some. They left me and the other husband in charge o' the children, and away they went, got what they wanted, and walked the four miles back again, carrying their heavy purchases. We tried it for the first time, and after that we often had some.

Well, it happened that we had got some for tea one day when old Jack Small came to our house to kill a pig for us; he was one who had declared against it, and said 'his stummick 'ould 'eave at the very soight on it'. He had been at work all the afternoon, cutting up the pig and so on, and he always reckoned to get his tea into the bargain. So at about the time that I was expected home from work, my wife cooked a lovely thick foreign beef steak, about three pound and a half, enough for all our teas. Small used to ask his hostess if she would get him something different to pork, as he had too much pig as it was when he was killing.

When the tea was ready, my wife put the steak, surrounded by lovely gravy, on a big dish, and placed it in the middle of the table. Then she called Small to come for his tea. He come—he sat down at the end of the table, and drawing the whole dish towards him, began to eat ravenously. Me and my wife looked at one another, a bit flabbergasted at seeing our tea as well as his'n disappearing, but none on us never said nothink. After a minute or two my wife pulled herself together, and asked me if I should like a bit o' cheese for my tea. So that's what we had, while he went on eating the steak.

'This is a beautiful bit o' steak,' he said, 'a bit o' the best as I'm ever tasted. It's different from that there foreign stuff as some people 'ev so much on now; I coul'n't touch a mossel o' that. I could tell it anywheer, afore I could get near enough to taste it, b' the smell on it.' He went on eating,—I caught me wife's eye, and I thought we should 'ave t' laugh, but we never said a word.

When he had finished it all except a tiny little bit, he laid down his knife and fork, and said 'You've done too much at me, missus; I really can't eat that last little bit.'

'Ah,' said my wife. 'I'm glad you enjoyed it. Do you know what it is you're had?'

'Ah,' said Small. 'That a-dew. I'm 'ad as good a bit o' beef steak as I'm ever 'ad.'

'You're had the first bit o' foreign beef as you're ever tasted,' said my wife.

His eyes nearly popped out of his head. He made as if to reach, and said 'Aughrrrrr. I could spew it all up again.' I thought then, and I still think, that that is just what should have happened to him. I were allus a fairly good eater myself, when I'd been to work all day, but I never had much use for that sort of a glutton.

He was a great pillar of the chapel, and when they used to hold a chapel tea, he would be at work all the afternoon, getting ready, serving, fetching hot water to fill up the urns, and clearing away afterwards. From the moment he arrived he would start eating cake from the tea provisions, and he would go on eating it continually all the time he was there. I used to marvel at him, then, for one slice of that 'shop cake' would give me indigestion for hours. But he used to say that nothing would ever turn his stummick, and if it did, it were just the same the other side.

I mustn't do Jack Small any injustice, however, by dwelling on his capacity for eating without mentioning some of his good points. He worked for the chapel as few other men have ever done. He was Superintendent of the Sunday School, and in the days when there was no organ at the chapel, he went on, undaunted, to teach the children their new hymns for the Anniversary. He did not know a single note of music, but he walked the four miles there and back to Ramsey, where he learned the tunes and the words. Then he would teach his Sunday school children by ear, and a very creditable job he made of it, year after year.

He was the district molecatcher, and had thousands of acres of land to keep clear of moles. He would sit up at night, hour after hour, making his mole traps, till he fell asleep from utter weariness, and would rest where he sat, still in his clothes, till he woke, ready dressed to be off to work the next morning.

He had 3d. per acre per year, for this job. He earned more money than any other man in the fen, for he worked like distraction, and it was said of him that 'he ha'n't a lazy bit o' flesh on him'.

I've said a good deal about eating, but very little about drinking. Land work is very thirsty work, and most men took a bottle of something to work with them in their flagon baskets. It would be cold tea, generally, but in harvest the women used to make a special effort to provide something particularly 'squenching'. We used to grow horehound in our garden to make horehound drink, while some folks had a sort of homemade beer. We had all sorts of other herbs in our garden as well, to be used in the preparation of homemade medicines and salves. Wintergreen ointment, adder's tongue ointment, and rue tea are some that I can remember, the last being the bitterest physic I ever tasted. But worse than any other I hated the brimstone and treacle, with which we were regularly dosed, and I shall never, never forget having the whooping cough, for mother's cure for that were to make me eat a fried mouse. I don't know why I should care about eating a mouse, but I did, and now, arter seventy odd year, like old Jack Small and the foreign beef, I could cag at the very thought on it.

9

I 'M bin a-thinking about what we used to get up to a-Sundays.
There were a church at St Mary's, against Hitson's Bridge,
built by the goodness of Lady de Ramsey, right opposite the
school we 'ad to go to. Some families in the fen went there,
mostly the big farmers, and as they were the on'y ones as kept
maids, their maids used to have to go to church. So very often
us young men 'ould go to church more to see the gals than to 'ear
the preacher, after we got growed up a bit. Besides, it made us
somewhere to get dressed up and go to of a Sunday, and I daresay we needed a bit of instruction. It wasn't an old church, by a
long chalk, but I used to sit there an' wonder however folks ever
got clever enough to build such a place: and when I used to see
a real old church, like Ramsey's, or like Ely Cathedral, it real
used to make me feel queer to think how ordinary men ever come
to think o' such places, let alone ever start on 'em and carry 'em
through. But 'our' church di'n't get used a lot by my gang of
associates, on'y for weddings and funerals, 'cos we had the
Wesleyan chapel a sight nearer, for one thing, and for another, it
seemed as if we 'ad more aright there than we 'ad in church, what
was run by the big farmers and the rich folk. I used to like to hear
the parsons at the church talk, with their eddicated voices and
their long words, but they were a queer lot, all the same, and
thought theirselves a lot better than the folk they were supposed
to serve in the Lord's name. Whenever we met old Parson Harper
or his wife, we had to stop until they'd gone by, and touch our
caps and bow our heads, and the girls 'ould 'ev to curtsey. I'm
sure now, looking back on it, as they thought they were doing
their duty by us, but though I were never proud, I hope, and am
allus been willing to give credit where it's due, I could never
bring myself to understand how it come that people who were
supposed to be following the Lord's example could be so 'ikey':
and I used to remember how Peter and Andrew and James and

John were fishermen quite as ig'orant as I was, and though they were chose from outa the whull world by Christ his very self, they never got to making other poor folks bow down to 'em. Perhaps they did get above theirselves now and again, like when they rebuked the children, but they soon got put in their places again.

We had to use the parish church for getting married or buried, 'cos it were many and many a year afore our chapel 'ad a licence to marry anybody; but at all other times we went to chapel. It seemed more in keeping with us, somehow. My family were all Weslyans, so of course I went there as a child, an' I dare say that's got a good deal to do with my feeling about it. I were allus connected with it, and the Sunday school there, and I were a trustee right up to the time 'Itler moved me, and after, until they wrote an' asked me to resign. I were 'urt about that, not 'cos I didn't see their p'int, but becos I thought they might a-knowed as I ha'n't left the fen o' my own accord, and they might let me die in the 'arness I'd wore for so many year. It 'ould be good for a lot o' young folks to remember that old 'uns have pride left even when their usefulness is over, and though we're willing enough for 'em to take over the job o' holdin' the reins and whipping the world along, we still like to sit where we can see the road in front.

I used to be frit to death at the old men who run the chapel when I were a child. For one thing, my mother were so strict with my upbringing that any grown up made my knees tremble and a lump stick in my throat when I tried to speak. But the leaders in chapel were associated in my mind with the tales they used to tell us littl'uns at Sunday school about hell-fire and the bottomless pit, and the Angel of Death coming to fetch good children to heaven and the Devil coming to fetch bad children to hell, and so on. I used to sweat all over wondering which one on 'em 'ould come to fetch me, for I used to come out o' Sunday school convinced I coul'n't live till the next Sunday. This warn't much to be wondered at come to think on it, 'cos a lot of children did die. I suppose they died because they warn't fed well enough, and ha'n't got no strength to fight against any ordinary children's illnesses. Then they were allus wet through, dragging along with

94

'A moment's time, a moment's space
Shall waft you to that 'eavenly grace
Or shut you up in 'ELL!'

mud up to their knees or else through long grass down the dyke-sides, and its no wonder they died o' consumption, or 'went into a decline' as it were called then. Things like diptheria made a lot o' gaps in families, and of course, there were allus children a-getting drownded, falling off planks or playing too near the dipping holes. When I had children o' my own, I used to say to my wife 'If you miss one on 'em, don't stop to look or call, run straight to the dipping hole', but thank goodness she never 'ad no need to, though my son tells me that he fell in the Catchwater once and would a-bin a doner on'y for his little friend Willis, who got a bit o' stick and pulled 'im out with it. Willis's little brother Ailwyn wasn't so lucky as to have a friend there, and he were drowned. To get back to the chapel, though. It did mean a lot to the folks in that old fen. They believed every word they were told there, and I think most 'on 'em tried to live as good lives as they could accordin' to their lights. My old grandad used to go in his half-high-hat, and when he got to his seat he'd put his hat upside down on the floor and swack his handkerchief down in it afore buryin' his face in his hands and praying into them. All

95

over the chapel there'd be folks a-doing the same, groaning out loud as they confessed their sins o' the week and pleading for the folks they loved as were bad at home, and so on. There were none o' the death-like silence that there was in the church, especially at the prayer meeting that very often followed the normal service. Of course in theory the youngsters warn't expected to stop to the prayer meetings, but my father and mother used to stop, and I 'ad to wait for 'em. That was another time I used to be scared to death. The old men used to come out to the front, one after another, to 'testify'. Sometimes they'd tell us what sinners they'd been till they found the Lord, and make my hair stand up with tales of what might 'ave happened to them if they han't been saved in time. They'd get excited and shout and rave, sometimes, and sometimes they'd get overcome with emotion and not be able to speak for a minute or two. All over the chapel the others 'ould be a-sitting, and exclaiming and groaning as they listened. 'Ah!' ''Tis so!' 'Thank the Lord!' 'Amen to that!' 'Praise be!' and so on. They may a-bin a poor, ignorant lot by modern standards, but what they lacked in knowledge they more'n made up in feeling. I should like to see anybody now showing such penitence, or such a desire to testify to the God he believed in. There's one thing, if the poor old folks o' my fathers and grandfather's times ha'nt 'av 'ad something to a-believed in, they'd never a-got through life at all. But after a Sunday spent praying and praising they were rested and comforted, and filled with enough strength in body, mind and spirit to tackle the next hard week.

Talking about how frightened I used to be, I remember one occasion particularly, when a preacher had come from a long way off to preach. I were sitting at the back o' the chapel with a lot o' other old boys, all on us twelve or thirteen year old, and we couldn't believe our eyes 'ardly when we see a man come in who were a reg'lar 'out-n-outer', an' ha'n't no religion on'y beer and bacca and using his fists on his missus and kids. We wondered whatever 'ad made him come to chapel, and thought he must be turning over a new leaf: but we soon found out, 'cos when the preacher started to preach, this 'ere chap got up and shouted out loud 'I say, Mister, who made God?'

In the shocked hush that followed the question, I were so frit that I darn't move to see what were happening up in the pulpit. I couldn't believe but what God would strike the man dead where he stood, that the chapel would crash down on top of us all, that we should go up in flames like Sodom and Gomorrah, or be changed to pillars o' salt. When nothing happened, I begun to raise my 'ead and see the chap what 'ad asked the question loungin' out o' the door. I were ready enough to do as the preacher said and get down on my knees to pray for 'our poor misguided brother'. I felt as we'd all been spared a terrible calamity and we'd got a lot to be thankful for. It appears as somebody 'ad bet the chap a pint o' beer that he darn't come in an' ask the question. He'd won his pint o' beer alright, but I shouldn't be surprised if his knees didn't shake as much as mine did, in spite o' his not believing in nothing.

Most o' the services were took by 'local' preachers, though it depends what you mean by 'local'. They were lay preachers from the other villages round about, but some on 'em come from as far away as eight or nine mile, and ha'n't no way o' travelling on'y Shanks's pony. One man I knowed walked eight mile or so each way nearly every Sunday to take a service somewhere. The congregation used to take it in turns to have the preacher to tea, and a great occasion it were for the family. The child'en 'ould all be schooled for days aforehand about minding their manners, and then they'd all sit round the table scrubbed and washed and not daring to speak while the stranger were there. One poor woman what 'ad come from a better family but 'ad married and had a big family, and 'ad got very poor—gone down hill, used to look for'ard to having the preacher. She'd go to such a lot o' trouble to save and pinch to get a few special things together to eat for the great day. Once when it were 'er turn, she'd got the table all set and the visitor just ready to sit down when one of her older child'en come 'ome unexpectedly and stared at the table and then said 'What a' yer got a sheet on the table fo' mother?' Poor woman were confused, but the ol' boy didn't know no better. He'd never seen a white tablecloth affore, if 'ed ever seen one at all. The best a lot o' folks had were sacks cut open, made of a sort of grey linen stuff, what the farmers had seed in.

The preachers used to have their favourite places to go, and no wonder. They deserved whatever little bit o' recompense they got, for they were good, faithful men for the most part. Some on 'em couldn't read at all, and had to learn by 'eart everything they were likely to want for the service, hymns and psalms and readings from the Bible and all the lot. Some on 'em could only put two or three words together at a time, and talked 'in stelches' as we allus said, and some 'ould be so thin and weak you'd think they wouldn't have enough strength to get up the steps to the pulpit. There'd be them as would use a lot o' long words as they di'n't properly know the meaning on, but then, more di'n't we, so it di'n't matter, and them 'as 'ould get so worked up they'd lay across the front o' the pulpit and hammer it wi' their fists and shout and then sink their voices down to a whisper and make your flesh stand up all over with goose pimples.

Us children were allus very much in awe of 'em, as I'm said afore, but when we growed up we used to laugh and make fun on 'em a lot more than we ought to a-done, for they were doing what they thought they ought to as well as ever they could, and that's more than we were, most on us. Still, there were some cures amongst 'em, and there were times when you really had to laugh.

There were the time when one poor old chap got took back when he found that the Bible in the pulpit had only got Roman figures in it. He'd learn't off by 'eart the psalm he were going to 'read' for the lesson, but 'ed forgot what number it were. He could read just well enough to find his way about the Bible, when he knowed what 'e were looking for, and 'e turned over the pages in a hurry to see what number to announce. There it were in front of 'im 'Psalm CIV': so he spelt it out to hisself and then announced 'We shall now read Pislam Siv' by which name the beautiful hundred and fourth psalm has been known to my family ever since. Then there were the one who allus told some sort of a story with a moral, if you could find it. He came from a family o' three brothers as were all local preachers, and they all talked in stelches, even in ordinary conversation. In the pulpit nervousness made them worse, and what George had to say on one occasion come out about like this.

Now—there were a man—weren't a good man—in fact—'e were a thief. One night—went to rob—another man's—orchard.—Took a lantern—'ad to climb—over a wall—dropped his lantern—went out—couldn't see where 'e were going—run into a hive o' bees—knocked it over.—Bees come out—stung 'im—begun to run—come to the wall—Jumped over the wall—into a pond—deep pond—couldn't swim—got drownded—that were th'end on im—Hymn fower hundred—fowerty four.

If there's any eddicated folks as read this they'll wonder what we went to chapel for to 'ear preachers like this: but for every queer one there were five as 'elped us all to find some sort o' belief, and most of us who thought at all honoured 'em for doing what we ha'n't got the courage to do, stand up in front of a lot of other folks and testify to our faith.

Of course, there were a few who done it for the wrong reasons, because it brought 'em trade, if they were shopkeepers, or because they liked to show off, perhaps. There were one man who used to come round the fen from Peterborough, regular, selling things to the women at the doors o' their houses. We used to call him Jeremiah. He were a local preacher on our 'plan', and when he got up in the pulpit he really could preach a good sermon. It stood him in good stead in his business, because apart from saving their trade for them, any o' the families as could afford it 'ould invite 'im to a meal. He nearly allus used to get to our 'ouse when my wife were dishing up the tea, and nine times out of ten 'ed share anything we 'ad. We begun to notice how regular this got, and specially when we found out by chance 'as he mostly used to manage to be at our best friend's place for dockey time. We talked it over and decided not to be quite so liberal, 'cos 'ed lower as much grub as the rest of either family put together. One day when it was his day on our 'round' with his suitcase, my wife got our tea early on purpose, so we'd finished it when he come: but she were just putting a bit of jam roly-poly away for one o' our children who were coming in late. His eyes nearly dropped out when he see we had finished, but 'e caught sight o' the pudding in my wife's hand and offered to buy it. We didn't like to think of 'im walking back to Peterborough 'ungry, so she give 'im it, and when he'd had it, my wife had a bright idea and produced a missionary box we allus kept, and stood it in front of him. 'If you want to pay for your tea' she said 'you can put 3d. in there.' He were took back, for he never thought we should take anything for it: but he never give way. 'No, thank you, missus,' he said, 'I never did believe in missionary work. I like to do my little bit to my poor fellow creatures at home.' So he got it for nothing after all. The friend at whose house he mostly had his dockey warn't a chapel going man at all, but Jeremiah used to talk so earnestly to him that at last he promised to go to chapel next time J. preached. He did, and he were so impressed that he started to go regular. Then one day he were on his way 'ome from work, along the river bank, when he stumbled on J. lying in the long grass with a girl what had a very bad reputation. My poor old friend were upset and shocked, and come up to tell us about it. He summed the situation up, as fenmen usually do, in very few words. 'He's no Christian' he said. 'He's more for guts than God.'

10

TURNING the turf was an agonising, back-aching job. Turning all day long,—about twelve thousand turf in a day,—made the worker feel sick and bad with the pain in his back. A good many real old turf men growed to stoop so much that in their later life they looked more like four-footed animals than human beings. I can remember a good many of them, 'Bent' Townsend, Bob Carnell, 'Sosh' Chapman, 'Bam' Moore, 'Smooker' Etherds—(Edwards, my grandfather,)—and Old Henry.

Henry spent nearly every summer of his life in the turf fens, and most of the winters at work in the dykes; and gradually his

back became more and more bent, till his head were lower than his back were. He used to walk with the help of two sticks, and really, he did look like a quadruped. One day during the first World War, I were a-standing on the road outside my farmyard, when Old Henry come along the road with his two sticks. He'd bin to Ramsey to fetch his Old Age Pension. When he got to me he stopped and spoke. He were too bent to stand upright at all, so he turned his face sideways to speak to me.

He pulled a red pocket-handkercher out of his pocket and wiped his face. 'It's 'ot, Bill,' he said.

'Ah, Henry,' I said, 'It is 'ot.'

He said, 'It's a long way for me to 'ev to walk to fetch me pension, fower mile each way, but it's wuth it.'

I told him I thought there ought to be some sort of arrangement made about getting the old chaps like him their pensions, so that they di'n't have to go all that way.

He said 'Ah, well. I think I'll be a-poking me way orf 'um. Good-day Bill.'

So I said 'Good-day, Henry.' And away he went with his sticks about three mile an hour.

A few minutes later, while I still stood out there, up come a young fellow with a hoss and cart. 'Whoa,' he hollered, when he see me and stopped. 'Did you see Old Henry?' he asked.

'Yis,' said I, 'I'm just bin a-talking to 'im.'

'Well,' he said, 'my 'oss were frit at it. I am had a job to keep 'im on the road.'

So you can imagine what a sight poor Old Henry was after all the years of turf-digging.

In 1921, we had a very dry summer. The main drain in our district, running up to our oil engine, were dry. I was the district Drainage Officer at the time, and I thought it were a good time to get the drain cleaned out. So I got together a gang of men to do it, and Old Henry was one of them. One day I were doing something a little way away from the rest of the men, when Henry left the gang and come up to me.

He said, 'I wanted to git yer by yerself Bill, fer a minit or tew, 'cos I'm got som'ink to tell yer. Yairss,' he said, 'I'm in trouble.'

'A-yer, Henry?' I said.

'Yairss, Bill,' he said, 'I'm done wrong.'

'Ah. There's a good many on us as is done that, Henry,' I replied.

'Well,' he said, 'I'm bin a-working over at the "Mollo", and I'm bin a-drawing me old age pension an' all. I'm got to appear at the bench a-week-a-Wednesday. I'm got me a blew paper. I don't have no peace o' mind in the daytime, an' I don't 'ev no sleep o' nights. I dew 'ope they w'u'nt gaol me.'

'They woul'n't gaol an old man like you, Henry,' I said. 'You ain't stole nothink, as far as I can see. You worked for what the "Mollo" paid you, and arter all they give you the pension.'

'Well,' he said, 'I never looked at it like that. It's a little over sixty pound. You're the fust one I'm told. I'm sure I feel better fer what you're said'—and away he went to work again.

(The 'Mollo' was the nearest approach the old man could manage to the name of a large firm, who during the first war, bought some turf land and experimented with the peat, mixed with mollasses, as a type of cattle food.)

A-week-a-Wednesday came and Henry appeared 'before the beak'. The chairman of the magistrates, one of Ramsey's mighty men, addressed poor Old Henry, and reprimanded him severely.

'The magistrates have taken a very lenient view of your case,'

he said, 'as you are such an old man. But you are a very wicked and dishonest old man, and although we shall not punish you in any other way, you must pay all the money you have had dishonestly, back again. You can either pay it all back now, and then go on drawing your pension as usual, or we will have your pension stopped, until all you owe has been paid off.'

Henry had saved some of the money he had earned, so he paid off what he could, and then his pension was stopped until he had paid off all the remainder. He said he didn't care, so long as they didn't punish him. Poor old fellow. I reckoned up that as he had walked over eight miles every Friday for that pension, it made it well over a thousand miles he had walked for that sixty pounds he had to pay back. I'm afraid I shou'n't never a-bin no good as a magistrate.

A few years after this episode, the magistrate concerned, who had called Henry 'a wicked and dishonest old man', became a bankrupt. He owed several thousands of pounds in all, and many small local tradesmen many times the amount that poor Old Henry got into such trouble about. The bankruptcy brought the magistrate to an untimely end, however, while Henry lived on for another twenty years or more, and died somewhere about halfway between ninety and a hundred.

Henry lived long enough to become quite a character of fen life, very near a legend. He was a staunch Methodist, and never missed chapel or Sunday school all the years I can remember. He always fancied hisself as a bit of a musician; he could play a concertina a bit, and whenever there were any sort of an outdoor function where any music was required, Henry and his concertina supplied it between them. By this time I'm talking about, his back was quite horizontal, and his head even lower, so he found it difficult to keep his balance at all without the aid of his two sticks. But nobody can play a concertina with a stick in each hand, and the poor old chap would be a minute or two a-struggling to maintain his equilibrium before he could begin to play the Doxology, or whatever the required tune were.

I remember one incident that took place in the chapel. The American organ had gone to St Ives to be repaired, but the services went on as usual. On this particular Sunday, Henry had offered to start the hymns off by singing the tune and giving the note. The preacher give out the hymn, and Henry, standing at the back of the chapel, where he allus set to keep 'the old boys' in order, struggled to his feet. After his usual balancing trick, he started to sing. The congregation picked up the tune and joined in. But Henry had chose the wrong tune, a common metre tune

to an irregular metre hymn, and they found that they had a line
or two of words to spare. The singing faltered and stopped, and
Old Henry's voice was heard, from the back of the chapel,
remarking that 'That there wou'n't dew.'

The parson did his best to calm Old Henry's discomfiture, by
remarking 'Our good friend may be a bit out of tune to-night,
but I am sure we shall all be in tune in Heaven.'

One Sunday afternoon my family and I all went off to the
house of another old friend who was laying bad a-bed. When
we got there, we found as several other people had done the
same thing, and among them was Henry. We were all asked to
stay to tea, and our hostess soon prepared quite a spread. When
we set down, Henry said 'I think we had better sing grace.' Now
Henry allus had a habit o' wearing out one tune at a time. On
that day he had in his mind the tune of a real old Methodist
hymn. The words of the hymn are:

> O, Love Divine, how sweet thou art.
> When shall I find my willing heart
> All taken up by Thee?
> I thirst, I pine, I die to prove
> The greatness of redeeming love,
> The love of God for me.

Then, according to the swinging old tune, the last three lines are
repeated again.

Well, Henry started off the grace that begins 'Be present at our
table, Lord,' to the tune of 'O Love Divine'.

All went well for the first three lines.

> Be present at our table, Lord.
> Be here and everywhere, adored.
> Thy creatures bless, and grant that we
> May feast, may feast, may feast, may feast,
> May feast, may feast, may feast, may feast,
> In Paradise with Thee…

But by this time the assembled guests were in great straits to
keep from busting out a-laughing, and could not face the repeat.

The singing broke down, and Henry said 'Ah well, that'll 'ev to dew,' and sat down to his tea.

I never think of this incident without thinking about a grace that one of the wits used to say when we were at work in the turf fen.

> One word's as good as ten.
> Leather away. Amen.

Henry was a bit of a wit hisself. One day he was gaulting for another farmer. By gaulting, I mean digging out the buttery clay to spread on the surface of the land, where the peaty soil were so light that it would blow away. The clay was dug out of a hole, or pit, that would be six to ten feet deep by the time they had finished. Henry was down in a gault pit, throwing out the clay, when the farmer went to see how his men were getting on.

'Hullo, Henry,' said the farmer. 'How ayer gettin' on?'

'Oh, orlright, Mairster,' replied Henry. 'On'y it's me woife as I'm a-thinking about.'

'Oh dear,' said the farmer, all concern. 'Why, whatever's the matter with her?'

'She broke her arm, larst night,' said Henry.

'Oh, that is a pity,' said the 'mairster'. 'However did she come to do that?'

'Well,' said Henry. 'Yer see, mairster, this 'ere job makes me so 'ungry that she broke her arm a-gittin' the pudden out o' the pot fer me tea.'

Poor Old Henry, though he had to work hard enough, never had any real will for it. He did love to be off home to his pipe and his fireside, and any little shower that most men wouldn't have noticed would make Henry think about leaving off. One cold day he was at work with a gang of other men, when it started to snow, just a few small flakes. Henry called out to the others, asking them if they didn't think it was too rough for them to carry on. The others didn't agree that it was bad enough to 'knock them off'.

'Ah, well,' said Henry. 'Let there come *one* more flake, and I'm orf.' Henry was always very forward to do or say anything, and had great confidence in himself. In spite of this he was really a very simple old chap, and he did hate to have to admit that he didn't know about anything that was new. He was at work, one day, with his near neighbour, an old pal of mine, who is blessed with a good deal of humour and a real sense of fun. When 'dockey time' came, they sat down together to eat. Now George had some sandwiches made of pork haslet, a very delicious dish, I always thought. I don't know what Henry had, but anyway, George offered Old Henry some of his sandwiches.

When he had finished it he said 'What war' that there as I'm just had, George?'

'Why,' said George, 'don't you know, Henry? It were Bala-clava Sow. Ain't yer ever had any afore?'

Henry thought for a minute in silence. Then he said slowly, 'Yairss, George, I 'ev. My missus brought some 'um from Peter-borough, and very nice it warr, tew.'

11

I 'M bin out to-night, a-watching my neighbour pulling a old
root out o' one o' his fields. We allus call 'em 'roots' but in
some cases its more like the whull tree as 'as to come out afore
ploughing can continue. I'm talking about the black oaks what
lay buried under the peat, o' course.

Most people don't seem to think much about things as they
have knowed all their lives, but I'm thought a goodish deal about
them old roots, and though as I keep on a-saying, I never had no
schooling and I ain't much of a scholard, I know I'm right about
some things when the gentlemen from Cambridge and sich
places are wrong, with all their book learning.

'The fens' is a pretty big area, and peat forms only a small part
of it. Now all the buried trees lay under peat. I think I'm safe in
saying that, but at least I can say as I *know* its the truth with regard
to the thousands and thousands o' tons o' wood as lay under
Huntingdon and Cambridgeshire.

Round Ramsey, for instance, there's several fens, but not all
on 'em are peat—at least all the *fens* are, but all the land ain't.
Lotting Fen, New Fen, Woodwalton Fen, Sawtry Fen, Holme
Fen, Bury Fen, Upwood Fen and Raveley Fen are all peaty: but
Ramsey Mere, Hall Mere, Ugg Mere, Brick Mere, the Delph,
Middlemoor, Glassmore and Whittlesea Mere are not.

In the fens, the depth o' the peat may vary from about two feet
in some places to as much as twenty in others. Since the fens were
drained, the peat has shrunk down so as you'd hardly believe it
if it weren't for bits of evidence as can't be disproved. One such
bit is in Holme Fen, and I'm seen it many a time. In the year
1852, a column were set up in Holme Fen, and by 1932, eighty
years later, the peat had dropped 10 ft 8 ins away from it, so
as it stuck that much farther out o' the ground than it did at
first. Then in Venturer's Fen, in Cambridgeshire, a gate were put
down so well in the last century that it stands there to this very

day—on'y now the 'osses and carts go underneath it instead o' through it.

A lot o' learned folk have writ books about the ol' fens, an' I never miss a chance o' reading what they have said about 'em, in books like *Fenland Past and Present* and *Fenman's World* and so on.

In *Fenland P. & P.* the author says as these buried trees were all killed by the moss and vegetation what growed in such profusion in them days. Then, he says, the prevailing wind broke 'em off, and the peat growed so fast over 'em that it covered 'em up and preserved 'em. He states that they must have all died in September, or in the autumn at any rate, because of all the nuts, acorns and so on as can still be found with 'em.

Dr Ennion, on the other hand, is of the opinion that a great forest were all laid low by a terrible tornado, and what a crash that must a-bin, he remarks.

Dr Lucas thinks that at one time the whole area of the fen were at least ten feet higher than it is now. It was of a stiff clay what could support trees of gigantic size and heighth, and among which strange animals roamed, because bones have been found resting on the clay. He suggests that there were a sudden subsidence of the whole fen area, of about ten feet, and this would be followed by an inrush of water like a tidal wave. These terrific forces, he thinks, 'ould carry down everything standing in their way: gigantic trees measuring from 80' to 100' tall were torn down and laid flat on the clay, not torn up by the roots, he says, but 'snapped off like a weaver's thread!' He also states that all the trees lay flat on the clay in a N.E.–S.W. direction, and he even says that this is uncontradictable.

He puts the time of the catastrophe as during the Roman occupation, 2,000 years ago or so.

Dr Ennion also thinks about 2,000–3,000 years was the time they fell, approximately, but the authors of *Fenland Past and Present* thought 70,000 to 80,000. On this point I ain't got nothing to say, for the simple reason as I'm got nothing to go by, so I shan't even guess. But I'm got plenty to go by to form my own opinion of what happened, whenever it happened, and I don't agree altogether with any o' the authorities I'm been talking about.

Dr Lucas were a Drainage Commissioner for thirty years, and had to be conversant with all levels and changes of level, and he made his own observations and drawed his own conclusions. So did I. I'm bin connected with fen drainage all my life an' all. I were in charge o' two fen pumping stations at different times: I'm bin a fen farmer, on and off, all my life: I'm bin a Drainage Commissioner, and a Drainage Officer. I'd better explain this last job.

All the fen is divided, for drainage purposes, into districts, and each district is managed by its own drainage commissioners, land-owners and farmers being eligible for election. In our district, you were eligible if you owned twenty acres or farmed thirty. Our commissioners met on the second Friday in April every year, to lay the drainage rate, discuss the work to be done in the coming year, and to appoint a Drainage Officer. This officer then became secretary and treasurer to the board, collecting all the rates, and settling all accounts: but he also had charge and complete oversight of all the work in hand, as well as looking after all dykes and drains, keeping 'em clear o' weeds and reeds and so on, and keeping 'em cleaned out to a depth of 8 to 10 ft.

This is the position I held for more than twenty year. During that time, we enlarged one o' the dykes into a main drain. The new drain had to be cut 8' to 10' deep, with a 12' bottom, for $1\frac{1}{2}$ miles across the fen. The depth brought us right down on to the blue clay, where the old trees lay. And during the whole o' that operation, I took particular notice o' every one as we came across and I drawed my own conclusions, as don't fit altogether with them as I'm mentioned.

For one thing, I don't believe the trees were ever killed by moss and vegetation, because if that had been so, the trees would have rotted as the process went on, and by the time they were dead they'd a-bin beyond preservation. Besides, if it were like that, it must a-bin a long old process lasting many and many a year afore a tree died. Why did they all suddenly fall in the autumn then? Then *Fenland Past and Present*'s authors say that they were broke off by the prevailing wind. In my own experience, the number of trees I'm see *broke off* is very small indeed, and in the majority o' those cases, when the stump has been found, the trunk has disappeared. Well, if the trees was already rotting and then were broke off by the wind, you'd expect to find the trunk a-laying beside the stump —but as I said, most of the trees I'm ever see fell whole and were'nt broke at all though I have seen trunks where no root had bin in evidence.

Now for Dr Ennion's theory, that they were laid low by a mighty rushing wind, and the peat growed up and covered them. This 'ould mean that they all fell at the same time. Well then, why ain't the huge limbs and branches that such big trees must have had, to be found with or at least near the trunks? I can't believe Dr Lucas altogether, either. If, as he says, the whole fen area was, until the subsidence, continuous with and on the same level as the surrounding highlands, then I can't see no reason for supposing that the whole area weren't covered by these great forests —but it's bin proved as there ain't no buried trees more than six mile from the edge o' the high land.

So I shall give my own opinion o' what happened, though it is only a guess, same as the others. I reckon that these trees were part of a big forest as covered the entire country. The land sloped towards the Wash, and the water at that time come up as far as the trees growed so of course they couldn't grow no further. Then some sort o' phenomenon occurred, causing an inrush o' water, probably about ten feet as Dr Lucas says, and just covering the six mile area under which all the trees are to be found. Standing in the water, the trees all died. Their branches rotted off, and the roots got loose in the clay. Then come the strong winds, and they fell one by one before it into the water surrounding them. As the rotten branches fell off the standing trees, they dropped into the water and floated away. You can still find some o' the biggest on 'em, but generally apart from the main trunk. By far the greatest number of the trees lay with their heads to the north-east, as you would expect, seeing as the south-west wind is the prevailing wind. But they don't all lay that way, by any means, proving, or so it seems to me, that they fell before winds from all quarters, one at a time, many and many a year after the inrush o' water. They fell on to the hard blue clay, which o' course 'ould be on the surface then.

I think the water did come in in the Autumn, because o' the hazel nuts and acorns as can still be found. There they lay, perfect to look at, but too soft to handle. I had about a pint o' them at one time, but I've give so many away that I'm only got a handful left, now. When we were at work in the drains, I carried a tin with me, and when we come across any good specimens, I hooked 'em into my tin with my finger, mud and all. Then when I got home, I put 'em in a bowl o' water and cleaned 'em, and very gently lifted 'em out and allowed 'em to dry. They soon hardened, and could be handled, with care. There are many acorns to be found, they must a-growed a lot bigger than the general run o' acorns now. The kernel's gone from them when you find 'em, but the skin and cup is still perfect. I've heard some old men what have worked in the dykes all their lives, say as how they've found walnuts, whole and complete. But I never had the luck to find one, though I looked for twenty year. I think the nuts fell into the water off the standing trees, and floated till they became saturated and sank, though acorns 'ould be heavy enough to sink straight away.

Some o' the trees fell from the south-east. Two trees fell from the south-east beside each other across the corner of a field where the drain turned in a right-angle bend, from north to east. They crossed the drain twice, the middle o' the trees being in the corner of a field. So each tree had to be sawn off four times. In another case I found one what had fell from the south-west, laying right across another as had fell from the north-east.

I'm never found any bones nor anything else to show that either man or beast was alive in the forest: and I shou'n't expect to either: for according to my theory, any animal 'ould have time to reach safety, only six mile away, when the flood occurred. But bones have been found, there's no doubt about that. Only I don't think they need a-died at the time o' the inundation, even if they are found resting on the hard clay. I once see a bullock as got in the dyke in Woodwater Fen. We coul'n't get it out nohow, and it just sunk into the soft bottom o' the dyke and disappeared, poor thing. How far it went down we could only guess, but I hold that if its bones are ever found, they'll be below the peat.

I realise as the bit o' the fen as I know so well is very small, but I'll describe the layers of earth there. Of course, people will say that the fens are all perfectly level 'like a billiard table' they say. In fact, there's considerable differences in the level o' the land. If the layer o' peat is thicker, and the layer o' 'buttery clay' not so thick, there is more shrinkage, and that place gets lower.

On top, the soil is about 15″ thick: then ther's a layer o' peat, usually about 2′ or 3′, though it may be a lot more. Next comes the layer o' 'buttery clay', usually about three feet. After that there's a layer o' the peculiar peat known to us as 'bear's muck', on account of it being so difficult to work. It 'ould stick to all your tools, and the only way to deal with it were to use a wooden scoop called a 'sluff' (or slough—I don't know). The bear's muck varies in thickness, but there's allus a screed of it, no matter how thin, atween the two clays, the hard blue clay and the buttery clay. This screed may be as little as an inch in some places, but its allus there: and it's in this bear's muck as the nuts and acorns lay.

It's the shrinkage o' the peat as brings the trees nearer to the surface o' the land. It's a terrible nuisance to the farmer, because the plough comes into contact with 'em when ploughing deep for celery, potatoes or other root crops. The ploughman used to carry a little bundle o' reed with him. He had a spring foot chain attached to the plough, so that when the plough hit a root off 'ould go the chain and let the horses free. Then he'd get his plough clear, and stick one o' his reeds on top of the place where the root were, to mark the spot so as the old root could be dug up. Strangers 'ould wonder, no doubt, to see reed stuck about all over a fresh ploughed field. Getting the roots out were done in the slack time, generally in winter. The trees have to be split up into lengths and got out somehow. The stumps are allus the worst, 'cos they won't split. We used a beetle and wedges to split the trees, or else a sledge hammer. We never could decide which were more economical, to use the beetle (a large wooden mallet with iron hoops round it), or the hammer. If you used the hammer, you knocked your wedges to bits, and if you used the beetle, you soon knocked that to bits.

The wood o' the trees is carted into heaps where it lays for years, till somebody gets sick on it and burns it out o' the way. The trees are as sound as they were when they were a-growing. They soon split or rift while they are still wet, but if they lay a year or so above ground, they get so hard and tough that it's quite impossible to split them, or even to drive a nail in them, let alone a wedge. They used to be begged for nothing, and hacked up for fuel. Fen folks say as black oak has one advantage over all other fuel. It warms you twice, once getting it a-pieces, and again on the fire.

Old Jackson, as lived in Jackson's Fen, had, at the backstock of his hearth, a strong hook what had a pulley hanging from it. He used to fetch in a whole tree, with a horse, and lay it across the floor, with one end on the hearth and the other under the table. It 'ould last for weeks, being hitched up with the pulley and iron bars as it burned away. You could see the same sight at the 'Speed the Plough'. The landlord there had a lot o' children, and the old tree stretching away across the floor made a real convenient seat for 'em all, and with the help of a few cesses, the end that were

on the hearth blazed away and kept the tap-room a warm and pleasant place, at least as far as warmth were concerned.

Some o' the old stools are terribly difficult to get out o' the land. I've had a many as three tractors on one stool, but couldn't move it for hours. It were as big as the body of a cart, and it still lays there in the corner o' the field where we put it when at last we could get it out. I've read about trees being found that were 80 ft to 100 ft long. Most I've seen 'ould be atween 50' and 60', but I did have to deal with one as were 90' long.

There don't seem to be no use you can put them to, except to make posts when they are split up. They are used for building pigsties and rough hovels, but nothing else. I have seen a few nice walking sticks made of it, but furniture etc. will warp out o' shape and not be worth the trouble it takes to do it. When it is used as posts, it won't last above two or three years at the most. It will last forever under the ground, or above the ground: but a post set upright will rot off at ground level in nearly no time.

I'm sure people havn't any real idea o' the amount o' black oak there is on some farms, but it's nothing to see an advert, in a local paper saying something like

> For Sale. 300 Tons of Black Oak, Suitable for Fuel.

—all from one small farm.

12

I'M allus regretting that I din't get a bit more education than I did: I reckon the tenth commandment is as easy to transgress as any on 'em, but it's the one as I'm never found much call to break. It's allus seemed to me to be one o' the silliest things anybody could do to worry their gizzards with envy or jealousy, and grizzle all the while about something they ain't got and ain't ever very likely to get. And it caps my behind when folks covet what other folks have got, not because they want it, but just 'cos they don't like the other chaps having it. But education's a different thing: there's enough o' that for everybody to have, and nobody need suffer any shortage of it just because more and more folks are getting a bit, and if I'm ever envied anybody anything, it's folks who 'ave got time to read and find out about things as they're interested in, and to go to places and see for theirselves. When I were young I used to think that one day I'd be well enough off to have a boat o' my own and go up and down all the rivers and canals in England for the rest of my days: and if I got through that, I thought, I'd start and walk right round the coast of Great Britain till I got back to where I'd started. But the farthest I've ever got to doing either of these things is in imagination or between the covers of a book. Ah well—I'm very nearly forgot what I were saying. It were about not being as well educated as I should a liked. I suppose I hadn't ought to grumble though. I know how many beans make five.

> Two beans,
> *And* a bean,
> A bean and a half,
> And half a bean.

I know how to count, an'all, like we used to when we went to school,

One's none,
Two's some,
Three's a few,
Four's anew,
And five's a little hundred.

But even the lucky ones who 'ave had all the education they could take, right up to the university at Cambridge, don't get everything right.

I never miss an opportunity o' reading anything anybody else has wrote about the fens, but I do get aggravated with the authors sometimes. They are all eminent, educated men, usually graduates of Cambridge and quite often natives or residents of that county, too, so of course they know it better and are more interested in it than any other county. They nearly allus suggest (and in some cases, even state as fact) that Wicken Fen, in Cambridgeshire, is the only one left in its natural state, and without artificial drainage.

I can hardly believe that these gentlemen have never heard of the existence of Jackson's Fen, Wright's Fen, Payne's Fen and Mowbray's Fen, all lying together in, and part of Woodwalton Fen, in Huntingdonshire. The whole area, covering about six hundred acres altogether, is three times the size of Wicken Fen, and is drained naturally or not at all.

Jackson's Fen is 60 chain long and 40 chain wide, or thereabouts, and covers 240 acres, approximately. It is bounded on the east by a magnificent row of poplars—'the ole popples' we call 'em—about a mile and a quarter long. I'm heard folks say as this is the finest row o' popple trees in all England, but I reckon that's claiming a lot. The river called Raveley Drain runs right alongside these trees on the east of them, and very pleasant it is to be gliding down the stream in a boat, in the shade o' the popple trees, when the sun begins to get round to the west, of a summer evening. The worst about that would be the swarms of mosquitoes hovering about over the water, and biting you whenever they got a chance. They'd fetch up great bubbles on you within a minute or two of them attacking you, and that were all the while, because there'd be so many on 'em you'd just have to

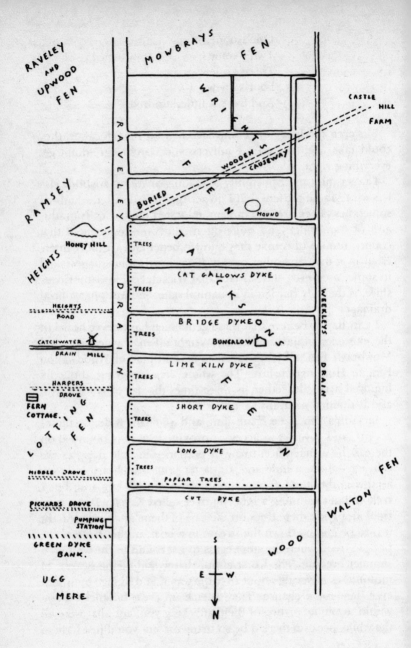

RAVELEY AND UPWOOD FEN

MOWBRAYS FEN

RAVELEY HEIGHTS

RAMSEY

RAVELEY DRAIN

E. PITS

F E N

WOODEN CAUSEWAY

BURIED

MOUND

CASTLE HILL FARM

HONEY HILL

TREES

J A T

TREES

CAT GALLOWS DYKE

C K S

HEIGHTS ROAD

CATCHWATER DRAIN MILL

TREES

BRIDGE DYKE

BUNGALOW

WEEKLEYS DRAIN

HARPERS DROVE

FERN COTTAGE

LOTTING FEN

TREES

LIME KILN DYKE

F E

TREES

SHORT DYKE

E N

MIDDLE DROVE

TREES

LONG DYKE

POPLAR TREES

PICKARDS DROVE

PUMPING STATION

CUT DYKE

WOOD

WALTON FEN

GREEN DYKE BANK.

UGG MERE

S

E — W

N

fight your way through. If we had any visitors stopping with us they'd all want to go and see the turf-fen, but they'd soon wish they hadn't gone and be a-wrapping their legs up in brown paper or something to keep the mosquitoes off. We used to say they never bit real Fen Tigers, and certainly never worried me a lot.

When I first remember, this fen (Jackson's) belonged to the Fitzwilliam family, and a man named Jackson were the tenant. I used to hear tales about this old man when I were a child. It appears that he tried to farm the land, and for quite a little while he had a fair amount o' success. But he were a heathen who actually harvested some of his corn on a Sunday, and after that the land wouldn't grow nothing, never no more. 'What could he expect?' my elders said to each other, when telling the tale. They thought it a just retribution for breaking the fourth commandment, and I've no doubt that hearing this tale in my early youth helped to form the strong reluctance I've allus had about doing anything to further my own interests on a Sunday.

Anyway, old Jackson couldn't farm the fen no more, so he dug it for turf. He had five boat dykes cut through it, and as everything that was took out of them was peat and could be sold, they didn't cost him much and he were well paid for his outlay. He cut the dykes ten chain apart, and invested in five lighters (barges) and sent millions o' turf from his fen to places all over East Anglia. Of course, this lowered the level o' the fen considerable as the time went on.

Old Jackson were 'a bit of a cure' by which I mean that he were a strange, eccentric old fellow. At this time, the day of the cloth-sailed windmills, was just a-drawing to its close, and these old mills were being demolished on every hand. Whenever he heard of a mill being condemned, Jackson made a point o' either buying or begging it.

He'd go and dismantle the mills himself, and bring them home in his lighter when he was returning from a turf-boating trip. He accumulated such a great pile of wood, iron and lead in this way that after his death it took an auctioneer the best part of a week to sell it. It were a queer hobby for him to have, and not a very happy one, as it turned out, for this passion he had for windmills

were the death of him. He were taking a mill down, all by himself, one day, when he were crushed in the water lane, and killed.
Then all his treasures fell under the hammer—such a collection
o' lead and solid oak as would be worth a Jew's eye, nowadays.

When the sale were all over, his son, John, carried on the turf
business, and millions more turf were cut and carried away. Then
after a goodish while, the fen were sold to one of the Rothschild
family, who let it go back to nature. It were made strictly private
then, and kept as a moth sanctuary.

This upset us locals: we didn't like it a bit. Besides, we couldn't
help being suspicious of folks who didn't keep reasonable hours
—'up with the lark, and to bed with the fowl' like other God-
fearing men, but were often a-hollering and a-shouting about in
the fen all night, making everywhere look horrible with their
great torches. No doubt they were only collecting specimens of
moths, but we couldn't believe anybody could be soft enough to
stop up all night to do that. And I don't suppose for a minute,
that they realised how far their excited voices carried in the still-
ness of a fenland night. But I tell you, we didn't reckon nothing
to such carryings on.

There was an old house where the Jacksons had lived, but after the old man died it was let to another man who had a large family, and a jolly good place it was to live, too. Pheasants and other game just strolled about everywhere, asking to be poached, and fish didn't cost nothing but the pleasure o' getting them.

We had several ways of fishing, though we rarely used rod and line. When I had been pumping, and the water in the drains was no more than a trickle I used to go with my 'pilfer'. I can't find that word in no dictionary, nor one anything like it, so I don't know whether I'm spelt it right or not. It was a sort of five or seven-tined fork, with a handle ten to twelve feet long, and three of the prongs had arrow-head shaped blades at the end.

You just walked along the bank of the drains watching for any sign of life in the water or mud. If you saw anything moving, you just jabbed your pilfer at it. You never knowed what you might bring up, a-wriggling atween the tines of your pilfer, for all sorts of fresh-water fish abounded, and eels by the thousand.

For catching eels we used an eel-glaive—we allus pronounced it 'gleeve' and for larger fish, such as pike, we had a bow-net.

One day I had my bow-net in the mill drain—always a good place for fishing, because the fish were pulled up with the water. I had covered the hoops of my bow-net with wire netting, instead of string netting, because I found that easier to handle.

When I pulled it out, on this particular day, I had only one fish in it. I intended putting my net back in a different place, but something or other called me away from it, and I left it lying on the bank.

Later in the day, I thought about it again, and went back to it. I had a catch that I didn't expect, for inside my bow-net, squeaking, squirming, and fighting, I had a fish, a rat, a cat and a little dog. I can only suppose that in the manner of the old tales we used to hear, the rat went in after the fish, the cat after the rat and the dog after the cat. I were very amused with this incident, and on the way home, like Samson, I made up a riddle about it:

> A fish and a rat,
> A dog and a cat,
> Now tell me where I found them.

I told that to a good many—and a lot who wouldn't believe as it were the truth. I allus liked a bit of a rhyme, and many a time I'm wished as I could remember and set down the rhyme we used to say when we were children. We had such a long way to get home from school, we played any game that would get us along quick. We used to play one called 'Gi-gi-gi- under the water bridge', where two children held their arms up and the others skipped along under them singing:

> Gi-gi-gi- under the water bridge—
> It is so dark, we cannot see,
> To thread the tailor's needle.

I know there's more to it than that, but I can't remember it now. There were a family o' boys as couldn't talk very well, and they'd play it on their way home, sounding something like this:

> Titho dark, tannothee,
> Tithew, tathew, nithoo.

after which we allus called it 'Tithew-tathew-nithew!'

We used to have a ritual for going over planks, or through gates, or anywhere where we had to get into single file. We used to scramble for first place or second, because each place in the line had a name:

> King, Queen, 'Baccabox, Shit-shovel, Lick-it-clean.

Many a little old boy has gone home roaring because he had to be 'Lick-it-clean' over the plank.

To return to Jackson's fens when the Rothschilds took over the fen. They pulled the old house down and built a bungalow on the site. They built it on concrete pillars standing right down on the hard blue clay and extending four feet or so above ground level, so that the bungalow was on stilts, like the natives of other swampy and snake infested areas build their huts.

It goes without saying that there were plenty of snakes. We never took much notice of the ordinary varieties of grass snakes, though once I saw one that made my flesh creep. A poor old woman who lived on the edge of Jackson's Fen disappeared. Soon all the able-bodied men were out looking for her. I was going across the wilderness, looking and calling all the time, when I come to a boat-dyke. I took a run and jumped, but as I stretched out my hands to land on the other side, I see the biggest, blackest snake I ever did see, just where I was going to put my hands. I didn't want to fall in the dyke, because although it looked perfectly dry, I knowed from nasty experience that there was nothing but ooze and slime under the crust, and to get into that by yourself with no one to help you, might very easily be the end of you. But I couldn't have put my hands on to the reptile for all the gold in China, so I sort of fell up the side of the dyke and the snake slithered away.

It was my pal Bill and me who found the poor old soul in the end. She had been out more than twenty-four hours, but she was quite cheerful, engaged in building a little pile of stones. When I spoke to her, she said she was making a fire to boil the kettle to get Mr Hussey (local squire) a cup of tea.

Needless to say, we all had a healthy respect for adders— nobody only a born fool would want to be too familiar with them. They abounded in the fen and were a common sight to the turf diggers, who couldn't be said to be frightened of them, even if they didn't make pets on 'em. They had their own particular way o' dealing with 'em. They'd take off their silk neck 'ankerchers and rustle and shake 'em in front of the adder, and then it would strike out at the 'ankercher. Its fangs would penetrate the silk, and try as it would, it couldn't disengage them, and there it would hang dangling, wriggling and writhing but caught fast by the fine, strong shreds of silk. This was the recognised way of catching adders, and I once saw an old turf man with a red neck-handkerchief spread in front of him, on which were no less than eleven adders at once.

There has always been a superstition that an adder has no

power of hearing. 'Deaf as an adder' is a common saying in the fen, and

> If I could hear as well as see,
> No man would be the death o' me.

When an adder appeared to a turf-digger at work, he would tease it with his spade, the blade of the spade being worn as bright as silver with constant use. When the adder was penned it would show fight, and strike at the bright blade glistening before it. Wherever it discharged its deadly poison, the silver would turn to brilliant blue-green in an instant.

The flies and mosquitoes would have been a nuisance, but the turf men had their own way of dealing with them, as well. They just tied a bit of rag on to a long pole and stuck the pole in the ground: the silly, deluded flies buzzed round a bit of rag all day, instead of bothering the sweating men.

Wright's Fen, covering from a hundred and fifty to two hundred acres next to Jackson's Fen, was dug twice all over for turf in my lifetime. I wasn't old enough to help with the first digging, but I did on the second. A depth of fourteen inches was cut each time, lowering the whole fen two feet four inches altogether. At the time I'm talking about, this fen were owned by a man called Thomas, from Cambridge, who let it out in half acre lots. The agreement was that not more than fourteen inches should be cut, and that the land should be left level. The lease expired after two years, but in that time a digger could expect to cut approximately four hundred thousand turf from an acre of ground.

I dug several acres of it on the second course, and I were very much interested in a find we had there.

We came across a buried road (no doubt, a Roman causeway, for the passage of troops). It lay about 2 ft under the surface of the peat. It was made of fir trees, packed very close together and pegged down with stakes six or seven feet long. They had got so soft that a turf spade would cut right through them without a digger noticing. I dug down to the bottom o'several pegs, and found them all pointed with some sort of edged tool.

I always presumed that this causeway crossed the fen from Honey Hill, Ramsey Heights, to Castle Hill, Woodwalton, and it could still be traced quite easily. But I don't suppose it ever will, for I should think Charlie Mason and I are the only two men who know of its existence.

There was a big mound in Wright's Fen, too, that was a problem I need to try and solve. It was made up entirely of peaty earth, without stone or bricks or mortar or anything similar. It interested me because of the numberless tobacco pipes that could always be found round the outside of the mound. When I was a little boy my gang of confederates and I used to spend days digging round the mound in the hopes of finding 'a whull 'un', but we never did. They were very small in the head, and were always flourished with a tree or something similar on each side of the bowl. The stems were mostly broken off about an inch or two from the bowl, but I found several three or four inches long.

Spade for clearing dykes

I have always wanted to know how they came there, but like the old road, that's another thing as I suppose will sink into oblivion, when me and my generation of old codgers are underground as well.

13

THE old song says: 'Never be born on a Friday, Choose some other day if you can,' but on the other hand the old saying says 'Always be born in the morning.' Well, my mother told me that I were born on a Friday, June 2nd, 1870, at 10 o'clock in the morning. So although I was born on an unlucky day, it may have been set off a little by my being born at a lucky hour. I had three sisters, but no brothers. My oldest sister was ten years older than me, and was married by the time I were ten year old. She married a man named John, and a very long life they had together, for they lived to celebrate their diamond wedding, and even lived a year or two after it.

John had one characteristic that allus made me fond of him, and that was that he did so love a bit o' fun and a joke. He could think o' things to do, and when he had thought of 'em he had the power to carry 'em out, right to the bitter end. I should fill a book if I tried to tell half the things he got up to, but I shall have to content myself with one or two o' the most outstanding ones I remember.

My mother had a friend who could get her soldier's tunics what had been discarded, bright scarlet, for about a shilling each: she used to cut them up to make the design in the rugs that she pegged for the floor. John happened to call at mother's one evening when she was busy rug-making, and one of these red tunics laid on the table. So John tried it on, and it fitted him a treat. He looked in the mirror that allus hung over the mantel-shelf, and the idea come to him. 'Bill,' he said to me, 'fetch us your old sealskin cap, will yer?' So I did, and it really were surprising how different he looked in it.

'Now I want a little cane,' he said. Well, mother still had the little penny cane she used to chastise us with when we were small children, though we were all on us well beyond that stage by then. So I went and got it for him, and there he stood, well enough equipped as a soldier to take anybody in as di'n't look very close.

It were in the middle o' winter. A real hard frost had set in, and the evening was a bright, keen, moonlight night. Away went the soldier from our house, swinging his little cane, and off he went to his own parents' house. When he got there, his father was messing about outside, feeding his pigs. He were in the little outhouse place where he kept his pig food and cooked his pig 'taters, so John went in to him.

''Ello, Mr Oliver,' said John, 'how are you?'

'Orlroight, my boy, orlroight, my boy,' said his father, peering at the soldier in the dusk. 'But I don't know as I remember you, my boy.'

'No,' said John, 'I don't suppose you do, Mr Oliver. I am what they call a recruiting sergeant, you know; there are several young men about here we should like to get into the Army, and your son William, who didn't like the job himself, has asked me to break the news to you that I have enlisted him.'

'Who? Who? My son Bill? 'Listed in th' army? O, dear, O dear, Mother! Mother! Mother!' and away the poor old fellow went, swinging his arm to help hisself along, like he allus did, towards the house. The recruiting sergeant followed him inside.

'Mother! Mother! Our Bill's 'listed in th' army.' Nobody doubted his word, for this upright young soldier in the red coat seemed to confirm it straight away. The younger members of the family began to howl and wail, and of course his mother was in a terrible state to think as Bill should leave 'em all and join the army.

'Do compose yourself, Mrs Oliver,' said the sergeant. 'It's the best thing any young man can do; if he stops here he will allus have to work hard; now he will see the world, and allus have a good living found for him, and besides, think how smart he'll look in his red coat.' But none of these advantages seemed to carry much weight with Bill's mother, who was so genuinely upset that John could see she would soon be doing a faint. So he had to run to her and snatch off his sealskin cap and show her who he really was. What a relief! His father said he was

127

pleased John had played such a joke on them, 'cos o' the pleasure he felt when he found out that it were on'y a joke.

Then John pacified his mother and the rest of the family, and turned towards his own home. His success at his parents' house made him feel pretty sure of not being recognised, so he continued his little game.

He had to pass his next door neighbour's house about a hundred yards before he reached his own. 'I may as well give them a call' he said to himself, so off he went and knocked at the door. One o' the young men who lived there answered the knock.

'Dad, 'ere's a soldier.'

'Come in.'

'Thanks.'

A chair was pushed forward and the soldier sat down.

'I have been told that a young man, named George Berridge, but nicknamed Tim, lives in one o' these three last houses down this drove,' he said.

'So 'e does. So 'e does,' the whole family said, all at once.

Now I ought to have said, afore this, that John had got his own little dog with him, and of course it kept following wherever he went, and he was very much afraid it was going to give the game away. The dog jumped up to him wheer he was sitting. John patted him on the head, in the way a stranger allus does to a dog he don't know, and said 'You're a nice little doggie, you are. What's your name, eh?'

'NELL' yawped all four on 'em, each one bawling as loud as he could in his anxiety to be in first. ''E belongs to them people wheer you're a-gooing. Ain't it funny as he should jest come in like that? It seems as if 'e's real took ter you.'

'Yes,' said the sergeant, 'most dog's do take to me, some'ow.' So he got to know where Mr Berridge lived, though of course he didn't need the information, because Tim Berridge was his own sister's husband, and they all lived together in the very next house. He prepared to go, saying 'Thank you, goodnight; goodnight, thank you.' But they warn't going to part with him as easy as that. The breadwinner o' the family had an idea.

''Erbit and Jinny, goo down to Mr Oliver's 'ouse wi' this 'ere young soldier. I know 'e ain't much used ter these 'ere droves; 'e's the very fust soldier I'm ever see down 'ere, anyway.'

John had a bit of a job to shake Erbit and Jinny off, but at last he got away without them, and when the door shut behind him he crept back under the window to listen to the commotion he had caused.

'Well, who d'yer 'ccount 'e is?' he heard.

'I know who 'e is' (from 'Erbit), 'tha's Jimmy Tibbs, that is; I should 'a knowed 'im anywheer.'

(Jimmy Tibbs were a young man from the other side o' the fen, who had enlisted some two or three years previously.)

'Well,' said the father o' the household, 'if tha's Jimmy Tibbs they're made a different man on 'im to wot 'e was afore 'e went.'

'Ah,' said the little know-all, Erbit, 'they dew make diff'rent men on um wen they git um into th' army.'

John went off to his own house, then. He knocked, and Timmy opened the door to him.

'Would you be kind enough to direct me to a village called Walton? I believe it is really called Woodwalton, but nobody seems to call it that.'

'Yis, it is Woodwalton by rights, Sir,' says Tim, 'but we allus say Walton. Nobody can show you the way better than I can, 'cos my father and mother live there, and I orften goo to see 'em. But you needn't goo the same way as I goo, as it 'appens. You are very lucky, the river is safe to walk on.' (Recruiting sergeant looks a bit dubious, as befits a man not used to fenland water-ways.)

Timmy saw the look, and answered it. 'There's no fear o' yer gittin' in, Sir, 'cos yew coul'n't git in if yer tried; it 'ould bear a 'oss an' cart. Now yew want ter goo along the river till yew pass three butt-dyke ends. Then goo down the fourth butt-dyke to the end, and yew'll come out on a good road as'll take yew roight into Walton.'

'Thank you. Goodnight.'

'Goodnoight, Sir. Goodnoight,' said Tim. John watched him go into the house, and then slipped round to the window.

'Who were that?' asked Harriet, (John's wife, and my sister.)

'A soldier bloke as wants ter get ter Walton,' said Timmy. 'I shoul'n't loike 'is journey. I don't believe 'e'll ever git there. 'E looks ter me as if 'e's 'alf boozed. But I got shut on 'im, so tha's all I care.'

Of course, John heard this, so it gave him a fresh idea.

'There's somebody else coming to the house,' said Harriet.

'I do believe it's that fella coming back again,' said Tim. It was.

'Sorry to disturb you again,' said the soldier, 'but I forgot which boat dyke you told me to go down. I didn't want to get down the wrong one.'

'I'll take you to the river, Sir, and put you right,' said Tim. 'Yew'll soon trip along to Walton. It's allus good walking on th'ice.'

They set out again, and John remembered that he was drunk. When they got to the bank of the river, he stumbled and nearly fell over. Timmy was real worried. 'Let me 'old your 'and, Sir' he said. 'Mind the dippin' 'ole. That's wheer we git our water from to drink, and fer the cattle in the yard. O' course, they allus drink more in frosty weather than they dew at other times.'

'Oh, do they?' said John. 'I didn't know that afore.'

The conversation turned to Mother and Father living at Walton, Timmy talking all the while, and they soon slipped along the ice till they come to the place John was supposed to turn off at. 'Thank you,' says John. 'No bother,' says Tim.

Tim went back into the house again. 'I think that's got out on 'im this time' he said to Harriet. But before many minutes passed Tim said, ''Ere's that 'umbuggin' fella a-coming back agin. I should like ter shoot 'im.'

The soldier didn't stop to knock, this time. He walked straight in and sat down, with his feet sprawled out in front of him, towards the fire, and his arms on the table.

'Coul'n't yer find yer way?' said Tim.

'Well,' said the soldier, more drunk than ever. 'I dare say I could have found it if I'd wanted to.'

'I wonder where John is' said Harriet, looking perturbed.

'Who's John?' asked the soldier.

'My husband' said the soldier's wife.

'Well,' said Timmy, 'I should 'ev thought as yew'd a-liked to a-bin a-startin' on your journey. It's a jolly long way you're got to goo.'

'I don't want anybody to tell me where to go, nor when to go, so don't you dictate to me.'

'I don't expect yer dew,' said Tim. 'On'y as I thought as it's a long way ter goo…'

'You thought,' said the soldier, witheringly. 'What business is the likes o' you got to think in front o' one o' the Queen's non-commissioned officers?'

The sergeant here began to sing, in a lawless, lither sort of a way

> It's the soldiers of the Queen, my lads,
> Who've been, my lads,
> Who've seen, my lads,…

but just casting his eye round to Harriet to see what effect his music was having on her, he noticed as she was just making preparations to get out o' the situation by having a fainting fit. So he called out 'Ain't yew a couple o' ninnies. I should a-thought you'd a knowed me afore now.'

'It's *John*,' said Tim.

'John? John who?' said Harriet, preparing to come round again.

'Why, *your* John,' said Tim.

Harriet was too relieved to be cross with her soldier husband. But she didn't like having to admit that he had fooled her so completely. So she said 'Ah, I knowed it were *somebody* as I'd seen afore.'

'Ah, so did I,' said Tim. But it were many a long day afore he were allowed to forget the recruiting sergeant, especially 'Mind the dipping-hole Sir' and 'Shall I take 'old o' yer 'and.'

There's one more little episode about my brother-in-law as I should like to tell, and if it ain't very thrilling, it'll all help, as the famous old woman said. As usual, I shall have to go round by Will's mother's to begin it.

They used to say that if we had three foggy mornings in succession in March, there'd be a flood in May. Well, whether or not that is so I can't say, 'cos there were allus such a lot to do atween

131

March and May that I allus forgot to connect the two. A-many's the time I'm said to myself after the third successive foggy morning in March, 'I'll remember this 'ere, an' just see if we do git a flood in May.' But if there did come a flood in May, as there very often did, it were such a disaster that I di'n't bother my head about proving any old weather saying right or wrong.

A May flood were disastrous because turf-digging started in March, and by May a lot of people would have dug and ricked anything from ten to twenty thousand turf. Altogether hundreds of thousands of turf would be washed away by a May flood, and would float away all over the turf fen and up all the rivers, and come to rest on the banks. It is an ill wind as blows nobody good, though, and anybody as liked could go and pick them up. The people who had dug them picked up a few and had to make the best o' things, though they had done all the work for nothing, and still had their ground rent of a shilling a thousand to pay.

After the flood had receded and the water went down to normal, tons of fish, mostly black bream, in shoals, would be in the river.

Now as soon as the news broke that the black bream were 'up', we would make up a party and go a-fishing. The bream weighed as much as two or three pound apiece, and with our nets we could soon land half a ton of fish. I can't think why we ever bothered to get so many, for any fool knows that nobody will eat fish when there is plenty. Besides, we were poaching, of course, and in any case the fishing season didn't start till June 15th. But the bream wouldn't wait, they'd all be gone within a day or two, so we had to have them—and our bit of sport—while they were there to be had.

Well there 'ad bin a May flood, and the black bream were up. I were soon one of a party, and off we went to the house where my brother-in-law lived.

'Ain't yer coming fishing with us to-night?' we said. Much to our surprise, he declined.

'No,' he said. 'I'm got a lot o' little jobs I'm got ter dew as must be done to-night. But yew might bring us a few fish in as yew come back.'

'Ah, a'right,' we said, and away we went to the river and soon had our nets in operation, a draw net and a stop net.

We were no sooner ready, however, than a strange gentleman came stepping briskly towards us on the opposite bank.

'What are you men all doing here?' he said 'Are you FISH-ING?' The man who happened to be nearest to him felt bound to answer.

'Well, Sir,' he said, stuttering-like, 'we was on'y trying to git a fish or tew fer our own eating,' and with that he begun to walk sideways and back'ards so as to slive off and away. But the gentleman had him.

'Don't go away, Bunnage,' he said, 'That won't do you any good at all. I've been to the "True Briton" and talked with the landlady there, Mrs King. I know the name of every man here.'

Bunnage di'n't stop to hear any more. He come a-clawing up to where me and another fellow called Tommy who was the acknowledged leader o' the gang, were busy with our nets.

'Tommy! Tommy!' said Bunnage, 'We're 'AD.'

''Ad?' said Tommy, astounded. 'Wha'd'y'mean, "'Ad"?'

'Thar's a gentleman up there,—says he's copped us at last.'

'Weer?' asked Tommy. 'Werrrr' (I can't spell this particular ejaculation), 'Werrrr, I don't take no'count o'rim. Goo an' tell 'im ter 'ommux orf 'um, Wag.'

(Bunnage had been christened Charlie, but all Charlie's were alike to us,—Wags.)

'Ax 'im what it's got ter dew with 'im,' added Tommy.

'I daresent,' replied Wag. 'I can't tell 'im that—'e's a perfect gentleman, I'm sure.'

'Well,' says Tommy, 'Yew goo back an' keep 'im a-talking while we git these 'ere nets out. We don't want to lose 'em.' Of course we were on the opposite side of the river from Wag and the stranger.

Very reluctantly Wag returned. The gentleman was prepared for him.

'Bunnage,' he said, 'Get your men together and let me get their names booked in order.'

'They ain't MY men, Sir,' said poor Wag.

'You are head man, arn't you, Bunnage?' asked the 'perfect gent', 'The ring leader, so to speak?'

'No, Sir,' wailed Wag. 'I'm sure, Sir, I ain't no wuss than any o' the others, an' I'm got a big fambly ter keep, an' I don't want ter git no summons.'

'I know you have a large family, Bunnage. I know that you have seven children, and that's all the more reason, in my opinion, why you should be more careful and not get into trouble like this.'

('That bee-ing ole woman at "The Briton"'s tole 'im everythink,' spluttered Wag. 'I'll niver 'ev another pint in 'er 'ouse as long as I live.') By this time the nets were all out, and the rest of the men had gathered round to hear the explanation. One by one their faces lost their apprehensive looks and several wore broad smiles.

'Ah, well' says the stranger, 'I should go and let your nets down again if I was you. I dunno as I shall say anything about it this time arter all.'

Wag was just a-taking off his cap to thank the gentleman for his leniency when the faces of the rest of us give the game away. He took a closer look at his perfect gentleman. 'Why,—it's JOHNNY OLIVER' he said, and so, of course, it was, disguised only by an old fur cap and a commanding voice that he could allus 'put on' when he wanted to.

I had good reason to be annoyed with John many a time before he died, and he did me more than one dirty trick in business; but I allus liked him for his wit and humour, an' I know how it would please him to think I were a-laying here in bed and writing it down after all these years.

I call him to mind as he was the last year or two of his life. He and my sister had a bungalow built close to my farm, and there they lived till they died. Between them they had, or said they had, every disease known to medical science except one as I shan't mention, but in spite of it all they both died of old age and nothing more.

John got very stingy and was allus a-lapping hisself up in bits of old flannel, and bandages, and anything else he could find. He had a bad leg once about ten year afore he died, and had to have a crepe bandage put round it. He never left the bandage off afterwards because he said his leg got cold without it. When he died it was taken off, and we found that the continued tightness of the bandage had reduced the size of the leg until it weren't no more than half as big as the other. He used to wear two or three 'ganseys', one a-top o' the other, and allus had his cap on. I don't know as he slept in it, but when he got too bad to get up he used to sit up in bed with it on, and he smoked his old rank baccy to the last.

Both him and his wife had great faith in brandy as a cure-all. At first they used to have a bottle in the house in case of emergency, and they kept it in an old ottoman at the foot of the bed. But it was surprising how many times a day John would remember something he had left in the bedroom, and after fetching it would come out smacking his lips. When my sister 'smelt a rat' as the saying goes, she would also make a trip to the bedroom as soon as he came out. And as she told a niece who looked after her at that time 'took a little drop out o' the bottle, about as much as he had had, and filled it up with cold tea'.

But as the niece afterwards remarked, what did she do with the little drops she took out?

This caused the system to break down altogether, and soon afterwards they agreed to have a bottle apiece, and paid for their own out of their Old Age Pensions.

They used to have their supper about eight o'clock every night, sitting one each side of the big table in front of the fire. Harriet would have her bit of supper and then get out the big family Bible and read aloud to John while he finished his. There they would sit, Harriet wrapped up in a bright green wool shawl and mumbling out some genealogical chapter of Genesis, John smothered in wool weskits and with his old cap covering his thick mass of curly snow white hair, carving off chunks of bread with his knife, then transferring the bread to his mouth with his knife still clutched in his hand, missing his own ear by a fraction of an inch every time. While Harriet's eyes were cast down at the Bible and her voice droned on with 'And Adam begat so-and-so,...' John would reach for the carving knife, and with the help of its longer blade, sneak an extra knob of butter from under

Harriet's nose. Then how his merry old eyes would twinkle to think he had 'done the missus down'.

I know he'd a-laughed to read this 'ere chapter, specially after it has been typed out.

'Seems to make it all the better, Bill, ter 'ev it put through that there thing,' he'd a-said, pointing at the typewriter. Ah, and how vividly that does bring him back to my mind's eye, for I allus laughed at the way he pointed at anything, not in the usual way, but by jerking a very long, curved thumb towards it. Asked the whereabouts of anything he would reply 'Over yinder,' and jerk his thumb back'ards over his shoulder towards it.

14

TALKING about my bro'-in-law John, has made me call
to mind some o' the other cures as I'm knowed during my
life time in the fen. There were all sorts and sizes on 'em, now
I come to think about 'em, and looking back at a lot on 'em who
are dead and gone, I can't 'elp but think as I laughed at 'em a
good many times when I ha'n't ought to a-done. Like me, they
were most on 'em born and brought up where they never see
nobody only their neighbours and relations, and never 'eard
nobody talk on'y the local preachers at the chapel. A lot on 'em
cou'n't read and di'n't want to, and a few on 'em were so isolated
where they lived that they were frit to be in company. But in
spite o' that they'd git through life somehow, and very often
they'd make more of a success on it than a lot who had better
chances.

I should think it were because our lives were so simple and we
were so ignorant that we talked and listened to each other so
much, but I'm often wondered if other folks used to go away
laughing at me an' at what I'd said, like I used to when I'd bin
a-talking to some o' my old pals and acquaintances. There were
them as looked funny, and them as acted queer, and them as
said things as 'ould make me laugh. There were some as were a
bit simple by nature, and some as thought theirselves too clever,
and tried to 'hang it on'. There were them as knowed they were
saying funny things, and them as said things meant to be took
serious but were really so amusing that you'd have to get away
as quick as you could afore you busted out a-laughing. Then
there were the times when somebody 'ould say something so
simple to you as for a moment or two you'd be deceived into
thinking it were funny, till you got to turning it over in your
mind and realised just what the simple remark were a-covering
up. I allus were touched easy, and I very often went away having

to gulp a lump down in my throat and a bit ashamed at having to draw my hand acrosst my eyes. Sometimes it were good for you, though, to see as you ha'n't got all the troubles yourself.

When I were about sixty, I suddenly got the gout come that bad as I cou'n't stand, let alone walk, or hold anything in my hands, and the pain were terrible. I used to have to cling to the table wi' my elbows to get my balance to stand up at all afore I could start to stumble along, and if I fell down I darsn't put my hands down to catch myself because my wrists were gone stiff and felt as if they'd break off, so I used to let myself go and roll over like one o' these acrobats you see sometimes. I were born as I'm said, in 1870, so by the time the gout got at me it 'ould be about 1930, and anybody as knows anything at all about farming history knows what that means. So what with one thing and another, I were a miserable creature; I'm allus bin a bit of a pessimist, at least so my wife tells me, and it really did look as if I ha'n't got much left to struggle on for. I got so down with my own lot as I di'n't bother much about nobody else. Then one morning I had a lesson. I'd struggled up early, like I allus had to, and gone out to the yard to try and do something to help, but it di'n't seem to matter where I went or who I spoke to, I were on'y in the way. I see the postman, Tom, come up to the 'ouse, so I made my way back to see what 'e'd brought, but I di'n't get a very warm welcome there either. My wife 'ad just got up as full o' rheumatics as I were o' the gout, an' her knees wou'n't hold her up any more 'n my ankles 'ould 'old me. None on us could lift the kettle to make the tea, and when anybody done it for us, we cou'n't pour the tea out, that morning. All Tom had brought were a lot o' bills as I cou'n't pay, and when I started mourning about things my wife got savage with me and told me to clear out where she cou'n't see me. So I got up again and staggered back out to the yard. I went to the big gate as led out on to the road, and leaned up against it, very nearly roaring wi' the pain and misery o' one thing and another. Right opposite to me were the gate o' the little farm opposite, and I ha'n't bin there above a minute when my old pal from across the road see me and come across for a chat. We stood there for a few minutes a-talking, when a pain struck me as nearly knocked me down, an' I clawed at the gate to keep myself from falling over. Alty looked that surprised, as if he ha'n't see me afore for many a year, an' said 'A-yer got a bad leg or som'ink, Will 'En?'

In spite o' the pain, I could a-laughed. I said 'Coo, Lor Alty, I'm got the gout so bad as I can't walk nor nothink else,' and I started to tell him all the details. When I got going I warmed to my job, and told 'im 'ow it 'ad bin coming for two year, and getting worse all the time, and the doctor said as there were no cure as he knowed on, and I should on'y go on getting wuss till I died. Then I said about the farm going downhill 'cos I cou'n't work no longer myself, and how I were a-gooin' bankrupt, an' about the bills what I cou'n't pay an' the fields I'd 'ad to set wi' my own seed 'taters 'cos I cou'n't afford no new seed, and all the while Alty stood there looking up at me sympathetic with his 'ead o'-one-side, 'cos he were a short, plump man and I were tall and thinner than usual, just then. When I cou'n't think o' no more miseries, I stopped, and Alty spoke.

'Ah well. I s'll 'et to be a-gooin' an' a-gittin' on wi' som'ink, Will 'En,' he said. '*But I'm sure I'm glad your better*', an' away he went. For a second or two I di'n't know whether to squeal out loud or laugh, when I looked across the road at Alty going in at his own gate. I'd seen him there three or four times a day for about ten year, but I'd never really looked at 'im till then. If I were a poor old mess, he were worse. He'd had gout or rheumatics, or something, for so many year that I'd real forgot he'd ever bin an ordinary figure of a man at all. He weren't just stiff and in pain, like I were: he were twisted and crippled till there wern't one single bit of 'im that resembled what it ought. You could a-run a wheel-barrer atween his poor old legs at the knee, though his heels were close together: but his feet splawed out till they p'inted sideways altogether, and he had to walk by liftin' 'em sideways. His poor old bald head were pulled all shapes by the same rheumatiz as his legs, and his hands were quite as bad, if not worse, than my own. What's more, I knowed as he cou'n't a-got twisted to that shape without a sight more pain than I'd 'ad yet, and that 'e'd got quite as many money troubles and farming troubles as I 'ad, for his farm warn't nothing like so good to start with, and for another thing 'e ha'n't bin half so well established as me when the slump set in. I could see very well why he ha'n't bin a-botherin' about me having a bad leg, an' why 'e ha'n't bin a-listening when I'd told 'im my troubles. But it made me laugh and cheered me up to think on us both being just as blind to everybody's misery except our own. Poor old Alty: he's bin dead a-many-a-year now, and here I am at seventy-nine well enough to get about without sticks again, and still with enough sense to remember that incident and write it down, when the gout don't keep a-snatching the pen out o' my hand.

It were different, an' 'arder to bear, when I met another old pal a-gooin' 'ome down a drove one night. I stopped for a chat, an' 'e told me 'e'd bin to Peterborough to the doctor's, and they'd told 'im as 'e'd got an incurable growth, a cancer. He said 'It ain't very nice, Will 'En, to et to goo 'um an' tell 'em that, is it? An' then when the mornin' comes an yer can't git up no more, to lay there an' know as yer got to lay there till yer die. I keep a-looking round me as I walk 'um, and I keep a-thinking as I don't want to leave none on it: and then I remember as I ain't the on'y one. *You've every single one on yer got to come with me.*'

But I never meant to start thinking about such miserable topics. It were the funny things as I'd bin meaning to remember. There were one farmer as lived a little way up the road from me what had a real gift for saying things you cou'n't forget, though he were a mournful sort o' chap with a high pitched voice and di'n't intend being funny, on'y sarcastic. His name were Al, and nearly every time you met anybody they'd start telling you the latest thing Al had said. He just cou'n't help exaggerating things. If his wheat straw were strong, 'e'd say 'It's the truth, Will 'En, you could use every single straw on it for a fishin' rod,' but if it weren't so good, 'e'd say 'Well, they ain't no stronger than cobwebs!'

One year when there'd bin a dry spring and things weren't a-growing as they should a-bin for want o' rain, somebody met Al and asked him how his wheat were a-doing.

'Not very well, t'tell you the trewth,' Al replied. 'I don't think it's quite as 'igh as it were when it fust come out o' the grownd.' Then, when this 'ad 'ad time to sink in, he added 'Well, I were a-gooin' acrorst the field th' other day, and I see as 'ow the mice are 'evin' to kneel down to nibble it orf.'

I'm said afore as our fen were on the edge o' the highland, and it so 'appened that Al had a couple o' highland fields. Like all of us real old fenmen, he ha'n't got much use for high land, specially in a dry autumn. When we ploughed the fen fields, they come down beautiful into a lovely fine tilth, ('tilt' we allus said) but the highland fields 'ould come up in great clots as you cou'n't break down properly whatever you done with 'em specially in the days when all our implements were drawed by hosses. One day Al sent his 'osskeeper, a man called Tuck, a-ploughin' in one o' his highland fields. At dockey time Al went to see 'ow 'e were a-getting on.

'I got orf me bike,' he said, 'and looked acrost the field. There were the 'osses wi' their nosebags on, stan'in' on the headland: but Tuck I cou'n't see no wheer. So I 'ollered, Tuck! Tuck! but 'e never come. I begun to be frit that somink 'ad 'appened to the man, and went clawin' acrost the field as 'ard as I could goo. When I got a good way inta the field, there sat Tuck, 'eving 'is dockey—*a-hint a clot*.'

141

I remember a dozen or more such sayings of Al's as are got to be real catchwords all over everywhere. I never did know whether he were aware o' the things 'e were saying being funny. He ha'n't got a lot o' fun in 'im, but I don't reckon as 'e could a-thought up 'alf the things he did do if 'e ha'n't a-enj'yed 'em 'isself. Not that they were said light-'eartedly, for they warn't. Very often we sh'd both be in despair about something, but 'e'd still come out wi' something witty. In May and June we used to get dust storms. I remember once when a storm lasted three days, and for all that time you cou'n't see no further than the end o' the garden for the soft black soil a-sweeping in a great black cloud over the fen. I'm 'eard tell as they 'ave sand storms in the desert, caused by the wind a-blowin' the sand. This is just what we have, only it's soft, black, silky dust instead o' sand. Arter it's all over, the dykes and drains are all level full o' soil, and when it comes afore the tiny plants like mangolds and sugar beet are well rooted, the wind clears 'em off as clean as if the land ha'n't bin planted, and there the little seedlings lay, tore up by the roots, among the soil a-filling the dykes. One year after a partic'lar bad storm, I went out to look and see what the effects 'ad bin, an' I met Al, who'd bin doing the same. We'd both lost all our sugar beet crop arter we'd paid to get it all set, and it were a blow. We stood a-looking down into a dyke near the main drain, and both on 'em were level full wi' muck and beet seedlings. But Al, as usual, 'ad something to say. 'Ah, Will 'En'' 'e said, 'Looks to me as if we'd better be setting orf for Denver Sluice if we want to single our sugar beet this year.'

Yes, Al were a real cure: but there were others who thought they knowed everything and loved to show off. Then we'd do our best to catch 'em out, and if we cou'n't, we'd make fun on 'em behint their backs. There were one feller as 'ad a son what 'ad gone to 'Americky'. One year when there were a long frost, some skating matches were being run at Bury Fen and on Cubit Wash, and the results were being discussed, 'cos of course we were all skaters in them days. One man were talking about the time a certain race 'ad been done in, and 'e added 'Somink like tew minutes, five and three-fifths seconds, but I dunno. It caps my

142

backside to know 'ow anybody kin measure up to a fifth part of a secont.'

'Werrhr—that ain't nothink' said the father o' the traveller. 'In 'Mericky, wheer my Bill is, they've got clocks as'll measure up to sixty-fifths.'

'Sixty-fifths?' said the first man. 'Well, 'ccordin-lye to my reckonin', that 'ould be twelve whull-uns!'

We 'ated anybody to show off. It were the one thing as we just cou'n't stand no 'ow. Now and again there'd be a preacher at the chapel as 'ould think 'e were a-coming to talk to a lot o' poor ignorant creatures as di'n't know nothink at all, an' try to 'lay it on'. I were in chapel one night wi' my old friend Stratt when one o' that sort were a-preachin'. He got to talkin' about the Bible, in his patronising way. He le'nt over the pulpit and said 'The Bible is full o' long words, my friends: words too long for some of us to read an' understand. I wonder, my friends, does any one here know what the longest word in the Bible is?'

This were too much for Stratty, who never could put up wi' fools and wern't afraid to say so. So while the preacher le'nt over the pulpit, a-pausing afore telling us ig'orant fen folks what this 'ere long word were, Strat got in first.

'I sh' think I dew' he bawled at the top of his voice, 'It's NEWRONSANIPONSKALIASKEREZER!'

Some really were simple. Then they got treated accordin' to the character o' the person they were a-talking to. Some folks love to think they're better than others, an' if they can feel superior they make the most on it, but I used to feel sorry when I met such real ignorance, though there were no way of helping. My mother 'ad a chap called Joe worked for 'er on the farm afore I took over. He laid rough very often, and never washed. One day I stood close to him, and looked at his neck. You could a-sowed onion seed in the muck in the creases o' his skin.

'Joe' I said, 'ain't it about time you 'ad a wash? Specially yer neck!'

He di'n't seem to care about me telling him 'e were mucky, but 'e 'ad his answer pat.

'I sh'd like to 'ev a wash, Bill,' 'e said 'but I daresn't. You see, if ever I wash the back o' me neck, it allus makes me nose bleed.'

He went to work at piece work one year for another dear old pal o' mine, a-chopping out 'taters. He worked 'ard, and at the end o' the week the farmer went to pay him. 'You've worked real well, Joe' he said, 'so I shall give you one-and-thruppence a hacre.' Joe were put out, and showed it.

'W'a's the matter?' asked the farmer, surprised. 'Ain't yer satisfied?'

'No,' says Joe. 'I ain't 'evin' no one-an'-thruppence a hacre. If I cayn't 'ev a shillin' like other men, I wou'n't wukk at all!'

I reckon we must all on us 'ad a good ear for a bit of humour, for there wern't much as passed us by in that line. When a woman was heard to say she ''ad a bout o' the ole touch', meaning an attack of 'flu, we never had 'flu again ourselves. We 'ad 'the ole touch' instead: during the slump, a knowall was heard to remark 'There wou'n't be many as 'll be able to 'old 'em this year' (meaning the deeds of their farms, because the bank would want them)—and from that time on 'Shall you 'old 'em?' became a catch-phrase and a greeting.

The exclamation of an old woman 'Your three sons are two beauties, if ever there were one' was repeated and enjoyed years afterwards, and as for this sort o' remark, we had a whole issue of 'em, all attributed to a chap called Fred Tatt, though he never said half o' the things as were laid to his charge. But if anybody said anything 'Irish', or back to front, we'd remember it, and tell it again and again, adding 'as Fred Tatt says'. Fred Tatt were a real man, and I knowed him, and 'e did say some peculiar and amusing things, none on 'em at all important, but enough to cheer us up. Looking at a ladder as were extra long one day, he was 'eard to remark 'The longest lather I ever went up were down a well,' and on another occasion he stopped work and gazed upwards. 'Look at them tew bloody ole crows!' he said 'They're so high they're right out o' sight.' 'We nearly 'ad a letter the smorning' he said, 'They 'ad one next door.' He were arranging with a friend to meet 'im on the way to work. 'How shall I know whether you're gone or not?' said the other fellow. Fred scratched his head and said 'If you git to the field gate fust,

144

lay a stun on the gate post: an' if I git there fust, I'll knock it orf.'

'You've got h'odd shoes on, Fred,' somebody said to him one day. Fred looked at his own feet for a long while, and then said 'Well, I can't make that out, 'cos I'm got another pair at 'um jest like 'em.'

Ah, there's no end to it! Fred 'ad a cat as 'e were very fond on. He cut a hole in his barn door so she could get in and out as she liked. One day a neighbour come across Fred busy a-cutting a little hole by the side o' the big one.

'Whadda yer dewin' Fred?' asked the neighbour.

'Why, don't yer see,' said Fred, 'my ole cat's got some kittens now.'

This 'ere chapter's got real out of 'and, because I'm sure as I di'n't mean to get on telling such silly little tales as I'm bin a-doing, except as it gives me a lot o' pleasure to remember 'em. I did allus love a man with a witty tongue, an' there's no mistake there were plenty on 'em in the fen. I'm remembered one more as I must tell.

There were a man in the fen what had a lot o' little children. He were supposed to have said 'e intended to 'ave as many as the Lord 'ad disciples, and when I last 'eard on 'im he'd got beyond that number. He started at the beginning o' the alphabet and named the first one Albert, and the second one B'linda and the third Claude, and so on, and 'e'd got a good way up it by the time I'm talking about. He worked with a threshin' tackle, and 'ould go here and there with it to carry out the threshin' for the farmers. If 'e were anywhere within strikin' distance at all, 'e wou'n't have a packed-up dockey, but 'ould order his wife to bring 'is hot dinner to him in the field or the yard where he happened to be. So the poor woman 'ould cook him a 'hungin dumplin' or a pudden' o' some sort and when it were done she'd put the last two or three children with his dinner, in the pram and drag the rest o' the tribe o' littl'uns miles across the fen with 'er to take their dad's dockey.

One day they were busy a-threshin', and Dan stood down against the engine, while up on the drum his mate Billy were beginning to want his dockey, but had to keep at work till the tackle stopped. From the top o' the drum he spied the cavalcade approaching two or three fields away. So over the rattle o' the drum he shouted down 'Time to knock off, Dan—'ere's your dockey a-comin',' adding, as he looked again at the trail of children 'Well, if it *ain't* your dockey, Dan, it's a bloody school-treat!'

15

WHEN you're a-writing something like this 'ere I'm bin attempting, it ain't a mo'sel o' use trying to think what you're a-going to put. You just have to git 'old o' your pen an' start a-writing, an' afore you know where you are, you've thought o' the next thing. O' course, when I start, I'm aware all the while o' two things. One is that nothing I'm writing about is any consequence, and the other is that there's no end on't: everything I write brings to mind something else, and starts me off remembering folks as I'd forgot, and things as I'm thought years ago when I'm bin at work by meself, and questions I'm bin meaning to ask somebody as should know the answer. When I were trying to write about the amusing characters in the fen, I kep' thinking about them as were sad ones.

There were one old fellow as lived in the fen as I'm often thought a lot about. His name were Al Elderkin, and he lived in a little hut in Wright's Fen, where all 'e 'ad to look at were the great wild bareness for miles and miles wi' 'ardly ever a house or habitation in sight. When I remember 'im, he were a real wild man. What few oddments o' rags o' real clo'es 'e'd ever 'ad were wore to shreds, and to cover his nakedness he wore sacks hung round 'im and tied wi' bits o' string. His boots were padded wi' scraps o' old sack as well, and 'e wore an old felt hat with a broken crown tied under his chin wi' another bit o' string. He never washed, let alone shaved, and his finger nails 'ad growed till they were like curved eagle's claws over the ends o' his fingers. He never 'ad nothin' to eat on'y what he could pick up as 'e went about. Some folks took pity on 'im reg'lar, and o' course 'e soon knowed where to go. But most folk ha'n't got much to give away, an' 'e'd be 'ounging about round doorways picking up crusts what the child'en had dropped, and round yards hoping for pig taters, and so on. He were part o' the landscape, an' we never took much notice on 'im. Women used to be

147

frit at 'im an' run in an shut their doors if they see 'im a-coming, but children 'ould be fascinated by 'im and stan' and stare at 'im wi' their eyes bulging out. If their dad were at 'ome, he'd know what the poor ol' chap were after, an' say 'Give us a song, then, Al' and Al 'ould shuffle up on the doorway and caper about for a minute or two singing, in a gruff voice from atween 'is lips buried in 'is whiskers

> Beeswax and teerpentine
> Sheepskin and plaster
> The more yer try to pull it orf
> The more it sticks the faster
> Skin-a-ma-link-a-doodle-doo
> Skin-a-ma-link-a-di-doe.

Then 'e'd get a bit o' bread and seam an' go away clawin' it down 'im as if 'e really were a two-legged animal.

He had another song as 'e'd sing at pubs for a drink. It were a mixture o' a lot o' songs as 'e'd knowed when 'e were young, I reckon, cos it di'n't make no sort o' sense.

> 'Appy-day, 'appy-day
> Jesus washed my sins away.
> Pluck pears down,
> Pick 'em up an' eat 'em
> Jane Shaw, Meg Merilees
> Bow, wow, wow,
> Bow, wow, wow.

The last lines were like a real dog a-barking, an' it were this the men in the pubs used to like 'im to do. They made fun on 'im, and I dare say it pleased 'em to think that as poor an' as ignorant as they were, there were somebody worse off still. I cou'n't laugh, though. Old Al were one o' the sights I had to try an' forget. Somebody 'ad told me that when Al fust come to the fen, he were a great, strong, handsome young fellow as sharp in his head an' as clart as anybody ever needed to be. The tale were as the girl 'e loved 'ad jilted 'im, an' 'e'd took it so 'ard 'e'd come out into the wild ol' fen to be by 'isself while 'e got over it. He never did get over it, and stopped there broodin' and grievin'

148

to 'isself until his money 'ad gone: then 'e ha'n't got no 'eart to work, so 'e started going without food, and that soon made 'im bad in health. What wi' one thing and another, 'is mind went, and he degenerated into what I'm just described. An' yet 'e lived on an' on, wi' no purpose to 'is life at all, till 'e were a real old man.

He'd bin out one winter's night lookin' for a bit o' grub no doubt, an' 'e fell down in one o' the deep ruts in the old muddy drove an' cou'n't get up again. Somebody found him an' sent for the doctor. O' course the doctor cou'n't do nothing for a man in his filthy condition, so 'e 'auxed 'im off to the Union.

When they got 'im there, they tried to undress 'im. They cut the old sacks off 'im, but 'is 'at they cou'n't get off. His hair had growed right through the breaks in the hat, and were long and matted over the top on it: and the string what 'ad 'eld it on in the fust place 'ad got buried in his whiskers, 'cos 'is beard 'ad growed over the top o' the string. They 'ad to cut his hair and his whiskers off to get his hat off, and then they put 'im in a bath an' scrubbed 'im clean. After all 'is years o' privation and cold, 'e cou'n't stand a hot bath an' such a change in 'is routine, an' he died the next day.

Well, there's bin many a song, an' many a poem, an' many a book, wrote on the same theme, but never a sadder one than I see wi' my own eyes in poor old Al Elderkin, as wasted 'is life an' died mad all for the sake o' a woman.

Another sad case were 'Old Carnell'. He'd come to live in our fen when 'e were younger, with a pretty young wife as 'e were proud on. They 'ad a little cottage kept spruce and neat wi' flowers in the windows, and they were both prosperous and appeared to be happy. They had got a bit more education than a lot of us 'ad, and Carnell 'isself were a real musician. He had a beautiful little organ in his cottage, an' 'e'd sit down an' play an' sing as 'appy as you ever did see a man. Then his wife died, and 'e begun to pine away. First 'e wou'n't work, and then 'e took to drink. Little by little 'e slipped down 'ill, till 'is money were all gone. But by that time the craving for drink 'ad got so 'old on 'im that 'e 'ad to have it, so 'e begun to sell the bits and pieces from his little home to get it. I went one night wi' some-body what wanted to look at some things 'e wanted to sell. Old Carnell were in bed, but 'e were just about to have an attack o' the D.T.'s. He told us 'ow the Devil come to 'im an' what a terrible fright 'e'd 'ad, and 'ow he were all the while threatening to come again.

'Ah,' said Old Carnell, 'can't you 'ear 'im how? Listen!' and he 'eld 'is 'and up for silence, an' we pretended to listen.

''Ark at 'im rattlin' 'is chains in the chimbley,' Carnell whispered. ''E'll 'ev me, one o' these days! 'E'll come with 'is chains, an' 'e'll 'ev me!'

We bought whatever it were we'd gone for, and paid him the money, about ten shillings in silver. Old Carnell laid it down, and a minute o' two afterwards went to pick it up again, but 'e'd forgot where 'e'd put it, and it wern't in the fust place as he looked. Carnell begun to swear and shake his fist at the chimney, and said

'It's 'im again! 'E's 'ad it! 'E's allus playing tricks on me like that. Th'ass who's had it—'E's 'ad it.'

Next moment Carnell found the silver in his pocket. 'There, the Old Sod's brought it back again' he said, growling, and as we left we could still hear him shouting at the Devil to clear off and leave him alone.

The devil did ''ev 'im' one night an' all. It were one black night when 'e'd bin to the pub and 'e were going home drunk. He had to cross a plank over the cut, and 'e missed 'is footing and fell in. He were wearing a great heavy old coachman's cloak with two or three capes at the shoulders, an' though the water wern't very deep, the coat were so heavy as soon as it were wet that in his drunk state he cou'n't lift hisself up, and were found drownded the next morning. They took him to a hut kept for such things by the side of a pub. There were nothing they could do for 'im, so they soon got 'im a pauper's coffin and shoved 'im in, just as 'e were, coat and boots an' all. He ha'n't got a soul to mourn 'im, an' as far as I could see, it di'n't matter a skerrick: but there were a few who were terribly upset about it, and among 'em were my father-in-law.

He were a regular out-an'-out character hisself, and one o' the last you'd a-ever a-thought 'ould a-bin upset by such a thing. But he cou'n't a-bear the thought of Old Carnell going to his grave in his boots and without being shaved. He went to the police and offered to go and undress the corpse and take its boots off, and shave it, so as it could be buried decent: but they wou'n't allow it.

My father-in-law were a sad man of a different kind, one o'

them as is his own only real enemy. He were of Irish blood, and it got the better on 'im. He were tall and very strong and handsome, with snow white silky hair and a long, snow white beard. They'd both gone white overnight when 'e were young, after his best friend had one too many and on the pretext o' throwing his arm round his shoulders, had cut a great gash in his throat with a razor. My father-in-law (always known as 'Rattles'), had the scar till he died. Perhaps the shock had some other effects on him, as well.

He were a difficult man, rather than a bad man. I married his daughter and I loved my poor mother-in-law as if she were my own mother, and because of his 'goings-on' I had a lot o' misery and trouble and expense and aggravation. But in spite of it I liked him, and cou'n't help meself. When he were in a good mood he were good comp'ny, and you never knowed what might 'appen next. He wou'n't work if 'e could get a livin' any other way at all, and he'd spend more time schemin' 'ow to do the man 'e were working for down than it 'ould a-took to do the job properly. He were a higgler with a hoss and cart of his own, but 'e'd go miles and miles out of his way to get a bob when he could a-earnt a pound by going direct. It's on'y fair, though, to say as 'e'd a-gone miles out of his way to gather a bit of a herb some old woman wanted, or to do any other little kindness for anybody like that. He were the most expert liar I ever did come across— on'y they wern't lies as 'ould do nobody much 'arm. He'd just invent 'em as 'e went along, an' tell his stories wi' such detail as made 'em sound real authentic. I had two young fellers working for me, once. They were brothers about thirty-five to forty, who run a carpenter's and joiner's business in the next village, and 'ad come to do some little jobs for me. We got talking, and it appeared that they'd just come from somewhere else where my father-in-law had been wasting his time and theirs by bladgin' to 'em as they worked. One on 'em said

'Ah, he's bin a wonderful man in his time, by all accounts. I could a-listened to 'im a-talking for a fortnit without stopping.'

'Wa'ss he bin tellin' you about?' I asked.

'Bout the time when 'e were young an' were a policeman in Australia,' one on 'em said. ''Ow 'e 'ad to goo out into the bush arter some escaped convicts, wi' nothing but a dog to 'elp 'im track 'em down, an' 'ow they got wind on 'im comin', and turned on 'im to ketch 'im. Then 'e 'ad to run for 'is life, and they captured the dog an' killed it an' ate it; but 'e got into a river bed an' under a culvert an' 'id there for three days, up tew his waist in water, till they gave up 'ope and went away so as 'e could escape an' git help to go arter 'em again.'

'Well,' I says, 'that ain't too bad for a chap as is 'ardly bin outa this old fen for more'n a day at a time since 'e were born.'

'D'yer mean as it ain't the truth?' one on 'em said.

They looked at me as if I were a real criminal a-takin' my own father-in-law's character away like that. But they belonged to a family as could allus take a joke, and they could see how they'd bin 'ad by his plausible old tongue. To tell the truth, I reckon a good many folks thought the better o' Rattles when they found he'd bin inventing his tales than they would a-done if all 'e said 'ad bin the truth.

His real trouble were his temper. He could not control it, an' once it rose up in him something 'ad got to 'appen, an' a terrible lot o' pain and distress that old temper caused everybody, specially his wife, who were one o' the gentlest and best women as ever lived. She got the brunt of all his awkwardness, an' there were no way o' helpin' 'er except with a pound or two in money when things got worse 'n usual. Most people shook their heads and despised him for his ways, and a few young 'uns encouraged 'im 'cos 'e done things they'd a-liked to a-done if they'd a-dared. He were a rebel against everything, so much so that I sometimes used to wonder if it wern't a disease as he'd got. It were as if 'e'd got a kettle a-biling inside 'im, and when the pressure got too high he'd got to blow off steam that minute, so whatever 'armless thing it were you were a-talkin' about, he'd turn on it an' there'd be such a row as you never 'eard. He'd double his great fists and bring 'em down on the table so as the oil lamp standing in the middle on it 'ould jump up in the air and go out: he'd roar and swear and threaten vengeance on anybody an' everybody 'e could think of, whether they 'ad anything to do with the matter or not, and the veins in his neck 'ould stand out above 'is red neck 'andkercher like ropes, and 'is eyes 'ould glitter like blue stars made o' diamonds with bright cold sparks o' light in 'em. Then his poor wife 'ould quickly gather the child'en up, while they were young, an' slip outside and spend the night in the barn or somewhere till it were all over. It were terrible for her when she got the brunt of it, but I must say it were a wonderful sight while it lasted, and I must confess that I wern't above rousing his temper a-purpose, sometimes, when nobody but me were going to suffer. I remember one night we'd bin somewhere together in his light cart wi' 'is old white pony, an' we were joggin' 'ome together slow, a-talking as we went. We'd made our minds up to stop for a drink at a pub on the Herne, where very likely one or two o' his brothers might be. Not that he wanted to *see* his brothers, for he hated 'em all like p'ison, so 'e said. I knowed this, an' waited my opportunity. He were doing most o' the talking as we jogged along, and as usual, he were doing a bit o' bragging about his strength and skill when 'e were younger. He started to tell me about how good 'e used to be with a scythe, an' how he allus could finish 'is 'land' first and 'ev to wait for the other mowers to catch up. I saw a chance, and took it.

'I'm allus heard you were pretty good with the scythe,' I said, 'but you warn't no match for yer brother, wa' yer?'

He straightened his back as if 'e'd bin shot.

'What der yer mean?' he growled.

'Wer'—I said, 'down the Ram one night one o' yer brothers were there—Steve, I think it were—an' 'e said as 'e could allus beat you anytime wi' a scythe...'

''E said WHAT? WHO DID? MR BLOODY STEPHEN HENRY?' he bawled, and stood up in the cart and laid the whip round the poor old pony till it broke into a gallop and the cart rocked from side to side till I had to 'ang on wi' both 'ands to keep from being pitched out.

I were delighted at the spectacle I'd caused, an' kep' it up.

'Ah,' I said 'Steve said as you never could 'andle a scythe quite as it ought to be done, so you cou'n't keep up with 'im, whatever you done.'

'Wait till I get to the Plough' Rattles snorted. 'I'll Mr Bloody Stephen Henry 'im then! Whoi, I could knock more corn down in a hower wi' a spile-peg than 'e could all day wi' a scythe! I'll 'andle a scythe round 'is legs when I get to the Plough...'

I began to wish as I'd chose a different spot to start a-teasin' 'im, for we were on'y about a mile from the Plough, and I could see as 'e warn't going to have time to cool down afore we got there. My on'y hope were that if any o' his brothers happened to be there, it wou'n't be Mr B—— Stephen Henry. But my luck were out—they were all there. There were no love lost atween any on 'em, and they allus behaved towards each other like strange tomcats, but this time the other two took Steve's part, and afore very long John Thomas and me were running for our lives to the cart, and as soon as we could climb aboard the ol' pony got another whipping an' we tore off down the road faster than we ever had done afore. Cur'ous family they were, and no mistake, all on 'em. When my father-in-law died, his brother Joe, what were the on'y other one left, come to the funeral. He wore a claw 'ammer coat and a glazed flat hat like a priest's, an outfit as 'e'd kept for funerals all his life. When we got back from the church for the funeral tea, 'e asked me if I wanted to buy 'is outfit. Apart from the fact that 'e warn't above 'alf as big as I were, I di'n't exactly hanker after it, so I said 'Well, Uncle Joe, you'll want it yerself, many's a time yet.'

'No, I shayn't Will 'En,' he replied, 'I don't intend to slip it meself, just yet, but this 'ere's the last time I'm ever going mortaring arter dead folks!'

John Thomas never 'ad no use for religion, either church or chapel, but in spite o' that 'e were superstitious. One thing as I remember about 'im were that 'e'd never 'ev a seed o' any sort planted on a Good Friday, an' another one o' his beliefs were that it allus blowed a gale on a day anybody were hung for a crime, to show God A'mighty's displeasure at the takin' o' a human life by other human beings. So 'e must 'ave 'ad some belief. In fact, I know 'e 'ad, on'y while 'e were strong and healthy 'e were too proud to admit it.

After his wife died, 'e lived by 'isself. The baker what used to call on him were a real firm Methodist, and a splendid local preacher. Now and again when he went to deliver the bread, 'e'd say as 'e left 'God Bless you, Mr Papworth.' One day 'e caught Rattles in a bad mood, and when he'd added this to his greeting, my father-in-law set about 'im, and said 'Keep your b—— prayers to yerself. When I want you to pray for me, young man, I'll ask yer.'

Now instead o' losing his temper, or preaching at the old reprobate in a sanctimonious fashion, the baker took it like a man, and replied 'Alright Mr Papworth: that's a bargain. An' if ever you ask me, whatever I'm a-doing, I shall come.'

So the years went on, and poor old John Thomas were took bad (it turned out to be a cancer, like so many other fen folks had). One Saturday when the baker were on his round, he found J.T. waiting for 'im at his door.

'Young man' said Rattles, 'do you remember me a-saying that if ever I wanted you to pray for me, I'd ask you? Well, I'm a-asking now!'

The baker turned on his heel and went to the gate. He called to his son who was in the van on the road.

'Son,' he said, 'take my basket and get off as fast as you can round the fen by yerself. I'm stoppin' 'ere with Mr Papworth.'

So they went in together, and every Saturday afterwards the baker stopped and prayed and read with him, till the day 'e died, which 'appened to be a Saturday. They have both been dead some years now, but I reckon that story does honour and credit to 'em both.

When he died, the parson at the church had had an illness, and was having to have somebody to take services for him. We were therefore very surprised when he declared that he wished to bury John Thomas himself for we di'n't think as 'e 'ardly knowed 'e existed. But seem'ly John T. had been in the habit o' going up to the churchyard, when it were getting dusk, and putting little bunches o' flowers on his wife's grave. The parson had found him there one night, and had talked to him, the first o' many such occasions. Poor parson Brown were going a bit strange in his own head, but he took to his late visitor, which accounted for him asking to be allowed to take the funeral service. They 'ad another parson there, just in case, and 'e were needed, because just as he got to the committal, poor Mr Brown began to mumble and sway, and stumbled and 'ould have fell into the grave atop o' the coffin if somebody ha'n't catched him. So Rattles were the last man as 'e ever buried, and very soon afterwards 'e went to 'is own outhouse, put a double barrelled gun in his own mouth, and pulled the trigger.

So we leave him with John Thomas, Old Carnell, Al Elderkin an' a lot more folks as I'm mentioned, in the churchyard down by the river. I don't reckon any on 'em has got 'eadstones, so quite likely nobody knows as they lay there, on'y them as read this. I'm often 'eard people remark, when walking round that churchyard, what a lot o' folks died young. So there were, what with drownings and diptheria and black-spotted fever and consumption and childbirth an' one thing or another. But that ain't the explanation. The truth is that when anybody dies young, they leave other folks o' their own age to mourn 'em, and it is felt to be such a tragedy as some sort o' memorial stone is found some'ow, even if people 'ave to go 'ungry to find the money for it. When old folks die, unless they've got children who want to show their love and their duty, or unless they are got money an' make their own arrangements aforehand, they are just let slip in the ground and forgot. And in my mind, that's how it should be. It won't be long now afore it's my turn to be laid there. I'm very near eighty year young a'ready, and I don't expect to live much longer. I hope nobody'll ever put no 'eadstone over me. Where my bones lay is no matter to anybody on'y my child'en, and they won't forget, I know. Who'll care about William Henry Edwards, born in 1870, in ten year's time? Will 'En, Bill 'Arry, Dad and Grandan may be remembered for a little while longer, though.

Per'aps this ere book'll be my memorial, instead of a bit o' marble, an' I'm allus loved books best, next to people. But if the love I leave behind me, inside all the folks I'm lived among ain't memorial enough, then I don't deserve one at all, an' in that case, I don't want one, neither.

MAM'S BOOK

1

I MARRIED Will 'En the day before Christmas, when I were twenty-two, and he were thirty-two. I'd knowed him for many a year afore then, though. He said he remembered me when I were seven. I were christened that year—me and my sister, and brother. We had a cousin as were born the very morning of the old queen's jubilee, so she were called Jubilee Anne, and when she were christened, we were all christened with her. My father were a curious man, and had all sorts of queer ideas, specially if they could be opposite to other folks'es, and he wouldn't have us children christened. My mother used to worry about it, and somehow or other she got her own way, so we were done with Jubilee Anne.

My sister and me had new black velvet frocks for the occasion, and I were as proud as a peacock 'cos I had a proper little bustle at the back. It were made like a little square pincushion about nine inches long and four or five inches wide, and I tied it round my waist afore putting my frock on. Then we had black velvet poke bonnets underlined with blue satin, and tied

underneath our chins with a big blue satin bow. We set in a row in a pew that were generally used by a big farmer and his family, and when old Parson Harper come down out of his pulpit we all got up and trooped down the church to the font one after the other like ducks to the pond. Mother took our bonnets off and laid 'em on the nearest seat, and there we stood with our faces all turned up while the old man christened our baby cousin, and then dripped the water on us. I remember it all well enough, and it seems that Dad (I shall have to call him that—it comes so ready after all these years) remembered it an' all. He'd be seventeen then, but he must a' bin a bit different from the general run o' young men, for it seems as he took notice of us little girls and has told me many a time that I never looked more beautiful than I did then.

I don't remember him, though, till I were about thirteen or so, when I see him at a School Treat. We used to go to the Methodist Chapel Sunday school (though we were christened church!) and every year on the second Tuesday in June we had our treat. We used to dress up in our best clothes and go off to the next field to the Heights Cluss, about three o'clock in the afternoon, carrying our mugs. Then we set down in a ring and the helpers brought tea round to us, and bread and butter and cake.

After tea, there'd be the scrambling for nuts and sweets. There'd be Basseloney nuts—about a stone in a big bag, and all sorts of hard, boiled sweets, and the Sunday-school super-intendent would pelt 'em about the field as far as he could all round him, and we'd all scramble for 'em, and we kep' all what we could get. It warn't a very healthy way o' distributing 'em, when I come to think about it for there'd be cows and horses in the field right up till the night afore the treat, and cow pan-cakes and horse pats 'ould be laying about everywhere. But I never remember that we were very worried about a bit o' muck: sweets were too scarce in them days.

After the scrambling we'd play games. There were the round games like *Jinny sets a-weeping* and *Green Gravel* and *There stands a lady on the mountain*: then there was *I sent a letter tew my love, and on the way I dropped it. One o' yew 'es picked it up An' put it in yer pock-et, Tain't yew, tain't yew, tain't yew, tain't yew, TIS YEW.* Then there'd be round tag and long tag, and when the mothers begun to come, they'd join in *There was a jolly miller* until it begun to get

dusk. That's when somebody 'ould suggest *Kiss in the Ring*. I
don't suppose it's ever played now. We used to stand in a ring
and somebody 'ould go round the outside o' the ring quietly,
till he 'tigged' somebody quick and then run off into the field as
hard as he could. The girl he tigged had to follow him and catch
him, and then they'd come back together into the middle o' the
ring and kiss each other, and then the man 'ould join the ring
and the girl 'ould go round till she tigged another partner.
Sometime the game 'ould get a bit slow, 'cos when a boy tigged
his sweetheart she'd run away into the dusk to the corner o' the
field and he 'ouldn't make much of a do o' catching 'er till they
were out o' sight o' the ring, and then they'd walk off and not
come back no more. Then them in the ring 'ould stand waiting
till they guessed what 'ad happened, and start the game again,
until so many couples had gone that there wou'n't be no ring
left. A good many weddings has started wi' *Kiss in the Ring* at
a school treat, and as far as I can see it were as good a way as any
other to pair off. At least you did know who it was you were a-
pairing off with, and you knowed all his family and his character
and his prospects and his temper and everything else about him,
most like.

The first time I ever had a new hat (not a bonnet), I wore it at
a School Treat. My hair were as black as jet, and I wore it hanging loose down my back. It had been washed the night before
and braided into dozens of tiny plaits, so that the next morning
it would be all frizzed and crimped. My new hat was a little straw
boater that sat on the top of my head and had to be kept on with
a long hat pin.

I'd been playing some games, when suddenly my new hat fell
off and went rolling away. I soon found it, but when I went to
put it on again, I'd lost my new hat-pin in the grass. I were in a
way, and started looking about for it—and then Will 'En come up
and asked me what were the matter, and helped me to look for
it. He were twenty-three, then, but he'd already got a reputation
for being the nicest young fellow in the district. I thought he
were very nearly a god, because apart from being tall and big
and handsome, he were so kind and patient and gentle and full
o' fun. My father 'ould come home from a pub and say 'Ah, that

Will 'En Etherds is a nice fella'—and so I thought when he helped me to look for my hat pin.

Four or five year later, I remember him again, when we had a horkey to celebrate the old queen's diamond jubilee. I should be seventeen, then. Some o' the leaders o' the village had had a collection round the houses to get some funds to spend. They'd erected a sort o' tent—a marquee sort o' thing, in the field next to the chapel. The field belonged to old Summers (the maister what kept the brickyard and the pub), and laid between the chapel and the pub. The young men put poles up and hung stack-cloths all round to make a tent. They arranged tables with planks on tubs all down the middle, and a little stage at one end. After the feasting was over, the tables were took away and the planks laid down to form the dancing floor. And there was Will 'En with his concertina, helping to make the music. Old Sambo White had his banjo, and Ponny had his accordian. One of 'em 'ould play 'Haste to the Wedding' while the others danced, and kept on taking turns. Then when it was Will 'En's turn to dance he came down and asked me to dance with him.

Between dances somebody would dance the Broomstick Dance, or sing a ballad. My mother loved singing and got up to sing 'Poor Old Jeff has gone to rest' but she didn't get on very well. Old Sambo White sang

> The Tay Bridge gave way
> And the train went ha-owling
> Dow-own in tew-ew thee a-ang-ree deep

That year there were a long, hard frost and nearly everybody spent their time a-skating. Will 'En were a beautiful pretty skater, but I were never much good at it, so he skated that year a goodish bit with my sister, Lizzie. Once soon after we were married we had just such another long frost, and he tried his level best to get me into the way of it. But I couldn't seem to get on, and at the end o' the day he said 'I don't reckon you really want a pair o' skatin' pattens at all. What you want is a couple o' pork pots!

Then I'd see him once or twice every year at the fair at Ramsey and the feast at Upwood. He had a penny-farthing and a tricycle that I tried to ride and I used to borrow his concertina to see if I could play it.

When I were twenty-one, I'd been away for a bit, and I come home at Easter. My sister and me walked to church on Easter Sunday evening, dressed in our best. As we drawed near the church gates, a gang of young fellows stood there.

'Cor! Look who's a-coming!' they said. 'Woul'n't speak to yew, so yew nee'n't worry,' said another.

'They'll speak to Bill 'Arry, if nobuddy else,' said somebody—and of course, we did. They followed us into church, and when the service was over, they took us home.

Not very long after this I walked along the bank to Walton to visit some friends o' my father. When I were coming back, there were Will 'En (or Bill 'Arry, he answered to both), coming along the bank to meet me, and that night he asked me to marry him. He had a beautiful home of his own and enough ready money to buy whatever we wanted to set up a home with—it were a rare thing, and no mistake, in them days! He bought me a ring the next week, and I went off back to my job at Huntingdon, where I was companion-help to a wonderful old lady. I never told my mother or father—I was afraid of what my father would say, as he was a violent tempered man.

One Sunday morning Will 'En went to see them, and mother was making some jam tarts. He sat down in father's chair and during the conversation said something about 'when we are married'.

'What did you say?' she said, startled.

'Why, aint Kate told you we're going to get married come Christmas?' he said.

Mother laid her rolling pin down, and sat down 'all of a heap', in tears. But they were tears of joy, for never had it entered her head that anything so wonderful could have happened as for one of her daughters to catch such a prize like Will 'En. She adored him, and he her, to the very end, and into the bargain he were the only man as couldn't do no wrong for my father. But things weren't so rosy for him at home, when he told them. His mother didn't want him to marry at all, 'let alone a school-gal' (a reference to my youth compared with him), and his sisters all felt that

they were a cut above my family, 'cos they were farmers, and my father only a higgler, with a queer temper, and a curious reputation an' all.

But it di'n't make no difference, and on 24th December we went to St Mary's church in a little trap, with my sister as bridesmaid, and my cousin as best man. My father had one of his awk'ard fits on and wouldn't come to the wedding, so Mother daren't come, and my brother had to give me away.

There weren't no spectators at weddings then, and we had it all to ourselves. We had to pass Will 'En's father's house on the way, but there was nobody looking out for us there, neither. They meant to, it appears, and sent out Bill's sister's little girl, Elsie, who was three, to watch for us. When we got there, we could only see Elsie, so we picked her up, just as she was, and took her to church with us; she was the only witness of our wedding except the official party. We stopped at Bill's father's house for tea, and Mother came up in the evening for a little while. We'd cleared the barn, and we kept up the wedding for the best part of the week, dancing and feasting. Bill lost his tie when he were getting ready to go to the church, and never did find it again—he had to wear an old one—the very same thing happened when my sister was married.

We stopped at his Mother's that night, and about six o'clock the next morning she came banging on our door yelling 'Bill, git up as soon as iver you can—the ole cow's a-calving', so although it were Christmas morning and the first morning of our married life into the bargain, he had to get up and be midwife to a cow.

Then after a week we went off to our own home in Lotting Fen.

2

THE house we went to live in were the one Bill had built when he come to the end of his boating life in partnership with Charlie, and were about a mile down one of the droves that run parallel to each other joining the high road with the Raveley Drain, across Lotting Fen.

I warn't born in the Lotting Fen, nor anywhere very close to it. My father used to live the other side o' St Mary's Bridge when he were a boy, and my mother come from Yaxley. They had a lot of adventures when they were first married, but if I start going all round by Will's mother's to tell you what happened to them, I shall never get to my own story.

When I were born they were living about five mile from Lotting Fen, in another fen, and as soon as ever I were born, father made up his mind to leave the fens and go and get hisself a job in a stone quarry somewhere in the North, near Manchester. I shouldn't be surprised if his going were a forced job, 'cos they did a moonlight flit in their old horse and cart. They took their bed and put it in the bottom o' the cart, and Mother and me and my brother, were put on it and away we went. That's how I never come to get vaccinated. I reckon Mother were glad about that— she never did hold with vaccination a lot. That warn't much to be surprised about, really. The doctor used to vaccinate one child from another all the while. When my brother had been vaccinated, the doctor at Ramsey sent for Mother to take the child to see him at a certain time on a certain day. He warn't very well 'cos his arm were paining him, and it were a pouring wet day, but Mother thought it were for his own good, so she carried him three mile and a half through the rain to the old doctor's. When she got there she found about a dozen other mothers with babies all waiting to be vaccinated from our baby.

She warn't very worried about me being vaccinated, but she were allus worried 'cos she said I ha'n't been registered in the hurried flight. It never worried me, though, until a few years ago, when I wanted to prove as I really were seventy. I thought I shoul'n't be able to get my old age pension without my birth certificate. But when we begun to make enquiries, my birth certificate turned up, giving all the correct details of my father being a higgler, etc. So I were registered after all: but when my sister Lizzie wanted hers a year or two afterwards, there warn't no

trace o' that. Mother must have got us muddled somehow. She had such a lot to put up with, and so many experiences of one sort or another it warn't much to be wondered at if the bottom had fell right out of her memory box.

Father couldn't have stopped long down at Manchester. For one thing, he got his foot crushed in the quarry, and for another Mother were bad, and they soon came back to the fens again. By the time I were atween three and four, we were living in a little house, one of a row of four cottages on the Herne. I remember living there. There were only one room downstairs, and two up. A ladder went from the downstairs room into the smaller room upstairs, and I remember my mother coming rushing up the ladder one morning when me and my sister were still in bed in a swing cot, laying one each end.

'Get up' she said. 'Be quick! There's a wild beast show going by!'

We scrambled out o' the cot in our bedgowns and rushed to the window. It was level with the floor, about two feet square, and we all knelt down to look out.

The animals were all just going past. There were a couple of elephants stumping along and swaying their trunks about—they were quite as high as we were and too close for my peace o' mind. I remember the camels, an' all, and then there were a lot more covered carts what had the bears and other dangerous animals in them.

They were on their way to Ramsey, where a Wild Beast Show was going to be held. By the time I remember actually going to see a wild beast show, the arch at Ramsey had been covered in and they used to be held in the Great Whyte in the street. But the one I see a-going by that morning wouldn't a-bin held there, for the river run right up atween the houses then.

When my husband first went a-boating turf, he used to hail his lighters right through the Gt Whyte up the river. The little old houses stood right on the brink, and as they sailed gently up, the old women 'ould come rushing out for some 'cesses' for their fires. They'd throw their penny into the barge and then the boatman 'ould nip up six turf in a row atween his two hands, and throw 'em as neat as you please into the old woman's apron, that she'd be a-holding out ready. So the business were done without any hindrance at all. The old turf men allus used to throw the cesses to each other six at a time, and one 'ould throw, and the other catch, so neat as they never hardly dropped one.

When the river were all arched over and made into one wide street, in Ramsey, it were about one o' the widest streets in England, and there were plenty o' room to have a wild beast show on it, then. It warn't a circus—there were no performing animals. It were just a chance for us country folk to see the queer creatures. They had a big tent and inside all the cages were set so as you could walk round and look at them. Outside the main door there were allus a big fire a-burning, with great long iron rods, red hot, in it. These were to control the animals if they got excited and out of hand. One year when the show were on at

Ramsey there were quite a bit of excitement. The lions suddenly begun to git so troublesome that it seemed they'd break out o' their cages. They roared and snarled and pounded their bars, that the men had to come a-running with their red hot bars, but even then they couldn't quieten 'em.

Then the manager come out and announced that he would have to ask the lady who was expecting a child, who was in the tent, to leave. He said 'e knowed what the matter was, because lions could allus smell a woman as was expecting, and then they allus behaved like this, though he ha'n't ever knowed 'em to be quite so bad afore.

Well there were a poor young woman there as were like to have a child soon. When she found the lions a-roaring at her and everybody a-blaming her and pushing her outside the tent, she were so frightened and upset that she fainted right away. I remember my mother and her neighbours a-talking about it, and if I remember aright, they blamed her a bit for ever going to a wild beast show in such a state. Of course, they thought such an experience would mark the child, and that it 'ould be born with a lion's mane, or something like that.

I know all these birthmarks are laughed at nowadays, as old wives tales, but we believed in such things. When I were a child, I had a white lock down the back o' my head—where it growed because my mother were frightened by a white bear at Peterborough Fair: another child had a slice of beetroot on his leg, because his mother slapped her leg when fancying a bit o' beetroot, and another one a bunch o' fly-blows on her nose 'cos her mother pinched her own nose when she found a bit o' meat fly-blowed and stinking. Then there's a man with a pair of greyhounds leaping up his back, and another with black pig skin and bristles on his head, because his mother looked at a black pig what had been burned to death in a fire.

Everybody as were expecting 'ould have 'fancies', usually fancying something they couldn't get. Then when the child were born, it 'ould be buttoning up its mouth and licking its lips, and the old women 'ould say 'He wants a little bit of whatever it were yew fancied. What warrit?' And if it were possible, they'd rub the baby's mouth with whatever it was, like a sour apple or a pickled onion, or whatever and say 'Now it'll be satisfied.' I'm heard my mother say that the first thing as ever passed my lips were a tiny bit of hare's brain.

The worst bit as I ever call to mind were a neighbour of our'n as were allus a poor, frail creature. She went out to pick some 'taters up one morning, and by mistake she picked up a fat, cold and clammy toad. It made her dither so much she shook her hands in horror to get rid o' the feeling, and when the baby were born, she see the result, for she'd shook all the poor child's fingers right off, and he had on'y little stumps on both hands.

It were a recognised part o' the daily round to go in and out of your neighbours two or three times every day. When a woman were expecting the neighbours 'ould take it on 'em to be interested and helpful. When the woman in question went in to see her neighbour, the neighbour 'ould say 'If you see anything you want on my table yew take it, an' welcome,' such store they set by having anything you fancied when you were carrying a baby.

There warn't very few as had a doctor for a confinement. There were allus a village midwife, 'the wise woman', as 'ould be in at the births and deaths, and she'd be in attendance. The mother wou'n't get much fussing up, afterwards, either. Her meals 'ould be a basin o' bread sop, with a mite o' butter and salt and pepper, or else a basin o' milk gruel thickened with flour and sugared.

Washing the new baby would be a bit of a problem, owing to shortage of water. I know most folks think there's too much water in the fen, but they ought to be there in summer time. Then the rivers and drains and dykes all dry up till there ain't a spoonful o' water nowhere, and it used to be all anybody could do to get enough to drink. Most houses 'ould have a rainwater tub, but that 'ould be green and shiny and full o' striddlebags, little wriggling creatures as 'ould turn into gnats afore long. That warn't very good tack to drink, but it were better than the muck from the dykes. Many's the time I'm seen a man or woman in the bottom o' the dyke, waiting for the water to seep into a tablespoon to be put into a kettle for the one cup o' tea o' the day. As late as 1921 we had a summer without water; it were so

172

bad that year that we could only have one bowl o' water a day in the house for everybody to wash in. The first up in the morning were the lucky one, 'cos he had it clean, but everybody else all day had to have the same water used over and over again.

The dyke water were hard and had to be softened somehow. We used to make a lea by mixing a quarter of a stone o' soda and a bucket-ful of wood ashes into it overnight. It 'ould be soft, this 'sody-lea', but it 'ould be the colour o' cider, and it 'ould take a nice lot o' blue-bag to get your clothes white in it.

The water for washing had to be got from the dipping hole—the man 'ould go and get it overnight with a pair o' yokes acrost his shoulders and a little jet to dip with. Then it 'ould be there for use the next day. Most houses had a water butt outside the door to catch soft water in, and while it lasted this were used to wash yourselves in. After it had stood for a little while in the summer, it 'ould be full o' little wriggling creatures, as thick as hair in the water. Ugh, how I hated having to wash in water full o' them striddlebags!

Nobody ever washed theirselves in the house more 'n once a week, when they had a 'bath' and changed their clothes. Other times they washed in a bowl what stood on a plank stool—about 2ft long outside the door. In the little house where I first remember living, there warn't no back door at all, so each house had its stool and washing tackle outside the front door, facing the road. There'd be a half a coconut shell containing a bit of yellow, strong soap, as hard as flint, and a square of an old shirt tail or a worn out blanket for a face flannel. Men didn't used to shave much, 'cos most of 'em had whiskers, either long or clipped.

All us girls had such long hair, it used to be a trial to get it washed. It were only washed about twice a year when there were plenty o' soft water. Then we should be sent to get two-penn'orth of 'air-ile', and mother would allus doctor it with a drop or two o' 'saint' (scent—usually lavender water). We used to wear our hair in one long plait down over our backs, and keep the snarls out of it with a little besom brush.

It were a job to keep children's hair free from lice, especially when girls whose mothers' couldn't be bothered, or hadn't time, went to school with their hair hanging round their shoulders. It may seem to you that they might a' done better than that, but on'y them as 'as bin through it knows. The families were so big. There'd be another new baby every year in some houses. (One woman as I knowed had four children in eleven months—two sets o' twins). The poor mother just couldn't keep 'em fed and clothed, let alone clean, very often, for she never had enough money and were allus carrying another child while she had two as couldn't walk. There wouldn't be enough seats for 'em to set down on, so they allus had to stand up round the table to 'ev their meals. Their beds were made of straw, so that when they wetted it, it 'ould all run through. Then when they got too bad, they could be burnt and have a fresh one. There warn't anything on'y straw beds in most folks's houses. Anybody as had chaff beds had a real luxury, and best of all were a bed of oat-flights 'cos they'd be free from thistles. These straw beds were a real breeding place for fleas, and the poor little kids 'ould be bumped up all over with flea bites. You could tell a child as come from a flea-pit, 'cos its neck 'ould all be spotted all over like a plum pudding.

Ah, poor kids, they didn't have a very good time. My mother 'ould allus have us dressed beautiful, whatever the trouble and effort to her. But even we could only have 'best' clothes very rarely, and our ordinary school boots were like other children's. We used to have to plough through mud up to our boot tops, and sit in our wet muddy boots all day.

If we were wet when we got to school, we had to stop wet all day. There were only one fire in the school room, and that were right up one end. The little children never got a look at it, let alone feel it.

Our boots were always wet, and they got as hard as wood. On Friday nights they used to be dried and rubbed with 'shoe-ile' to soften them, but it didn't do much good. Our heels were allus raw and the little 'uns would cry all the way to school—two or three mile—'cos their heels hurt 'em so. The boys had to have their boots hobnailed to make 'em last longer, but it made 'em so heavy they could hardly get one foot afore the other.

We used to clean our boots as well as we could with the equipment we had. The shoe blacking were a solid cake about as big as a 4 oz. bar o' chocolate, and we had to moisten it with spit and vinegar. Then it was applied with a rabbit's paw and brushed off with the one and only shoe brush the family possessed.

I remember one morning when I were about ten, I were a-cleaning my boots ready to go to school, spitting on the rabbit's paw and rubbing it on the blacking, when my mother came to me. She must a-bin a beautiful woman in every respect, tho' o' course a child don't stop to think about such things in the ordinary way. I can call to mind how she looked, though, that morning. For one thing I'd got used to reading her face, 'cos we lived in such fear o' rows and quarrels, my father being such a funny-tempered man. When I got home from school every day I used to look at her face to see what the atmosphere o' the day was, and I were allus afraid o' something terrible happening to my mother. When I were a tiny little girl still sleeping with my sister in our old swing-crib, I remember being woke up one morning with her tears dropping warm on my face, and when I looked up she were dressed ready to go out. She told me years afterwards, when I were grown up, that she had made up her mind to leave father that day, and had come to take a last look at us child'en afore starting. If I ha'n't a-woke up and looked at her, she'd a-bin gone, but when I roused, she knowed she'd never leave us of her own free will, whatever happened to 'er, so she took 'er hat and coat off and started getting our breakfasts instead.

Anyway, on the morning I were a-cleaning my boots, my mother were wearing her outdoor bonnet and a clean white apron, which was 'respectable' wear in them days. (Work at home was done in a 'hess'an eppon' [an apron made of hessian].) She had been weeping, I could see, and she had her face set with determination and her back as straight as a ramrod.

'Kate' she said 'you nee'n't clean your boots this morning 'cos you ain't going to school. I want you to stop at 'ome and put your father's pudding on, and see to 'is tea. An' if I don't ever come back, be a good gal and look after him well, and your brother and sister!'

Then she lifted up her apron and showed me what she had

underneath it. Tied round her waist, by a bit of coarse string through the hole in its handle, was the heavy hammer we used to break the big lumps o' coal with at such times as we 'ad any—mostly we burned turf.

'I'll either kill him or he shall kill me this day' she said, and away she went.

I knowed by what she said afore about my looking after my father if she never came back that it warn't him she were referring to, so I were left in a terrible anxiety till she come 'ome again, about $2\frac{1}{2}$ hours afterwards, with a triumphant gleam in her eye, and one corner of her mouth turned up like it allus was when she were pleased or excited. I had to wait a goodish while afore I understood what had happened that day. But I can tell it now.

It appears that one of the neighbours, a man called Wiggy, had a wife as were allus ailing. The poor woman cou'n't get up much, and my mother used to go back'ards and forrards to 'er many a time in the day, doing little jobs to help her and cheering her up a bit. Wiggy and my father were real cronies, birds of a feather in every way. They'd done a bit of unkisliding together, many's the time, but when a lot of valuable 'fossit' (phosphate of lime) was missing from a farmers' shed, my father really didn't know anything about it. But Wiggy did, and when the police come a-looking for it, it were found, covered up, in our pigsty. My father was as surprised as anybody about it—more surprised than most, I dare say, because he were a dog with a bad name and you might as well hang it and be done with it, and I sh'd think as soon as the stuff were missing at all, he got the blame in most people's minds. In this case he actually proved his innocence, and Wiggy wasn't suspected. The farmer got his fossit back, and the matter was dropped. But though Wiggy and Father went on much the same as they had done afore, there were allus bad feeling atween 'em afterwards, and they were allus waiting to 'do each other one'.

It appears that one night when Wiggy were in a pub and had had a drop too much, somebody else mentioned his wife, and how good my mother was, the way she went in and out to her. Wiggy took the opportunity, and told 'em all in the pub that it wasn't his wife she come to see, that were only an excuse to visit him. Of course it wern't long afore the tale reached Father's ears, and the night before the morning I'm talking about, he'd come 'ome and taxed her with 'carrying on' with Wiggy. There had been a terrible row that had gone on all night, and she'd had as much as she could stand, although she knowed perfectly well as he knowed there were no truth at all in the tale. Her life were too hard as it were, without such ungrateful beasts as Wiggy taking her character away.

She walked a mile and a half or so to the place where she knowed Wiggy 'ould be working. That were at the bridge opposite the church, next to the school. A gang o' lighters had come up from the fen loaded with turf, and Wiggy were unloading 'em and ricking 'em on the bank ready for 'em to be took away by whoever had bought 'em. Of course all fenland rivers run atween high banks and when the water were low the barges 'ould lay a long way down from the top o' the bank. So a plank 'ould be placed from the barge to the top, and the turf 'ould be packed on to a 'cess barrer' and wheeled out along the plank. When the cess barrow were loaded it held over a hundred turf, and to keep it steady along the narrow plank were a job as only a practiced old hand could do, and the best way o' keeping it steady were to go fast, like on a bicycle.

When Mother got close to the bridge she could see Wiggy at work unloading, and she told me afterwards that her courage very nearly failed 'er at that moment. There were a pub just the other side o' where Wiggy were at work, with a big yard leading down to the river bank, and a lot o' men, farmers and dealers and watermen, were already there, talking and drinking. One man had come in a pony and trap, and had tied the pony to the railings of the bridge. The whip stuck up in its socket at the side of the driver's seat, and as mother passed the trap she took the whip in her hand and went down to the river bank. Wiggy was quite unawares of her approach, and had just started running up the plank with his barrowload of turf when she went down the plank to meet him. She di'n't stop to explain what she'd come for, she just showed him. His hands were occupied with the barrow handles, and his feet on the narrow plank high above the river, so he cou'n't defend hisself, and she laid about him with the horse whip as hard as she could strike. He yelled and swore and cussed and screamed, till his cries brought the men out o' the pub to see what was going on. Most of them knowed both the people concerned, and the tale what had been going about, so it di'n't take much guessing what it were all about. I dessay they admired mother for taking the law into her own hands, and besides, it were just the sort o' situation they enjoyed. They stood round cheering her on—'Give it to 'im Missus! Now's yer chance! Give him another!' they called, slapping their sides

with excitement. Mother didn't need much encouragement and she wielded the whip so well that he couldn't stand it no longer and let go of his barrow to defend hisself. The barrow with its load, what had been between 'em, fell into the river, and mother lost no time in taking advantage of a closer range. She give him one final cut afore he could close in on her and 'ead over 'eels into the river he went after the barrow.

Then mother tossed the whip aside, dusted her hands on her apron, held up her chin as high as it 'ould go, and walked home again.

Nobody but me ever see the hammer hanging under her apron. I'm often wondered what would have happened if Providence hadn't sent the man with the trap to the pub that morning. It quite likely wouldn't have been a story with quite such a good ending to be telling seventy-five year later, if she'd a' bin forced

to use the hammer. Poor old mother, she'd allus had to set a
hard heart against hard sorrow, and it must a' bin hard that
morning for her to contemplate doing anybody a real injury.
But as it turned out, I think she enjoyed it—I still remember the
twinkle in her eye when she told me about it, years afterwards.

3

I WENT to the same school as Will 'En did, only of course he left when he were ten year old, and that 'ould be afore I were born. It were just as queer a place when I went as it were when he went, and conditions were much about the same as ever. I went for the first time when I were four, and we lived in the same little cottage as we did when I see the wild beast show going by. It were a goodish step to school from there, just about a mile, I should say, and I started after Christmas, when the snow were on the ground. I remember it well enough, because in the middle of the afternoon I had a pain in my stomach and went 'out the back' by myself. I di'n't know very well how to manage, and I got into difficulties with my buttons till it were too late, so I darn't go back into school. Instead, I went off towards home. When I got nearly there, I could see my mother and all the neighbours standing in the road outside the cottages, in the bright winter sunshine, listening to a German band playing in the snow on the side o' the road. Mother looked up and see me coming, and came to meet me.

'What's the matter?' she said, 'Why have you come home by yourself so early?'

I remember hiding my face against her because of the other women, and whispered 'I messed meself' and started to cry. Mother looked so surprised, I can see her face now. She turned up my skirts there in the road, to investigate, and then laughed and said 'That you havn't! You on'y thought you had' and led me back to listen to the band. Then when we turned to go in, the sun had melted the snow on the roof of our house, and it all slithered off the roof with a squelchy splash into the little garden in front of the door. Fancy remembering a little thing like that for over eighty year!

Soon after this we moved house and went to live about three miles from the school in the opposite direction. We were just inside the distance limit, so I had to go, but the journeys were terrible then, specially in winter. Most of the way was along droves, though the last mile-and-a-half was along the 'high way'. Walking is allus bad along the fen droves, up to your hocks in mud in the winter time and in dry dust in the summer. Even the high way had ruts in it you could lay down and hide in, and the only difference was that it had been 'gravelled' with great granite stones the size of a tea cup. They were all left loose on the road to bed down as best they might, and we did the best we could walking over them by keeping one behind the other up the smoother tracks made by the cart-wheels. The best walking we had were when the threshing tackle had been along. The tackle were free standing tackle drawed from place to place by horses, so when it had been along the road its weight had flattened the granites into the mud and made a path we could follow without stubbing our toes all the while. We did suffer on them journeys, specially with cold in the winter. Most of us had a good coat, and the girls had a clean print hood, starched and stiff, every Monday morning. The boys never wore no collar or tie, but they had a red and black check wool scarf round their necks, and caps with ear-lugs to keep their ears warm. We wanted something to keep us warm, because we coul'n't hurry no faster than the droves and the stones on the road 'ould let us, nor no faster than the pace the littlest ones of our gang could keep up. None of our clothes kept the wet out, and no stuff 'ill keep out a black-frost wind blowing across the fen. But worst of all were our sore feet. The boots we had were all made of strong, stiff leather to last a long while and to stand up to the stony road. They got stiffer and heavier through being wet and dried quick over night, standing on the hearth, and they chafed our heels raw. We had blisters and broken blisters and great cracks across our heels that wouldn't heal no matter how much shoemaker's wax was dropped into 'em to seal 'em. (Blisters were treated by drawing a bit or worsted through them with a darning needle, to soak up the water.) The little children 'ould start to cry with their feet afore they'd gone a quarter of a mile, and the slower they walked, the colder they got. Most of us 'ould be crying about something afore we got to school, sobbing quietly or grizzling or wailing or roaring out loud, according to the sort o' children we were. I used to have earache all the time as well, and were in pain at both ends. There must a-been something wrong with my ears, because I was very deaf by the time I were fourteen, and have been ever since.

When we arrived at school, after starting out as soon as ever it were daylight, in the winter, we were already exhausted and frez to the marrow or else sopping wet through, but there were no comfort there for us. Nobody had a change o' clothes or shoes, and there were no means of getting warm or dry. The school had two rooms, 'the schoolroom' (the main big room) and 'the classroom' (a smaller one for the babies). Both of them had a tiny fire place at one end, but no warmth from it ever reached us where we sat and we never got near the tiny fire. At dinner times the biggest children fit for the places near the fire as soon as the teachers had gone out and left us by ourselves, so the little 'uns and the weakest ones and the shy ones never got near it at all. We were never looked after at all in the dinner times, so nobody knowed or cared whether we ever felt the fire or not, though I remember envying one little girl I used to play with. She were a farmer's child, and I should think the teacher must a-give orders as she were to have a special place near the fire, because it were allus left for her. She were the only one of us as had proper sandwiches with meat in them for her dockey, and she used to bring a long knitting needle with her and hang a sandwich on the end of it and toast it in front o' the fire and make all our mouths water so that our own bit o' 'bread and seam' di'n't taste as good as it ought to a-done.

School in them days was a place where you 'learnt your lessons', and teachers di'n't do nothing only 'teach'. It warn't part o' their job to look after the child'en in any other way. So we set wet and cold and hungry and in pain and nobody took no notice at all. Outside the school building, they di'n't take no responsibility for us either. No wonder we stopped away whenever we could, and them as were outside the three mile limit took advantage of the fact and never went at all. My father were a very good scholar for his time, and were keen on us getting all the learning we could, and mother believed in it an' all, so we went whenever it were possible. It were a treat to be able to read, for there were a lot as couldn't read, and writing were useful even if it weren't needed a lot. Letters di'n't come often to such houses as ourn, but we had one occasionally. They were delivered to the village pub twice a week, and we soon got word that there were one for us and collected it from there.

When we got into school we had prayers, and then set down to the morning's work. There were no playtime or 'break', and even the little child'en worked through till dockey time without being allowed out. First of all we got our slates out and 'made pot-hooks'—practising our letters with a squeaking slate pencil. We used to love the job of spitting on our slates to clean them, and rubbing it off with our sleeve. I remember once when my brother had a present of a beautiful new slate and pencil, at home, and he sat drawing on it till it were full and then cleaning it in the usual way to start again. I did want to have a turn with it, but he wouldn't let me, so I set by his side and watched him enviously. Then it come to me how I could take part in his treasure, and next time his slate was full I leaned over with my mouth ready and said 'Do you want any spit?' After writing we gathered round a big reading sheet and read from it, one word or sentence each. Of course we knowed the sentences off by heart, but the words were harder. We used to chant the sentences as if they were poetry, specially as they happened to rhyme

Ann is ill.
Take a pill.
Do not cry.
A hot pie.

We used to sing songs because we had to get them ready for the day when 'the inspector' come, and we all had instructions to come clean and wear clean pinafores. Just before he come we learnt a lot o' songs to charm him with, like 'Home, Sweet home', 'The Ash Grove', and 'When Johnny comes Marching Home again'. There were others, less well known but not quite as puzzling to me

Daddy, dear daddy, come home with us now
The clock in the steeple strikes one.

You promised, dear daddy, that you would come home
As soon as your day's work was done.
Come—home, Come—home.
Dear daddy, come home with us now.

There were others a little bit brighter than this. One I remember
went

The fox and the hare and the badger and the bear
And the birds in the greenwood tree,
And the little bunny rabbit and the little black mole
They've all got a home but me.

and another:

The woodpecker pecked his hole in the tree
The blackbird piped his note so free
The wistful hawk and the bashful jay
Wished each other a happy good-day
Tra-la-la-la-la
Tra-la-la-la-la.

We had to get a lot of 'po'try' ready for the inspector as well. I
don't know whether it was because it were so drilled into us that
I'm remembered a lot of it ever since, or whether it were because
I enjoyed it. Most of it were mournful stuff for us little child'en
to be learning, now I think about it. There was 'I remember, I
remember', and 'The boy stood on the burning deck', when I
was very small. When I had left 'the classroom' and reached 'the
school room', there was 'The Old Armchair'

The years rolled by, and the last one sped
My idol was shattered, my earth-star fled,
I learned how much the heart could bear
When I saw her die in the old arm chair.

I've forgot now who 'she' was, but I used to think it were very
sad, and so was

If you're waking, call me early, call me early, mother dear
For I would see the sun rise upon the glad new year.

For it is the last New Year that I shall ever see
Then you may lay me low in the mould, and think no
    more of me.

and another one that ended

> Bury me where the lilies grow
> But don't bury me deep.

This warn't a very appropriate verse for child'en in the fen, now I come to think about it, because although there were plenty of chance of 'em being buried, there warn't much chance of 'em being buried deep. The church and churchyard were straight across the road from the school, and as I'm said afore, there were no supervision by the teachers at all during the dinner time. So as soon as we had ate our dockey, we were free till afternoon school started, to go where we liked and do just as we liked. In the winter we huddled in the schoolroom, or went down to the station to fill our pockets with carrots from the trucks. One pocket were allus full of carrots, and the other of cocksorrel leaves for chewing. Us girls used to love to collect pins to take to the station with us. We used to leave two pins crossed on the railway line, and wait for the train to run over them. Then they would be squashed together to make a pair o' doll's scissors.

In summer we played either in the river or in the churchyard. The river run right beside the school and there were a bridge over the road there. In the summer the water in the river 'ould be very low, and we used to play at running across the river under the bridge. The water 'ould come up round our knees, mostly, but now and again it 'ould be a bit deeper than we expected and come up to our waists. We held our skirts up as high as we could, but we never bothered to take our boots and stockings off, and of course our knickers used to get soaking wet. Then we went back to school and set in 'em all the afternoon. But we were allus wet, one way or another. No wonder so many on us are got rheumatics now. On the way home from school, or in the evenings, we played down the dyke sides getting wild flowers, and reeds and rushes, and we were more used to being wet than dry.

The churchyard were a different place to play in. It laid next to the river, with only the narrow road atween, and like all fen churchyards it were low and peaty. The graves weren't ever the proper depth, because it were impossible to dig 'em. After the first eighteen inches the water 'ould begin to seep in, and soon the grave 'ould be filled with water, so most folks 'ould be drownded after they were dead if they di'n't happen to die that way. The sexton 'ould do his best to disguise the fact, of course, and they'd pump the water out o' the grave all the time the coffin were in church, and right up to the last minute. Then just as the procession left the church door they'd sprinkle short loose grass into the grave so as it floated on top o' the water. It di'n't deceive nobody, but it made the relations feel a bit better than actually seeing the coffin lowered into water. Anyway, they were never buried very deep. Then, in a fine, hot, dry spell in the summer, the peaty ground all dried and shrivelled. The expensive gravestones people had saved and scrinched to buy all fell over because the peat wasn't strong enough to hold 'em up, and great wide cracks appeared in the graves themselves. Then us children had a fine time. We used to spend our dinner times laying down on the graves, shoving our arms down the cracks to try and touch the coffins. My arms coul'n't a-been very long in them days, but many and many's the coffin I remember touching and feeling through a crack in the peat.

Now and then something startling 'ould happen and we'd all tear off to see, with nobody to stop us. If it were a horse a-running away with its cart and load, we had enough sense to get out of the way afore the cart-horse a-galloping and a-blundering and its load a-swaying reached us. If it were a funeral, we got where we could get a good view, and stood and gawped at the coffin and the people in their new black, especially if it were a man being buried, and his wife walked after him all in her thick crepe weeds, with her tiny children, our own playmates very often, walking solemn and scared in front of her, after the coffin. When the mourners had left the graveside, we tore as fast as we could to it to see the coffin down in the hole afore the grave-digger could start filling it in, and if there were flowers we looked at 'em all afore leaving, making the most of the event. Occasionally when somebody of consequence were being buried, the old schoolmaster kept us in so that we didn't gawp at the mourners, but when it were one of the ordinary folk, we just joined in as we liked.

One dinner time, there were a fire at the farmyard next to the churchyard. It were in a dry spell and everything burnt like tinder and had gone up in smoke afore anybody could do anything. There were a lot o' pigs and horses in the yard, and as soon as the men see it they run to open the gates and let the poor creatures out. They were too late to save some of 'em, and the poor animals were roasted alive, but they did manage to get some gates open, and horses and cows and pigs, all mad and frantic with terror were a-galloping and a-rearing and a-gadding and a-squealing about while the men di'n't know whether to try and catch them or to try to rescue some more or to try to put the fire out. And there we were, a great swarm of us kids, all out o' control ourselves with excitement, getting in everybody's way and hampering the rescue operations as well as being in danger ourselves from burning materials and falling roofs and fire-maddened animals. I were there, and I know. When at last the school bell rung for us to go back to afternoon school, we went very unwilling. As I were running back across the littered yard, a bit o' paper blowed across my feet and I stopped and picked it up. It were a bit o' white paper with black writing on, and I tried to read it, but I coul'n't, so I tore it up into little bits and throwed it away. It were many a year afterwards that I see another like it, and realised that what I'd tore up and throwed away were a five pound note. At least, it looked the same to me.

When nothing out o' the way were happening, we played games in the school yard. The boys played fub-'ole with marbles and the girls played 'jinks' with five stones. Then there were round games like *There stands a lady on the mountain* and *Poor Jinny sets a-weepin'*. It seems to me now that whatever game we played used to have some sort o' words to go with it, else it weren't played right. We used to play *Fox and Hares,* a game child'en now call *Hide and Seek*. The party what were hiding went away to 'git 'id', and the other party 'ould hide their faces and chant

> When you're 'id, holler
> Else the little dugs 'on't foller.

Oranges and lemons had its own proper rhymes and so did another
game we used to play called *Thread the tailor's needle,* which were
a bit like oranges and lemons, the words being

> It is so dark we cannot see
> To thread the tailor's needle.

Not that we ever said it like that, because we had a family of boys
from our end as coul'n't speak properly, and they used to say

> Titho dark, tannot tee
> Tithew, tathoo, nithew.

so of course we copied them. Every night there'd be two big old
boys standing at the main gate o' the school yard when we come
out, to dub us as we went under their arms King, Queen, 'Bacca-
box, Shit-shovel, Lick-it-clean, and we used to hate it if we had to
be 'Lick-it-clean'. Then there were skipping games—specially to
find out who we were going to marry. You had to go and find
a five-leafed clover afore you could play that game, then you
could take part in *Tinker, tailor, soldier, sailor,* with all its other
details.

> Coach, carriage, wheel-barrow, muck cart,
> Silk, satin, muslin, rag,
> Big 'ouse, little 'ouse, pigsty, barn.

There were rhymes for everything—some just for the saying and
nothing else. We liked 'em better than the mournful poetry we
were teached at school. We cupped our fists, leaving a hole
between finger and thumb, and said

> Cobby's gone to market, to buy a new comb.
> Put your finger in cobby's 'ole, and see if 'e's got 'ome.

and another child would put his finger in the hole to see if it got
'squez': or we tapped our for'eads and pulled our ears and

188

ringed our eyes with thumb and finger, lifted our noses and put
a finger into our mouths as we chanted

> Knock at the door
> Ring the bell,
> Peep through the key-'ole
> Lift up the latch
> And WALK IN.

The rhymes we said were often about courting or getting
married, and the ones we loved best were the vulgar ones

> Polly went a-walking one fine day
> She lost her britches by the way.
> The girls did laugh, and the boys did stare
> To see poor Polly with her backside bare.

> Clover one and clover two,
> Put it in your right foot shoe
> The first young man that you shall meet
> Shall be your sweetheart all the week.

> *Reply:*
> If his hair don't curl
> And his teeth don't shine
> And he ain't good looking
> Then he shan't be mine.

> Mary had a pudding
> She made it very nice
> She wouldn't stick the fork in
> Till George come home at night
> Georgie will you have a bit
> Don't say no.

> *Reply:*
> Save it for our wedding day
> Ha, ha, ho.

I'm got a long way from what I were saying about school,
thinking about the games we used to play: so I shall have to go
back and get another start.

4

THE school were run by a family called Rigby. Old Daddy Rigby were the schoolmaster, and his family helped him. He were tall and had scraggy ginger hair round a bald place on top of his head, but mostly this were covered up by a red velvet smoking cap. He had a grisled red beard, and a straight leg, what he

used to put any poor child he were caning over and hold him down while he threshed him. He were a vicious old beggar, and no mistake. We were all frit to death of him, and no wonder. He lays buried just inside the churchyard gate, and I'll bet I ain't the only one of his pupils what has looked at his stone coffin tombstone many a time since then and been glad he were underneath it.

His wife were short and a bit dumpty, like old Queen Vicky, and allus wore a little mob cap. She only teached when they were a bit short of teachers. Then there were three daughters and two sons, and they all had a hand in the school. Miss Mary got married and went away, and Mr Rob went away after a bit, to be a schoolmaster somewhere else. Mr Fred bettered hisself by going to work in a draper's shop, and Miss Phoebe died after her mother and father. So that only left Miss Alice. She were like her father and wore a bright ginger wig. Years after, when the school had closed, she lived on by herself in the old school house, very poor and very fond of whisky, so she took to selling bits and pieces from the house to pay for it, until she'd sold pretty near everything as anybody 'ould buy. She were fond o' men, too, I'm heard tell, and the men 'ould call and see her because they were sure to get a good dose o' whisky. Once when a man called to see her, they both had a go at the whisky bottle till they begun to get merry, and then he pulled her down on to his knee; but Alice made a blundering do a-getting there, and somehow got her head on his weskit buttons, and when she went to sit up she left her wig behind her. My word di'n't he soon claw up and run, as soon as he could get the wig off his button. He never called again for no more whisky.

Of course we hated 'em all, every one on 'em. Teachers in them days were cruel to the children in any case, because they thought that were the only way to make 'em learn anything, and for all I know it may be so. But looking back on the Rigby's, it seems to me that they must have despised us all as poor, ignorant creatures of a different sort from theirselves, and treated us more like animals than child'en.

We were very poor, but my mother had had a lot better bringing up than most folks in the fen, and she loved to do things as well as she could. She had to work for us herself to see we had nice clothes, but she didn't care about that, and so we were kept as neat and clean and tidy and pretty as any o' the farmers' children. Perhaps that was why the Rigby women singled my sister and me out. Not for any favouritism, but for special duties. One morning after I'd answered to my name on the register and said prayers, Miss Mary called me out and took me through the door into the school house. There she set me to work, washing up the breakfast things and dusting until morning school were over. Next morning, it were the same again, only it were doing the vegetables and cleaning the shoes, and some days I went back in the afternoons as well. At the end of the week, she give me my pay, a quarter of an orange peel! This went on for weeks and months. Then one night at home we were all sitting round the table at home 'making pothooks' on our slates, and writing words, and Mother said 'I don't know why it is Kate don't seem to improve as much in her schooling as you others do,' and my sister, who was younger than me but a lot perkier, said ''Tain't likely she'll get on, 'cos she's never at school.' Mother began to ask questions, and soon found the truth out. But as far as I know, it never made no difference. Perhaps she di'n't complain, because she'd know we should be the ones that 'ould suffer. I still went on going into the school house, and got promoted to doing all the bedrooms out before I left. After that my sister were took on, but she were different from me and had a lot more pluck. She woul'n't do just as she were told as meek as I did, and she knowed she ought to a-bin in school doing her lessons. The Rigby's used to have an old boy about my own age in as well, to clean the knives and do the ashes, and so on. When my sister had to take over, her and the old boy who were helping her tried to get their own back—on the cat. They took the poor thing because it were the Rigby's pet, and tied a bit o' rope round it's neck, and hung it in one o' the apple trees in the garden. They were just making sure it were dead, by pulling the poor thing's back legs as hard as they could, when one o' the Rigby's see 'em and come in time to rescue it. I can't remember whether they ever had to go into the house again or not.

They very often kept us there until after the other children had gone home, and this were real bad for us, because it 'ould be pitch dark sometimes afore we got home. We used to play games all the way home to get us along, and it di'n't seem to matter how far it were quite so much when there were a lot on us to-gether. But if you were by yourself, it did seem a long way. Besides, it warn't safe for one little child to be out alone along the sides of them dykes on a slippery pad, and most child'en had to cross a dyke or a drain, on a plank, somewhere on the way home. We were allus warned about 'the old hooky-man' what 'ould get us if we played down by the dykes, but there warn't no way o' getting to a lot o' places except by crossing some water. Where there were a sleeper bridge, we felt safe, but though we were used to a sagging plank about ten feet long over a drain eight feet or so wide, we never liked 'em a lot. And there's no mistake that the old hooky-man did get a lot o' children, one how or another. I remember ever so many tragedies while I were still a child myself. The worst one were when two o' my own little friends, Fanny and Polly were drownded. The ice bore well, that year, and we were all in such a hurry to get home so that we could go sliding and skating. These two little sisters hurried off home and put their skating-pattens on, and away they went up the river. The ice were solid enough because it had been a long frost, but every here and there, there'd be a thin place where somebody had had to break it to make a dipping hole for the household water. If they had kept to the middle o' the river, they'd abin alright; but somehow they got to the side, and one of them got on a thin place and went under the ice. The other one tried to get her out, but the ice broke away from the side o' the hole and she went under as well. So both of them were drownded within twenty minutes o' leaving their house. It were allus the dipping holes as were the danger. One day when the railway first begun to run trips to the sea-side, there were a trip arranged for Hunstanton. Most people in our fen had never seen the sea till then, and a lot o' people went just once to have a look at it. One man were going to take his son on a trip one morning, and were busy getting ready, and all his family helping him. Then him and the old boy set out for the station, about a mile and a half away. But they never see the sea that day, after all, for while they were getting dressed, the baby o' the family, just toddling, had slipped outside without nobody noticing. As soon as her husband had gone, the mother missed him and started looking for him. She found him drownded in their own dipping hole, and a neighbour went after her husband and caught him afore he reached the station.

The worst case as I ever remember, and one as made the most impression on me, perhaps, was that of a little girl. Her mother and father had gone to America when they were first married, but they hadn't done very well, and they come back again. By this time they had this little girl called Polly, one of the sweetest and handsomest little things I'm ever seen in my life.

However, on the way home across the sea, the poor child's mother, what had been ailing, died aboard ship, and had to be buried over the side, and the young father come back by hisself except for his little daughter. He come to stop with his wife's sister and her husband, what hadn't got no children of their own, and they were so took up with the child they begged to be allowed to keep her. Her father had to get some work, so he willingly agreed, and her uncle and aunt coul'n't do enough for her. I remember they bought her a great big doll, the most wonderful doll as had ever been seen in our fen, nearly as big as she were herself, and she'd be about three year old when she come.

Then one day, about three months after she got there, her uncle, as were so proud of her, took her with him one day when he were going out with a horse and cart. Coming home, with the little girl sitting perched up on the front o' the cart beside him, they had to cross a sleeper bridge over the drain. Perhaps he never got the wheels quite straight for the bridge, or perhaps the horse shied, but however it was, the wheel got over the side o' the bridge and the horse and the cart and everything plunged down into the drain. The man jumped, or were throwed clear, but the little girl went into the water with the cart upside down on top of her, and the horse plunging about to get hisself out. There were plenty of help soon there, but the horse had to be got away so they could lift the cart, and the poor mite were drownded long afore they could move it. It nearly killed her uncle as well, he were so grieved. When they carried her little white coffin up to the churchyard, the big doll were in it an' all, which seems a waste in a place where nobody ever had no bought toys, but I think if it 'ad been me I should a-done the same, for I'm sure I cou'n't a-beared to see any other child with it if such a terrible thing had happened to one o' my little girls.

I wonder there wern't more on us drownded than there were, for in spite o' the old hooky-man, we played a lot down the dykesides. For one thing, they were a mass o' flowers all the spring and summer: there'd be wild violets and forgetmenots in the spring, followed by beautiful yellow 'flags' (irises) as you could gather by the armful. Then there'd be a tiny little pansy we called jonquils, and in the summer there'd be yellow water lilies and 'hen-and-chickens', the pretty pink clusters of flowering rush. Feathery reeds stood above our heads, and we used to pull the pointed leaves of 'em for two purposes. If you laid the flat leaf tight atween the two palms o' your hands, and blowed short and sharp on it in a certain way, you could make a piercing shriek of a whistle as 'ould tear your eardrums, and if you knowed how you could make a real little boat that 'ould sail up the dyke, out of one of the leaves. You took the leaf with its hard little stalk still on it and folded each end of it back. Then you split the folded ends into three and tucked one o' the outside ones through the other outside ones, leaving the middle one flat for the little boat to sail on, and the stalk 'ould stick up in the middle like a real little mast. Then you dropped 'em on the water as light as you could, and away they'd sail till they got washed to the side. We gathered the great brown cat-tail rushes to take home for our mothers, and the thin little dark green rushes for ourselves. These were full o' white pith. We stripped off the green covering, and got the long, bendy pith out as long as we could and about an eighth part of an inch across. Then when we'd gathered enough, we set down and wove it into baskets for our flowers, or into 'Annie Roony' flowers to wear ourselves. Of course we ate anything we could as wern't poisonous. There were one sort o' reed as growed white under the water and green at the top. If you pulled hard enough it 'ould come up whole with a sucking noise. Then you could put your thumbnail along the white part and squeeze the 'butter' out and eat it. Little flat mallow seeds we called 'cheeses' and I must have ate pounds of 'em. We dug up tansy roots to eat, and filled our pockets with buckwheat whenever we could. We sucked the taste of honey from the tip ends of the white dead-nettle flowers, and suffered agonies peeling thistle buds down to get at the little white nut in the middle. Then off to gather different sorts of flowers again to dress ourselves up in to play 'Kings and Queens'

—great pink-striped bindweed flowers on trails of green twisty stalks and leaves, as you could bind round your heads and waists and trail about in as if they were royal robes. When you'd got yourself dressed up, you could lean over the water and see yourself, if you could find a patch that wern't covered with growing things, or watch the beetles skimming about on top with their long legs trailing after them, among the floating water lily and arrowhead leaves, or run squealing away at the sight of the long blue, green and red 'darning needles' or 'sew-your-eyes-up', as we called the dragonflies. Now and again we had the luck to find a reed-warbler's nest slung atween three rushes, and everywhere there'd be a mass o' beautiful butterflies, but we were so used to them we never took much notice on 'em. Only the old iron-'ards defeated us, for try as you may you can't pick these flowers with your bare hands, though their great long purply-red flowers were very tempting. I'm heard my husband say as their proper name were 'purple loosestrife' and that they were called 'iron-hards' because the roots were so hard that when the men were doing the dykes out, if they hit one o' the roots o' this plant, it were so tough and hard it 'ould bend their shovels.

Our fen were close to the edge o' the high lands, and about three miles away there were a wood. In the early spring this 'ould be covered with primroses, and every Good Friday we ganged together for a walk to the wood, carrying a bit of a picnic there in a basket, so as we'd got the basket there to put the flowers in to carry home. We picked all the morning and then went off so as we'd have time enough to arrange our flowers, get washed and have our hairs done in time to go down to the tea at the Chapel which were allus followed by a 'Service of Song' to mark the Chapel anniversary. This were one o' the highlights o' the year for us, and Good Friday were a day we looked forrard to more than most.

Our mother's 'ould save up to take the whole family to the tea (6d. for grownups, 3d. apiece for the child'en) and soon the chapel 'ould be crowded with people sitting round the slabs o' wood resting across the tops o' the pews, with a steaming brass or copper tea-urn, polished till it gleamed like gold, at the top

of each one, and a rosy faced woman behind it, pouring out. A
lot of people 'ould come from villages all round, walking or in
farm carts with the child'en setting in the bottom. Then our
Mams and Dads would see old friends they ha'n't seen since the
year afore, and we'd shyly make new friends as we shou'n't see
again till the next year, per'aps. When the tea and the talk were

over, the chapel 'ould be cleared, and some singers from
Ramsey or Upwood or somewhere 'ould come to 'render' the
Service of Song they'd been practising. The chapel 'ould be full
and crowded to overflowing, and as soon as it got dark the oil
lamps 'ould be lit and the doors and windows shut, and the
preacher would go up to the pulpit. Then he'd announce the
opening hymn for all the congregation to sing, and read the first
verse out loud

> Praise ye the Lord! 'Tis good to raise
> Your 'earts and voices in 'is praise
> 'Is nature and 'is works invite
> To make this duty our delight.

It were a delight to us, and no mistake, and there we all set like
little mice listening to the singing and the reading till we got to

joining in the 'dog's 'oliday' (doxology), and sleepy and tired we stood up with the rest to sing

> *Praise 'im* from—whom—all—*bless—sings flow*
> *Praise* 'im—all—creatures—'ere be—*low :*
> Praise—'im—above—ye—'eaven—lee—'osts
> *Praise Far—ther, Son and Ho—lee—ghost.*

Then we stumbled out into the pitch-dark night and clinging to mother's skirts, went up the road in gangs led by a man with a lantern, till we dropped out one family by one as we reached our own gates.

5

LIVING where we did and how we did, we used to make the most of anything a bit out o' the ordinary, and we looked for'ard from one special day to the next. Looking back on it now, I'm surprised to see how many high days and holidays there were during the year that we kept, and we certainly made the most of any that children could take part in at all.

Just after Christmas, there'd be Plough Witching to look for'ard to. This were Plough Monday, and of course I know that that is still kept in churches all over the land. But our Plough Monday ha'n't got nothing to do with church as I knowed. There were two or three different things about it. For one thing there were the pranks the young fellows got up to, playing tricks on their neighbours. Very often these were real nasty tricks, and they'd wait until Plough Monday to get their own back on somebody what had done them some injury during the year. Perhaps they'd take a plough in the middle o' the night and plough the other fellow's doorway up, or move the water butt so as it stood resting on a bit of its bottom rim, a-leaning up outside the door. Then when the man o' the house opened the door afore it were light, next morning, the tub 'ould fall in and the water slosh all over the floor o' the house-place, for the poor woman to clean up on her hands and knees afore the children could come out o' the bedroom. Very often a gang o' young men 'ould go round the fen taking gates off their hinges and throwing 'em in the nearest dyke, so that all the horses and cows got out. This sort o' nasty trick gradually died out during my young days, and a good thing too, I reckon.

Then there were the Straw Bear and the Molly Dancers. The Molly Dancers 'ould come round the fen from Ramsey and Walton all dressed up. One would have a fiddle, and another a dulcimer, or perhaps a concertina and play while the rest danced. This were really special for Christmas Eve, but o' course the dancers cou'n't be everywhere at once on one day, so they used to go about on any other special day to make up for it. They'd go from pub to pub, and when they'd finished there, they'd go to any houses or cottages where they stood a chance o' getting anything. If we ha'n't got any money to give 'em, at least they never went away without getting a hot drink. Sometimes it 'ould be hot beer. In pubs they used to hot the beer by sticking a cone-shaped metal container down into the glowing turf fire, with the beer in it. Then it would be made syruppy sweet with brown sugar, and spiced with ginger, served with a long rod o' glass to break the sugar up and stir it with, for 2d. a pint. At home it might be done in the same way, or it might simply have a red-hot poker plunged into it. Sometimes the Molly Dancers got home-made elderberry wine, well sugared and made scalding hot and spiced with cloves. A lot of the fen women were very good at making wine, and their elderberry would be so dark and rich as you could hardly tell it from port wine. So a good tumbler full of that, all sweet and hot and spicy, were worth dancing for, and kept the cold out till they got to the next cottage.

The Straw Bear were a sort o' ceremony that took place on Plough Monday when I were a child, though my husband says it used to belong to some other day once and only got mixed up with plough witching time by chance. A party of men would choose one of their gang to be 'straw bear' and they'd start a-dressing him in the morning ready for their travels round the fen at night. They saved some o' the straightest, cleanest and shiniest oat straw and bound it all over the man until he seemed to be made of straw from head to foot, with just his face showing. When night came they'd set out from pub to pub and house to house, leading the straw bear on a chain. When they were asked in, the bear would go down on his hands and knees and caper about and sing and so on. Some parties used to do a play about 'Here I come I, old Beelzebub', and there were another place where one man knocked another one down, and then stood over him and said

> Pains within and pains without
> If the devil's in, I'll fetch him out
> Rise up and fight again.

My sister, who is very nearly as old as I am, says it were the straw bear party as used to perform this play, and she remembers it the year when our father were the straw bear. I say it were the Molly Dancers what used to do the play, and I never remember my father being the straw bear. There's no accounting for what tricks memory'll play, so we shall never know which on us is right. I do remember hearing about the year when Long Tom were the straw bear, though. His mates had spent the whole day from early morning getting him 'dorned out, and they were just about ready to start when he were took short and they had to pull all the straw off him quick to let him go to the closet. They wern't half savage with him, I can tell you, and they di'n't let him forget it for a goodish while.

What us children liked best were the Plough-Witching, 'cos we could take part in that ourselves. We dressed up in anything we could find and blacked our faces with soot from the chimney to disguise ourselves. Then we went to our neighbours' houses and capered about on their doorways, or sang a song till they opened the door and let us in. There were a special song as we sung while we shook our collecting tin up and down

> 'Ole in yer stocking
> 'Ole in yer shoe
> Please will yer give me a penny or tew
> If yew ain't got a penny
> A a'penny'll dew
> An' if yew ain't got an 'a'penny
> Well God bless yew!

> Just one! Just one! Just one for the poor old ploughboy!
> Just one! Just one! Just one!

This went on right up to the time my own children were little, and for all I know there's still some places where they don't let Plough Monday pass without somebody going a-ploughwitching, but I dessay folks are all too educated and clever to take pleasure in such simple things as that, nowadays.

Valentine's Day were the next thing we 'ad to look for'ard to. You wou'n't think it 'ould a-made much difference to us child'en, but you must try and remember that we ha'n't got much in the way o' toys or books, and it wer'n't like it is to-day when a child can't go down the village street with its mother without grizzling for something to be bought for it at every shop they pass. We never had a penny to spend for ourselves except on special occasions. Just afore Valentine's Day, you could buy cards of all sorts for about a penny each. Some of them would have pretty pictures and hearts with arrows through 'em, and verses we could read again and again, like

> Run postman, run
> And do not tarry
> Take this to the girl
> I want to marry.

But that wer'n't the only sort of Valentine card you could get in them days. The thing was that Valentines went without being signed by the person what sent 'em, and this were took advantage of if you wanted to insult somebody what you'd fell out with. So there'd be really nasty cards, as well as pretty ones. Sometimes

you'd open the card and a great long paper snake 'ould unfold
itself and instead of a nice greeting there'd be a message like

You are a SNAKE-IN-THE-GRASS

or perhaps a black man with a terribly ugly face would stick his
tongue out at you when you opened the card. If we could get a
penny to buy one we were delighted, not to send to anybody, you
understand, but just to play with. Of course, when we begun to
grow up we longed to get Valentines for the proper reason, and a
lot o' fun we had guessing who they'd come from. My sister and
me were never short of admirers, so we got our share.

Pancake Day were soon after Valentine's Day, as a rule, and
that made us something else to think about. We di'n't have pan-
cakes very often, because milk were in such short supply. We only
had a penn'orth o' skim milk once a week, on Sunday, to make a
baked pudding with. All the rest o' the week we drunk our tea
without milk, though sugar were cheap and we could have it as
sweet as we liked. So we had to save our milk up from Sunday till
Tuesday if we wanted pancakes on Pancake Day. Next day were
Ash Wednesday, and we had to go from school to church. Even
this were something out o' the ordinary, because we went to
chapel o' Sundays and the church seemed a big, important place
to me. We dropped our curtseys to the old parson's wife as we
went by her, and sat like scared little mice till the service were
over. Then we got a half-holiday and went home. I never understood a word o' what went on in church and di'n't know no more
o' what it were about than if I'd bin deaf (which I was) and blind
as well. It were just all a mystery as a child mustn't question. As
I'm said afore, we all knowed plenty about death, enough to give
us bad dreams and make us frit to death ourselves if we woke up
in the dark at night; and church seemed to do with death to me
then. At chapel you got some relief when it were time for a
hymn, because everybody sung so hearty, though the words were
enough to scare anybody, even there

> A moment's time, a moment's space
> Shall waft you to that 'eavenly place
> Or shut you up in 'ELL.

In church nobody sung loud enough to be heard, and it made the cold seem colder and the roof seem higher and the dead all round seem deader because the living people inside acted so unnatural.

All through Lent we looked for'ard to Good Friday, that I'm already described, and on Easter Monday there were sports and races at Ramsey. We had to walk to get there, and after it were over we had to walk back, but we di'n't care. One custom I remember was that just before Easter there'd be a distribution of money to widows and old maids, and they gave away loaves of bread at the church. I don't know how they decided who was to have it. When Christmas was over, there was another chance for the poor old women, on Gooding Day. This was the day after Boxing Day, and the old women would put on their best clothes and go gooding. They called on any such o' the better off folk as they had worked for in the past, or on friends and neighbours who were a bit better off than they were theirselves, and the custom was that they were given any left-overs from Christmas. I think it used to be like that once upon a time, but when I remember it were a better custom as di'n't smack quite so much o' 'charity'. Instead of the left-overs, most o' the well-off folks 'ould give the poor old souls a shilling or two in money, and their acquaintances would have half a pound o' tea or a bit of pork ready for 'em when they called.

May Day were kept in our village, but not like it is in most places. We di'n't have no May Queen, and we di'n't go gathering may 'cos there wern't no may to gather right down in the fen, though if we'd a-wanted to gather it, no doubt we should a-took the trouble to go to Biggin Fields, where there were plenty. All we had a-May Day were a sort o' May garland. It were in the form of a doll, an old rag doll. A couple o' tall posts were set up, one each side o' the high way, with a clothes line stretched tight between them. Then the May doll were pegged on the line, over the middle o' the road. Our mothers spent hours making us little sawdust balls to pelt at the dolly, to see if we could turn it over the line. Old women who kept shops did a good trade in these sawdust balls at halfpenny a time, in the evenings when the young men and women who had a few pennies they'd saved for the occasion come to join in the fun. Then the doll on the line only served to get the crowd together, and it wer'n't long afore they'd forgot all about her and started playing the usual games like long tag and round tag and *Fox and Hares* and *Kiss-in-the-Ring*, which were really what they'd come for. But by that time the little ones had been took home to bed.

The last high day of the year, except for Ramsey Fair, were the Sunday School anniversary. This were the child'ens very own day, when the grown ups at the chapel celebrated the start o' the Sunday school. The chapel itself were different on that day, because planks were set up on each side o' the pulpit so that all the child'en could sit up there facing the rest o' the congregation. The tiny tots set in the front row and the next biggest on the next, right up to the back row where the biggest set—girls on the right side o' the preacher, boys on the left. The Sunday school teachers had been teaching 'em special hymns for weeks, and between the hymns such children as dared and could learn their 'piece' said recitations or sung little hymns in pairs or even an occasional solo. It were a terrible ordeal to stand up facing all the people and 'say your piece'. We used to practice it for days and nights at a time just before 'the anni', but when you stood up there wer'n't a single word of it left in your head. Some child'en 'ould cry and have to be told to sit down, and their poor mothers in the congregation 'ould be upset. I remember one 'anni' when a boy called Joe, about my own age, got up to say his bit, but he only got the first line out afore he stuck. One o' the teachers tried to help him, and he said the first line over again, but he cou'n't get no farther, and busted out a-roaring, saying 'Mammy, my big toe 'urts me.' Perhaps it did, 'cos it were quite likely that he'd got a pair o' shoes on as wern't half big enough for him, in honour o' the day. Every mother, however poor she was, had to get her child'en looking smart for the anniversary, and if they couldn't buy new clothes for their families every child had to have one thing new. Among the girls, the secret o' what they were going to wear were kept as if their lives depended on it, and many a mother has dragged out to work for weeks in the field to be able to buy the new things for the anni. This were the part we loved best, because although we were as poor as anybody there, we knowed we could trust our mam to get us the prettiest frocks as well as better quality ones than anybody else's there. The villages all round used to make a bargain with each other not to have their anniversaries on the same day, so each village visited the 'anni' at all the other chapels round about. We loved this, because we made friends with children from the other places for the four weeks or so of the anniversary season in the middle of the summer, and perhaps didn't set eyes on them again till the next summer. Occasionally, though, there'd be 'revivals' when a preacher from away 'ould come and stop in somebody's house, and have meetings night after night in the chapel. Then the regular chapel-goers from nearby villages would make the effort to come. They used to come regular to us from Upwood for these revivalist meetings, and I can see 'em now, in my mind's eye. They'd have a big farm trolley, with four wheels, all cleaned up and pulled by two beautiful horses all brushed and polished for the occasion. The side boards o' the trolley would be put on, and the bottom covered with clean straw. Men and women, dressed in their best clothes set all round the sides as thick as they could be, and at their feet the children with their hair brushed and combed and crimped set on the straw. When the meeting were over they'd climb back in the wagon again and go home, filled with new spirit that often made 'em go on singing as they drove away. So after all the goodbyes and wavings between the women were over and the driver had clucked his horses off, one o' the men 'ould give the note and the visitors would roll away singing

SWEE-ping through the gates of the new Jer—u—sa—lem.
Washed in the blu—hud of the La—ha—hamb,

till they were out o' sight and hearing.

Come to think about it, this visiting atween chapel congregations played a big part in our lives. We had another way o' doing it, besides a farm wagon, and beautiful it was too. On summer evenings we had a turf barge for the same purpose, and when we could visit places like Holme, by water, as were too far away to get by road. One of our members had a little harmonium and he would bring this and put it in the barge. The men erected seats made of planks, resting on gallon beer barrels borrowed from a pub, all round the outside of the boat, and the children sat in the bottom. Then away we went, pulled by a slow and lazy old horse on the towpath, singing all the way. The land were so flat on both sides of us that where the banks wern't too high we could see for miles and miles, and there were nothing to stop the sound of our singing, either, so that our hymns could be heard all over the fen. When we were coming back we sung just as loud and clear, under the sky as were all colours of the rainbow, for whatever folks say about the fens not being beautiful, nowhere can there be a place where the sunset is more worthwhile a-looking at. I like to think about them evenings, singing, on the barge. I thought it were beautiful then, and I still think so now.

The village we went most to was Holme. Soon after the trips I remember, the chapel there were pulled down or had big alterations done to it, and while it were rebuilding, they had a floating church made on a big barge, as went up and down the waterways round the district. I know several people alive to-day as were christened on it when they were babies.

Of course the main outing o' the whole year were at Ramsey Fair time, but there's so much to tell about that, I shall have to leave it while another day.

6

THERE were another occasion when we made use o' the farm wagon for transport, and that was Ramsey Fair. Our fen were about 3½ miles across the fields to Ramsey, and mostly we walked it both ways and made nothing of it. If we wanted anything in Ramsey, or if we wanted a bit of an outing, we walked across Biggin Fields. As a child I made this journey every Saturday, to get our ye'st for the next week's baking. When I first remember, an old man called Hooky Bellamy come round the fen selling brewers ye'st. He had it in a can like the milkman used to have at one time to deliver milk in, what 'e used to carry on his hook, and a long dipper to serve it with. It 'ould be all froth and bubble in his can, and the women would take a basin to the door and he'd put a measureful in it for 2d.—about half a pint. It were a long way round the fen, and if he ran short the people at the end of his round were unlucky. My sister swears that he see to it that he never did run short, but the folks were still unlucky, though what the eye don't see, the heart don't grieve over, as the saying goes. My sister tells the tale of how she watched him one day take his can down the side of a dyke, where he thought he were well hid, and make water into it. That 'ould make it froth up again, and no mistake, so there were plenty to go on with for the rest of his round. When he stopped coming 'cos he got too old, we had to find another way o' getting ye'st, so us children had the job o' going to wait for the brewer's dray delivering to the pubs. The dray allus carried a barrel o' ye'st, and we loved to wait for the dray to rumble up with its four great horses all shining like satin, and their brasses all shining like gold, and rosettes on their bridles and the load of barrels behind them. The draymen sat up high in front o' the barrels, as proud as punch o' their horses. It were a beautiful sight to see, and when we'd all been served with our ye'st and the draymen's business at the pub done, there were allus just a chance that the dray might be going to another pub our way, and sometimes a kind man who liked little girls 'ould take us up with him and give us a ride home. But this source o' ye'st failed as well, afore long, because the draymen stopped bringing it, so then there were nothing for it but to walk to Ramsey once a week for German ye'st. This were dry, and 'ould keep better than the brewer's ye'st, but the women di'n't like it so well. We got that put up in a paper bag, and when we were out across the fields where we thought nobody could see us, we opened the bag and ate the ye'st like sweets.

We often done errands for other old folks while we were going. One poor old woman used to wait for us every Saturday morning with her money and a bottle for us to get her her week's supply o' 'lodmun' (laudanum). I should think the poor old creature had a cancer, like so many other fen folks, and took laudanum for the pain, though, I believe there were a lot who took it just because they liked it, and many a crying baby as I knowed of has been soothed for a few hours by being give a lump o' sugar with three drops o' laudanum on it. That 'ould put 'em to sleep and keep 'em asleep while their mothers got on with the work. The chemist di'n't seem to mind letting us children have as much as we asked for, but if we had stopped or took a swig or two o' that on our way home we should a-bin in difficulty.

Everybody went across the fields to Ramsey in the good weather, and a lot o' folks'll tell you tales about their adventures on the way. Sometimes you'd meet a bull (though more often only a bullock), and run for your life: or get caught in a terrible thunderstorm. We laughed about a man we knowed what said he were born when his mother 'ad gone out, but it were true, for when I growed up I understood that she'd bin took bad on her way to Ramsey across the fields and her baby had been born by the side of the path. There were an old ruined house called 'Biggin Malten' across there, and us child'en kept away from it because we had heard that Oliver Cromwell's haunt used to be seen there.

My mother and my sister did see a haunt once, across Biggin Fields, but it warn't Oliver Cromwell. My sister remembers it to this day. They were coming home from Ramsey one morning in the middle o' the day, with the sun shining bright and hot. They got in sight o' the second stile across the fields, and there were a man sitting on it. When they got near enough to see him properly, mother thought there must be a show or a circus or something on as he belonged to, because he were wearing such a queer garb. He had trousers that were criss-crossed and tied with leather thongs all the way up, and a short tunic above his knees.

Over it all he had a sort o' cloak, done up with a brooch on his shoulder, and a helmet sort o' thing on his head. He appeared to see 'em a-coming, and got off the stile, as mother thought, to let 'em get over; but when she were level with him he turned aside and walked off down by the side o' the hedge for about ten yards, then straight into the middle of a pond full o' water, where he just disappeared! They both see him as plain as plain, but it wern't until the moment he went into the pond that they suspected he wern't a ordinary man. Then mother took my sister by the hand and they run till mother were out o' breath and cou'n't go no further, but they were soon within sight of habitation again and she felt better.

We sometimes walked to the fair, but come back in the wagon. By ten o'clock at night the child'en 'ould all be crying with excitement and tiredness, and the women 'ould be carrying the youngest in their arms, tired as they were theirselves. So they were glad to take a lift in the wagon, though it wern't so pleasant a ride as it might ha' been what with the children crying and a lot o' the men had a drop too much, so they'd quarrel wi' their own shadows and swear and be sick over the side. It seemed a long way, even to ride, then, when the fair were over for another year, and the horse 'ould plod along slow. Talking about that has made me remember something else. There were an old couple, relations o' my husband's, what had a little old donkey and cart they used to ride about in. One day my mother were walking round by the high road to Ramsey, and she fell in wi' them. They had a word o' two o' greeting, and in a moment of unusual kindness for them, the old man said 'Will yer ride, Mis' Pa'per?' and without thinking, mother answered 'No thank yer, Mr Potts—I'm in a 'urry'. (My mother's name were Papworth, but it were allus called 'Pa'per', like Plamers were Pawmers, and Leplas 'Plaws', and Onyetts 'Ungitts', and so on.)

But however we got home, we enjoyed the fair. It were held on July 23rd, and come just at the right time for a bit o' jollification afore folks had to set in to the harvest. Everybody 'ould try to save up a little bit o' money so as to have something to spend. There'd be stalls all over the green where you could buy things to eat, like hot peas in a basin, or a dish o' whelks, or a packet o' brandy snap; but there were a lot more ways o' enjoying yourself than spending your money eating. For the grown-ups, one o' the main attractions were the dancing booth. This 'ould be a fairly level spot with some long boards laid down for the folks to dance on. At one end there'd be the foosterers, one with a banjo, one with a fiddle, and p'raps another with a dulcimer. You paid two-pence a dance, and waited your turn to get on the floor. The money were took by a man called 'Old Jesus'. He were one o' the ugliest men I ever did see, with a nose that looked as if it 'ould cover a half acre o' land, it were so long and so broad, and covered all over with 'orange-peel' skin, and red into the bargain. He'd say 'Take yer pairtners' and the couples 'ould form up one behind the other, waiting for the music to start. Old Jesus 'ould keep time and call out

> Up the middle, down the sides
> 'Cross the corner, stan' a'-one-side

for such dances as everybody knowed, like the *Cross-hand Polka* and *Haste to the Wedding*.

With Old Jesus there'd often be another man called George Augury; he had a reputation for being able to drink a pint pot o' beer quicker than anybody else ever could, and he di'n't mind how many times he tried to beat his own record, providing somebody else paid for the beer. Once somebody thought they'd play a trick on him, so they took a dead mouse with 'em, a-purpose. They dropped it into his pint o' beer when he were ready to start drinking. He never see it, and picked up his mug. O' course the chap what had put it in thought when he found out, it 'ould upset him an' slow him up. But he emptied the pot straight off, and never knowed as he'd swallowed the dead mouse an' all. It had gone straight down his throat with the rest. It ain't much to be surprised at that he di'n't notice a little mouse, for he had a mouth as big as the top of a sock, or so it seemed to me when I were a little girl. He'd finish his trick by turning the pint pot upside down to show the beer were gone, and then he'd open his great mouth and put the pot inside it, and shut his lips up over it. I'm seen him do it.

After mother had had a dance or two, there were all the other sideshows to be visited. There were the Fat Lady, all dressed up in spangles, a mountain o' flesh and blood, and a couple o' tiny dwarfs called Tom Thumb and his wife, as rode round the booth in a tiny little carriage pulled by a dog. Sometimes there'd be a pair o' Siamese twins to see, growed up, joined at the shoulder, and one year there were the Elastic-Sided Man, who could take hold of his own skin anywhere on his body and pull it out away from him for all the world as if it really were made of elastic. The 'Human Skeleton' ha'n't got no flesh at all atween his skin and his bones, for you could see every rib as plain as if he had been a skeleton, 'specially when he sucked his belly in to make hisself thinner than ever.

In another booth there were the conjurers, and in another the performing fleas, that I remember being in chains. Then there were a boxing-booth, and a waxwork show, where when I were ever such a little girl I see the sad sight o' Queen Victoria and all her children round Prince Albert's death bed. One thing I shall never forget, because it seemed so very wonderful, were paying 6d. to go into a booth to hear the first phonograph as ever come our way. Other music come from the hurdy-gurdy with its little monkey to collect the pennies.

Sometimes a booth 'ould be nothing but a trick, and the folks as kept it took money from the other simple folk, because they knowed them as 'ould bin tricked wou'n't tell others, but let them go and be had as well. It wern't fair to take child'en's pennies for such things, but I suppose they had to get a living like everybody else. I remember one of them. There were a notice outside the booth that said

Come and see what you never have seen—a horse with its
tail where its head should be.

All it was when you'd paid your penny and got inside, were a horse standing with its tail towards the manger!

Us children went wherever our mother went, of course, but there were some things as were meant for us alone. Mother 'ould go with us for a ride on the 'Sea-on-Land', as were nothing really but a boarded floor made to rock from end to end and from side to side. But we went in the 'swing boats' by ourselves. There were a queer old couple from Ramsey what had swing boats o' their own, and they used to come round the school treats as well as the fair, so we felt we knowed them better than most o' the fair folks. The poor old woman had had a stroke at some time or other, and it had left her with her face all pulled awry, and her mouth twisted down an' all to one side. She'd be there, taking money and calling out all the while from the corner o' her one-sided mouth

Come 'long, come 'long child'en! Long rides a penny!
Long rides a penny!
'Ave another go
Yer mother wou'n't know
Long rides a penny! Come 'long. Come 'long.

The 'flying-'osses' were another attraction, though they di'n't exactly fly, because they were only cranked round by a man by hand; and when I were a bit older, I see the Penny-on-the-Mat for the first time.

When I were growed up, it got to be the fashion to go to Peterborough Fair as well as Ramsey. We cou'n't walk there, so we 'ad to go by train. I had been once or twice when I were little, because my mother come from Yaxley, and we 'ad a lot o' relations all round Peterborough. I remember one or two incidents about Peterborough Fair when I were a child. One was the time when some fool started a scare that a bear 'ad got loose from its cage. All the crowd started to rush towards the gates, trying to get out o' the fair ground, and them as were in tents and booths tried to get out while them as were outside tried to get in for safety. Some o' the booths and tents got knocked over in the struggle and made things worse, and a lot o' people got hurt in the crush. I dare say it wern't half so bad as I remember it, but one thing I know was that my mother's beautiful new bonnet got knocked off and trampled on.

The other thing I call to mind was seeing tomatoes for the first time. They were on a stall, all red and shiny, and thought they must be some special and beautiful sort o' plums. I'd got some money to spend, and I went to buy some. The woman on the stall tried to stop me from wasting my precious fair money. 'They are to eat with meat' she said 'or cut up on a plate with salt and pepper and vinegar.' I really thought she must be mad, and I insisted on buying some. As soon as I got away from the stall I bit one, and it were so nasty (so I thought then) I spit it out and throwed the others down and stamped on 'em.

More and more people went every year till they had to run special trains to take them. One year even the special trains were so full that when we went to catch our train to go 'ome, there wern't another inch o' space anywhere in any o' the carriages. So they put some cattle trucks on the train behind the carriages and we were all herded in and jammed together in them. We had to stand all the way 'ome in the cattle trucks, but we were jammed so tight we cou'n't fall over. It wern't a very pleasant journey I can tell you, and we contented ourselves with going to Ramsey Fair and no other for a goodish while after that.

7

A man's work is from sun to sun
But a woman's work is never done.

THAT'S a rhyme I heard a-many a time when I was young,
and as far as the women in the fen, like my mother was concerned, there's no doubt it were a true saying. If life were hard
for the men, it were harder still for the women. They often worked
side by side with their menfolk in the fields all day, then went
home and while their husbands fed the pig or fetched a yoke o'
water, they'd get the meal going. But most men could rest a little
while after tea, at least in winter, but the mother had to set about
preparing for the next day, getting the children washed and off
to bed, and making and mending clothes and what bits o' furniture and linen they had in the house. Then they'd have to be up
with the lark in the morning to sweep and clean the house afore
it were time to go to work again. Of course, not all the women
worked all the time, but most of 'em worked on the land in the
busy times, and some of 'em boasted about being able to do as
much as a man at some jobs. There were a lot of jobs a woman's
quick neat fingers could do better than a man's, but I di'n't like
to see a woman gault-digging, though I have seen 'em a good
many times and a lot o' women 'set off' the turf for their
husbands in the turf fen.

Then they would always either be carrying a child, or else had
just had a new baby, and very often they would have two or three
that couldn't walk. They boasted about the size o' their families,
and would be ever so proud to say they'd got seven or eight sons
and four or five daughters. Feeding a family like that on ten
shillings a week, which was what the father 'ould bring home,
were a job in itself. The money had to cover food and firing and
dad's baccy, but it was mostly what the mother earned that
bought clothes and anything else they had to have. Of course, as
soon as any o' the child'en were big enough to earn anything at

216

all, they had to, and the families as were too far away from school for the child'en to have to go were counted lucky because the oldest could earn a penny or two instead o' wasting their time with books. They minded cows and horses grazing along the banks o' the rivers (about the only place there were any grass), fetched water from the dykes, and tended sheep. Then they could bring the turf in to put on the fire for their mothers to cook with. The turf fire had to be used for everything, and a pot-hook hung up the chimney over it, with a great big oval shaped boiler on it. On washing day the clothes were boiled in it, and meals were cooked all together in it on other days. Though there were some who did have a big separate boiler for washing. The boiler had a lid, and that were very necessary, especially on wash days. When you took the lid off to put your sheets in, though, that 'ould be the very moment when a great lump o' soot 'ould come tumbling down the chimney all over the washing. No wonder us child'en used to sing at Christmas time

> While shepherds watched their turnip tops
> A-b'ilin' in the pot
> A lump o' sut (soot) come tumblin' down
> An' sp'ilt the bloomin' lot.

It were real to us, 'cos we'd seen it happen many a time. There were another sort o' pot in use besides the boiler. That were a round, three-legged pot as stood over the hot ashes and glowing turf. Most women had a little side oven for baking. It stood at the side o' the fire on the hearth, and you pushed the fire underneath it where it stood on a few bricks to allow for this. Then a bit o' fire was put on top o' the oven as well, and it would roast things beautiful. So would the three-legged pot. We used to do a 'pot roast' as a special treat when things got a bit better—a good sized bit o' sparerib ('sparrib' we called it) o' pork, rolled all over in pork fat and then put in the pot in front o' the fire. You had to keep turning the pot round to get the meat cooked even, but it 'ould be roasted better than any meat I'm ever had cooked any other way, and it 'ould fill the house with a delicious

smell and make your mouth water all the while it were a-cooking. The last cooking utensils 'ould be a frying pan made o' solid iron with a handle over the top to hang it on the pot-hook by, and a griddle to stand in front o' the hot fire to cook herrings on. This wern't so pleasant as the pot roast, because the fat dripped from the herrings through the griddle on to the hot ashes and nearly stunk the house out. The main meal o' the day were in the afternoon—sometimes at about half-past-three, sometimes as late as five o'clock, according to what the father was doing and how far away from home he were working. So the pot went on the hook early in the afternoon, with the 'pudden' wrapped up in a pudden cloth, the potatoes in a 'tater-net' and the salt pork in the water, all together. This meal meant that tea wern't took as a meal very often at all, but the women who 'neighboured' 'ould gather together for a cup o' tea sometimes when they wern't out at work. They kept their tea caddies on the mantelpiece over the fireplace, and if they were only tins like what had had cocoa in, they'd shine 'em up once a week to make 'em bright. One caddy had ordinary tea in it, and one 'green' tea, and in one or the other there'd be a little jar o' 'sody' (bi-carbonate of soda), to put a pinch in the teapot when the tea were made. It brought the colour out and made the tea seem stronger, and give a smoothness to the water. I never did like this habit of putting 'sody' in the teapot, but most folks I knowed reckoned to do it. If it were a special occasion, the woman who were having the teaparty might make a 'nodding cake'. She'd hang her big solid frying pan up the chimney and let it get well hot, and then make a bit o' short crust pastry with good home-made lard and plenty o' sugar and currants in it, and make a flat cake of it to fit the pan. Then it 'ould be cooked to a beautiful golden brown on both sides, and be ready, when the visitors arrived, to be cut open and buttered and ate hot, straight from the pan. But butter were too much of a luxury for this to happen often. Mostly it were home-made lard we ate on our bread ('seam' we called lard). Even lard wern't allus to be had. In bad years when the corn got damp afore we could glean it, the flour 'ould be so poor that you cou'n't make proper bread with it. It 'ould be black, nearly, when it come out o' the oven, and the flour made from growed wheat with barley mixed wou'n't set properly. Very often, if you opened your oven door to see how it were cooking, you'd have to shut it again pretty quick, to keep the bread from running out, because all the insides of the loaves had oozed out o' the tins on to the oven bottom. It cou'n't be wasted, so you let it bake on the bottom of the oven to a hard flat cake, and there'd be nothing left in your tins but a thick black crust all round. Without butter or lard, the child'en 'ould get this for their breakfast or their supper spread with a little brown sugar or black treacle. The few people what had cows let their milk stand in big pans for about three days, and skimmed every skerrick of cream off it to be made into butter for sale. Then we used to be able to buy the skimmed milk at a ha'penny a pint to make a Yorkshire pudding for Sunday dinner. At other times o' the week we had to do without milk. Sugar were cheap and our tea were well sweetened, but we never had no milk in it till such time as I were married.

Women who had big families o' boys made pork dumplings every day o' the week except Sundays, like as not. These were just a lump o' dough about as big as an orange. The woman would push her thumb down into the middle o' the dough and make a hole. Then she'd put a bit o' pickled pork the size o' a lump o' sugar into the hole and close the dough up round it again. There'd be one o' these for each boy who went to work to take with him for his dockey. The old boys tending sheep played football with their dumplings very often afore dockey time, but it di'n't matter how mucky they got, because you could peel the thick skin off as if you were peeling an orange, and inside the hard dough 'ould be clean enough.

I had one aunt as had twenty-two child'en (though one or two of 'em died young), and another as had fifteen. Aunt Marthe, the one who had fifteen, had so many boys at work it were a job for her to keep pace with cooking for 'em. She made 'em pork dumplings to take with 'em to work, and then she had the pot on all the afternoon and evening waiting for 'em to come in one at a time for their meal. She made nine or ten roly-poly puddings every day of her life, and dropped 'em into the pot at intervals so there was allus one ready whenever one of her sons come in. My uncle used to wait on a Saturday night till the butcher's stall on the market were clearing up, and buy a sheep's head and pluck, or a bullock's head, for nearly nothing. The head and pluck (we called it a watch and chain) he'd sling over his shoulder without being wrapped up or anything, and Aunt would clean it, (or the bullock's head) and put it in the washing copper with any vegetables in season, for Sunday. If they could get an old hare or a couple o' rabbits to flavour it, they were in for a treat, with the whole copper full o' dumplings for the one meal they all had together in the week.

When the winter come, and frost and snow, food got scarcer than ever and very soon some o' the family 'ould be down with colds and sore throats and coughs. Then there were the same remedy for all these ailments—onion gruel, with plenty o' pepper in it. If this di'n't have the effect it were supposed to have, the next step was to give the sufferer's chest a good rubbing with a tallow candle warmed against the fire till it would melt.

When the chest were coated with the tallow, a heart-shaped piece of brown paper was stuck to the tallow and left there till the cold was better. I don't know what difference the shape o' the paper made, I'm sure, but it were allus a heart shape that were used. Prevention was better than cure, though, and all us child'en wore a little square o' camphor in a bag on a string round our necks to keep diseases away. Men who worked in the dykes stood in water up to their ankles day after day and were very prone to the rheumatics, but they believed that a pair o' eel-skin garters wore just under their knees kept the rheumatiz from rising any further. If growed-up men and women had a very bad cough as onion gruel wou'n't touch, the remedy they tried next was to boil some linseed a few hours until it was well cooked, then strain it and dissolve a stick o' black Spanish liquorice in the water and drink it. My old Gramp went one better than that. He used to eat the linseed as well, in a basin with the liquorice chopped up in it. He said if a linseed poultice 'ould do good outside, it 'ould do a sight more good inside. He were a firm believer in keeping his-self well by taking as much saltpetre every day as 'ould lay on a threepenny bit. One time his jar got empty and he found some more as they had had a long while. He said to my grandmother, when they were going to take their morning dose, 'I reckon this 'ere saltpetre'll 'ev lost its meaning by this time, my gel, so we'd better take a bit more on it than if it were fresh.' They did, an' took nearly a teaspoonful each. Oh, it did make 'em bad! The doctor said it 'salivated' 'em, and they were lucky to come round. As I'm said afore, laudanum were the only cure for pain, and it were used for everything. When us child'en suffered with our sore heels and chapped and gathered toes, mother 'ould put us a water-bitney poultice on. Dad 'ould gather the leaves out o' the river, and mother crushed 'em with a rolling pin till they were bruised and juicy, and put them on the sore place. They soon relieved the pain. I suffered most of all from earache, and mother were allus trying new remedies to relieve my terrible pain. One thing she used to do was to roast onions and squeeze the tiny middle right down into my ear while it was still hot. I were allus in misery wi' my ears, and by the time I were fourteen I were very deaf, so I should think there must ha' been something seriously wrong wi' them that none of mother's remedies could cure. But I were glad for her to do anything she could to ease me. She suffered from a sort o' stomach trouble herself—she said her 'lights were rising', and she'd swallow lead shot to relieve herself. Most women had sick headaches, and would go about for whole days at a time with a bit o' white rag soaked in vinegar round their heads. There were cures for everything, and every woman had her own special ones. It were very necessary an' all, because the doctors wern't for the likes of us. There were two doctors in Ramsey, and they'd be sent for when folks were dying and it were too late anyway, but there were all sorts o' reasons for not sending for 'em. For one thing, there were no such things as telephones, and somebody had to go the four or five mile to fetch the doctor. When bicycles become common a young fellow 'ould usually go, but until that time it meant walking there. Then the doctor 'ould be gone out, very like, five mile the other side o' Ramsey, and by the time he'd got back he'd perhaps stop to have a meal afore setting out again on his horse. Even a horse cou'n't get down the droves, as bad as they were then, sometimes, and the man o' the family or a friend 'ould have to wait for the doctor where the drove joined the high-road and light him down, across the planks, over the dykes and so on, by lantern. So it wern't much use wanting him in a hurry. But it were paying him that were the worst difficulty of all, because he charged so much a visit, and when it were the father o' the family as were bad, there'd be no money coming in for food or firing, let alone to pay the doctor with. My poor old mother died at sixty-two with cancers all over her, and suffered cruel. But she suffered as well from knowing how much she owed the doctor what attended her. Most o' the doctors were kind-hearted men who never pressed for their money, though why they should work for nothing more than anybody else, I don't know. Now and again there'd be one as took advantage of his position and do the poor folks down. Mother's doctor (ours as well, but we di'n't need him quite so much), were a queer man who could never remember from one time to the next what he were a-doctoring you for. He cou'n't remember whether you'd paid him or not, either, and poor old mother 'ould go to work afore

she were well to get the money to pay him, and then one day the
postman 'ould bring a letter saying she owed him £10 or more,
a sum it 'ould a-took her all her life to accumulate, and the shock
'ould set her back further than any physick he could give her
'ould ever do her good. I dare say there were a lot o' folks as
di'n't make no effort to pay him, but he had a way o' getting his
dues out o' people. He had an eye for anything what were specially old or rare and valuable: and if somebody what owed him
some money from his last lot of visits cou'n't pay him, he'd
grumble and put hisself out when they sent for him again. Then
the poor woman 'ould plead and promise to pay, and in the end
the doctor 'ould say 'Well, I'll tell you what—I'll settle your
other debt for that old clock—or that china teapot, or that old
carved stool.' And o' course, the poor folks what 'ad got a ailing
husband or a child a-dying 'ould be only too glad to pacify him
with anything he liked to take out o' their house, even if it were
something they were very fond of for sentimental reasons. When
he died he left a goodish lot o' money, so he must have had some
good business besides bad debts.

It were no wonder there were epidemics and things though,
considering the sort o' sanitation conditions most folks had.
Many and many a cottage di'n't have no W.C. at all (we called it
'the closet'). They just 'went broadcast' in the fields. Them as
did have closets wern't a lot better off. They had a vault dug
somewhere near the house, with a wood structure over the top.
In the seat there'd be a big hole cut, too big for any child to sit
over without being frightened to death, and there were even some
real danger. So the child'en di'n't use the closet till they were
nearly growed up. They'd just go anywhere, but mostly along by
the side wall o' the house. Once a week somebody 'ould take a
shovel and a barrow and clean the leavings up, but where the man
o' the house wern't a mucher, the heaps 'ould grow and grow
from one week to the next, and of course the more child'en there
were in the house, the worse it got. There were one family I
knowed where there were a 'whull hustle' of little child'en, and
in the morning afore they set out for school, they'd all go round
to the house end together. If you went past just at that time,
there'd be a row o' little white bottoms all sticking up. The vaults

wern't a lot better than nothing, though. They bred all sorts of horrible maggots that would come out and crawl about, and whatever you done with 'em, you cou'n't keep the smell down so they were fit to go into.

The women did try hard to keep their houses clean and tidy and neat. They were proud o' what they had, even if it were only a few odd sticks of furniture and one bed. Most o' the families with a lot o' child'en di'n't have enough chairs to go round, and nobody only the father and mother ever sat down to eat a meal. The child'en just stood round the table. The floors, always damp, 'ould be covered with rugs pegged from old coats and trousers etc. or with clean sacks, and perhaps a strip o' coco-matting when times begun to get a bit better. Mother and father would have a bedstead, usually the one thing they managed to get from somewhere when they got married, and a good mattress and even perhaps, a feather bed. But the child'en had palliasses made o' straw or hay or oat flights. Oat flights were best because they di'n't have thistles in 'em. Then if the child'en wetted their beds, they could soon have some other clean ones. In spite o' being so poor and so bare, the little cottages used to look clean and pretty. The women washed their brick floors every day, and the hearths would get special attention. Peat ash is white and clean, and don't black things up like coal does, so the hearth bricks would be done up twice a day, very often, with a little brush, and once a week they'd be done over either with white bathbrick or red ochre. Every 'house-place' window had a plant or two in it, such as a pretty ivy, geraniums, calceolarias or fuschias, and a pot o' musk. The musk 'ould scent the whole cottage out with its smell, and when the woman had finished her work she'd take her coarse hessian apron off (her 'hess'en eppen', she'd call it) and get washed. Then she'd do her hair afresh, perhaps putting it up in a chignon bag, and put a clean white apron on, ready for the rest o' the family to come home. I'm talking now about the better sort o' families, and the times o' the year when the women di'n't be out on the land to work. The old ladies wore a mob cap in the afternoons when I first remember.

Women expected to work hard, and I daresay they were just as

224

happy as folks with too much time on their hands. They were forever making and mending and washing and ironing, and took a pride in doing it. They knowed very well that what they cou'n't or di'n't conjure up out o' bits and pieces, their families cou'n't have. So sewing and mending took up any spare time they might have had. Unbleached calico were 3d. a yard, and they made their own underclothes, chemises and knickers, out of that. If it were cheap, they di'n't spare labour on it, and they'd feather-stitch and trim their garments with lace, and with washing often the calico would soon be white. The lace would only be ½d. a yard, and it meant a lot to the women to be 'nice' underneath. Nightdresses got the same treatment, and as the calico was strong their work would last for years. Every woman, however poor, had a 'red flannin petticoat'. This was a beautiful garment made of soft red flannel, and scalloped round the full bottom edge. They used a ha'penny to draw round for the scallops, and worked it all with fine black wool.

Most women made their husband's shirts. They ha'n't much shape about 'em—just the width o' the material, with the neck cut out and gussets under the sleeves to keep them from tearing. The backs were left with a good long tail to tuck in their trousers, and the bit cut from the shorter front was used for the collar, bands and cuffs, gussets etc. Horrockses striped shirting was what was mainly used, and a friend o' mine what was very poor, made many and many a shirt by hand for a shilling. The reel o' cotton to make it with cost her twopence, so she got tenpence for all her work. Men di'n't wear such new-fangled things as pants. Instead, they had calico trouser-linings that were took out and washed once a week, and long home knitted stockings up to their knees. The shirts would be made o' calico for work, or shirting with stripes on a white ground, and their trousers made o' white duck, even when the work they were doing were turf digging or dyking or gaulting. They reckoned to have a clean rig-out every Monday morning, and the women were proud to see that they had, though looking back on it now, I must say as it were a bit silly, specially when I think what a trouble it were to wash and what a difficult job ironing was with flat irons heated in the fire.

Children's clothes were made out o' their parents' old worn out ones. Father's shirt tail made aprons for mother, nappies for the baby, or 'stays' for the children. These stays had stitching rows, close together, holding two thicknesses o' material together, and then between the layers o' material, and between the rows o' stitching, thick white cord was run. This 'ould make them strong and firm and warm. Then buttons were sewed round the bottoms of them for the child's knickers or trousers to be buttoned to. Elastic wern't in use at all, then. An old sheet 'ould make the little girls' knickers for Sunday wear, and one best white napkin for the baby to wear on Sunday too. Children just di'n't wear knickers at home, once they'd left their napkins off. This made it a real difficult job to get the little boys into breeches when it were time for 'em to be 'britched'. They wern't used to wearing anything at all, and suddenly to be put into thick, stiff, rough material made 'em cry and be miserable for days. When their mammy's had left 'em, they'd do their best to get the nasty breeches off, and very often they'd manage to, an' all, and be trotting round naked again when she come back. Then she'd have to force the clothing back on again, or bribe the little boy with a 'sucker', or threaten him with a smack. One way many a mother has got her little boy's breeches back on him was to say 'Come on, let Mammy kiver it up quick. If you don't the ducks'll be coming, an' they'll think its a worm and gobble it up.' There wern't many little old boys but what would hurry up and get their trousers pulled up if a duck appeared close to 'em!

However poor they were, though, everybody had one outfit for Sunday, from the baby dressed in white muslin with pink ribbon at the shoulders, to mother in her silk dress and father in his clean trousers and hard hat, with his hair and whiskers brushed and oiled. Then the women were as proud and happy as many o' the rich farmers' wives and the 'gentry' in whose houses a lot of 'em had worked as maids and learnt by the hardest way of all how to make a little go a long way, and not to care about hard work, for little or no pay. But that's another bit o' the story altogether.

8

I T seems as I wern't ever a really strong child, though I don't remember much about anything only the earache as used to keep me awake, crying, night after night, and my mother's attempts to find something to relieve the terrible pain. I dare say I had all the normal child'en's complaints like measles and whooping cough, and so on, but they all passed over me without making much impression on me. The next thing as I do remember, though, were terrible gnawing pains in my legs, specially my thighs. This 'ould be when I were about twelve, an' I were shooting up tall and thin. Nobody took no notice o' such pains, because they were all put down to 'growing pains' and it was took for granted that everybody had 'em at some time or other, and in due course growed out of 'em again. But now I look back on it, I should think I must really have been queer at this time, because somehow or other I escaped being sent to service as young as most girls had to go. Perhaps my mother, as had had such a lot better upbringing herself than most o' the women in the fen, and had been the spoilt darling of her childless aunt and uncle that had brought her up, used my ailments as an excuse to save me from what she'd never had to put up with herself, for as long as she could. When things got desperate at home and there were no money from anywhere, I did have one or two short spells in service, but by that time I were sixteen or so, and so anaemic that I were no good to anybody, and were soon sent home again. Afterwards, when I were eighteen or so, I went off to 'good' service as a parlourmaid, and afterwards just before I were married, I lived with a dear, rich old woman, the daughter of a big banker, as a trusted friend and companion. She were very upset when I left her to get married, and were my son's godmother when he were born. Thinking about her has made me remember a tale we used to hear about a girl in the same sort o' situation. I don't think as it could a-bin a true tale, but all the same I don't really see why it shou'n't a-bin. This girl, like me, lived as a companion-help to a rich old lady called Miss Percy. Miss Percy were very deaf, and dependent upon her Sarah. Then Sarah's fenland sweetheart come along, and wanted to marry her and take her away from Miss Percy. The old woman were upset, and done everything she could to put the girl off. When she found she cou'n't do nothing with Sarah, she decided to try and frighten the boy away. One day she said to Sarah 'As it seems you are determined to make this foolish marriage, you had better let me see your John. You may invite him to supper with me on Sunday.' Sarah darn't do no other on'y obey her, and John come. Miss Percy thought she'd show the poor ignorant clodhopper the sort o' life 'e were takin' Sarah away from, an' at the same time make him feel so uncomfortable an' 'out o' place' that 'e'd take hisself off and not come near to bother her or Sarah again. So on the Sunday when John were a-coming, Sarah 'ad to lay the table as if it were for a lord a-coming to dinner, with a lot too many knives and forks and things, and everything what 'ould make him seem clumsy and countryfied. Sarah had to wait on 'em, and Miss Percy set at the head o' the table in all her high class finery. John set at the other end, frit to death but determined not to show it. When the meal were ready, Miss Percy, who 'ad got it all thought out aforehand, said, 'As John is the only gentleman present, per'aps he'd better say grace'. O' course, she thought this 'ould put the last straw on the poor boy, because she di'n't think as he'd know a grace to say, let alone 'ave pluck enough to stan' up an' say it. But b' this time, John 'ad seen what she were up to, an' 'ad got his monkey up. He could see the game she were playing, an' most fen men 'ave got their share o' pride and a wit to match it, when they're roused enough. So he stood up to say grace, an' held up his 'and, like 'e'd seen the visiting preacher do a-Sundays at his mother's tea table, for silence. He knowed 'ow deaf the old woman were, an' raised 'is voice so as she should 'ear the first line, an' then dropped it so as she shou'n't 'ear no more;

MAY THE LORD IN 'IS MERCY
Take 'old o' Miss Percy
An' sit 'er safe down on 'is throne

> Leave me an' my Sally
> To live down the alley
> 'Appy, contented, alone.

Miss Percy were so surprised at him daring to say grace, and so mollified to see that he knowed 'ow to do it, that she felt guilty at what she'd been doing, trying to separate this good young couple, so she give in. And when John 'ad finished his little verse, she capped it all by adding

> Amen. May it truly be so.

I said as I can't be sure this tale is true, and you may say it cou'n't be, because no fen clodhopper 'ould be able to make a verse up like that out o' his 'ead on the spur o' the moment. But there you'd be wrong. I knowed several old fen men who made 'po'try' up about one thing o' another, and took a pleasure in doing it. My own husband were allus at it. He'd make rhymes up about anything an' everything to make folks laugh. When my two oldest child'en were little, 'e used to read nursery rhymes to 'em, and they loved it. One day they were listening, and they got to 'What are little boys made of?' Gerald, who were on'y thirteen months older than Lois, were real upset 'cos she were made o' sugar an' spice and all things nice', an' 'e were made o' 'snips and snails an' puppy-dogs' tails'. Gerald got 'isself worked up about it, and Dad could see 'e'd 'ev to put it right, some 'ow. So he read again 'What are little boys made of? Snips and snails' and so on. Then 'e went on

> What are little girls made of?
> What are little girls made of?

And while Gerald were screwing up 'is face to cry again, Dad went on

> Grass and twitch
> An' thistles an' sich
> That's what girls are made on

—and that's the one we've 'ad in our family ever since. When our child'en had growed up an gone away, 'e 'ardly ever wrote to them, or them to 'im, except in rhyme, and they treasure these letters to this day.

Old John Woodward were another as could turn a rhyme out whenever 'e wanted, specially if 'e 'ad cause to find fault with anything and 'e could draw attention to it by this way. One day 'e called at the Ram Inn, where the sign were swinging back'ards an' for'ards in the wind squeaking at every swing. He went into the tap-room and said in a loud voice

> If I could call this beer 'ouse mine
> I'd fetch some grease an' grease the sign.
> I would not 'ev this constant squeak
> F'om day to day an' week to week.

'Fetch 'im a point o' beer, missus' said the landlord, but I can't recall whether 'e went an' greased the sign. On another occasion, Old Woodward 'ad noticed that the landlord's pigs ha'n't been 'mucked out' lately, and that they were suffering for lack o' clean straw. So he done exactly the same thing as afore, on'y this time 'e said

> As I were a-comin' I did espy
> A dear little pig in a little pig sty.
> It 'ad plenty to eat, and plenty to gnaw
> But O how it needed a bottle o' straw!

There were several others as I could mention who wrote rhymes about events as happened, or made up hymns, or rhymes to remember things by. Of course I'm saying 'wrote' when I mean 'made up' sometimes, 'cos there were a lot who cou'n't neither read nor write at all. That di'n't stop 'em talking an' singing an' enjoying telling tales.

I'm got a long way from telling my tales about goin' to service, though. What I were a-trying to say were that I di'n't have the worst sort o' experience o' service myself, in spite of us being so poor, on account o' my health, and somehow or other my sister managed to escape as well. But most of our friends did, and we heard all the terrible things that happened to them.

It were nothing for a girl to be sent away to service when she were eleven year old. This meant leaving the family as she had never been parted from for a day in all her life afore, and going to some place miles away to be treated like something as ha'n't got as much sense or feeling as a dog. I'm got nothing against girls going into good service. In my opinion, good service in a properly run big house were a wonderful training for a lot o' girls who never would ha' seen anything different all the days o' their lives if they ha'n't a-gone. It were better than working on the land, then, and if it still existed now, I reckon I'd rather see any o' my daughters be a good housemaid or a well-trained parlourmaid than a dolled-up shop-assistant or a factory worker. But folks are too proud to work for other folks, now, even if it's to their own advantage, though as far as I can see you are still working for other folks, whatever you're a-doing. Such gals as us from the fen di'n't get 'good' service though, not till we'd learnt a good deal the hard way. Big houses di'n't want little girls of eleven, even as kitchen maids, so the first few years 'ad to be put in somewhere else, afore you even got that amount o' promotion. Big houses expected good service, but you got good treatment in return. It wern't like that at the sort o' place my friends had to go to. Mostly they went to the farmers' houses within ten or twenty mile from where they'd bin born. These farmers were a jumped up, proud lot who di'n't know how to treat the people who worked for 'em. They took advantage o' the poor peoples' need to get their girls off their hands to get little slaves for nearly nothing. The conditions were terrible. One girl I knowed went when she were eleven to a great lonely farm-house 'on the highlands', miles from anywhere. The very next day after she got there, the grandmother o' the household died and were laid out on the bed straight away. Then the heartless woman of the house sent poor little Eva to scrub the floor o' the room where the corpse laid. She were frit to death, an' no wonder, but she 'ad to do it. When she were cleaning under the bed, the corpse suddenly rumbled and groaned as the wind passed out of it, and to Eva's dying day she never forgot the terror o' that moment. I can't think there were many folks as 'ould 'ave bin as cruel as that, but when I remember the general conditions o' such poor little mites, it makes me think again.

I 'ad one friend as I were particular fond of, called for some

reason as I never did know, 'Shady'. Shady's adventures at
service 'ould fill a book on their own. They lived close to us, and
we'd allus bin friends, so she were nearly like my sister. She went
to service when she were about thirteen, to a lonely, outlaying
fen farm in a place called Blackbushe. The house were a mile or
more from the road, and there were no other house near by. A
big open farm yard were all round it on three sides, and at the
back door, it opened straight into the main drain, about twelve
feet wide and ten feet deep with sides like the wall of a house.
There were no escape there. Her duties were as follows.

She were woke up at 6 a.m. every morning by the horsekeeper,
who had walked several mile to work already, and used a clothes
prop to rattle on her window to rouse her. She had to get up
straight away and light the scullery fire in the big, awkward old
range, that she had to clean and black-lead afore it got too hot.
Then she put the kettle on to get tea made for 6.30 a.m. for the
horsekeeper, who baited his horses first, come in for his breakfast at 6.30, and went out and yoked his horses so as to be away
to work in the fields by seven o'clock. While the kettle boiled,

Servant gal

she started to scrub the bare tiles o' the kitchen floor. This were
a terrible job. There were no hot water, and the kitchen were so
big there seemed nearly a acre of it to scrub—and when you'd
finished that, there'd be the dairy, just as big and the scullery

as well. Skirts were long an' got in the way as you knelt to scrub, and whatever you done you cou'n't help getting 'em wet. In the winter you'd only have the light o' candles to do it by, and the kitchen 'ould be so cold the water 'ould freeze afore you could mop it up properly.

At 6.30 the horsekeeper come in for his tea, and as soon as he'd gone Shady had to start getting breakfast for the family. When they'd had theirs, she could have hers, which was only bread and butter, and the tea left in the pot by the family. If there were little children in the house, she'd be expected to have them with her and give them their breakfast while she had her own. After breakfast she washed up, including all the milk utensils and so on from the dairy, and then started the house-work. Very often another woman from the farm 'ould be em-ployed to help with this and to do the washing, while the missus done the cooking and housekeeping duties. On churning days Shady had to get up extra early to make time to fit the churning in. There were no time off at all during the day, and after supper she had to wash up all the things and prepare for next morning. This meant cleaning all the family's boots and shoes, and getting things ready for breakfast next morning. Farmers cured their own bacon and hams, so she would be given the bacon taken from a side 'in cut', but the custom was to have fried potatoes for breakfast with the bacon. These were supposed to be the 'taters left over from supper, but there were never enough left, so one of her evening jobs was allus to peel and boil a big saucepan of potatoes to fry next morning. As I'm said afore, she was allowed only bread and butter for her own breakfast.

Then if she had any time before it was bed time, she had to sit by herself in the cold dark kitchen in front of a dying fire that she wern't allowed to make up, except in lambing time. In lambing time it were took for granted that any lambs as were weakly 'ould be looked after in the kitchen, and while the season lasted the old shepherd 'ould come in and set in the kitchen while he waited for his ewes to lamb. I'm 'eard Shady say 'ow she dreaded this. The Shepherd there were a dirty, nasty, vulgar old man as no decent girl were safe with; but at the best o' times he wern't very pleasant to have to sit with, stinking o' the sheep, belching and blowing off, and every now and then getting up and straddling over to make water in the kitchen sink. The only other choice she 'ad were to go to bed, once she were sure she wou'n't be needed again, but that di'n't offer such pleasant prospects, either. Maids' rooms were allus at the very top, at the back on the north side o' the house. There were nothing in them but a bed with a hard old flock mattress, a table by the side of it, and the tin trunk the girl had brought her clothes in. It was icy cold in winter, and Shady wern't the only one o' my friends an' acquaintances by a long way as told me they slept in all their clothes to keep warm at all.

Though 'the woman' done the washing for the family, she di'n't do Shady's. She wern't allowed to do it herself, but 'ad to send it home to her mother once a week by the carrier. This took most o' Shady's 'afternoon off', because she had to walk up to the high road and meet the carrier's cart, often hanging about an hour or more waiting for him, to get her dirty washing exchanged for clean. Sometimes her mother 'ould walk the five or six mile with the clean washing, just to see her for a few minutes afore walking it all the other way. On the first time she did this, she found Shady on her knees scrubbing the kitchen floor. Shady got up to greet her, and her mother lifted her skirt and said 'Let's 'ev a look at yer britches.' As the poor mother expected, they were wet through with cold water and black as a soot bag with the constant kneeling and scrubbing and blackleading. It were a sort o' test to the experienced mother's eye o' what sort of a 'place' she were forced to leave her daughter in. I don't know which of 'em 'ould suffer most, the mother or the daughter. But there were no help for it, and every girl as left home were one mouth less to feed. If she behaved herself and stuck it out a whole year, there did come a day when she'd draw her years wages, which stood then at £5.

After a month or two o' this it begun to seem as if there never 'ad been no different life, an' that there never would be. On'y the poor gels went on getting tireder and tireder and more an' more bedraggled, till they 'went into a decline' an' died, or got hardened and become 'bad lots', or like Shady, so rebellious as to run away. In her case, it happened like this.

One terrible cold morning, on the first day o' March, with the snow on the ground, she woke up so frez with cold that she just cou'n't force 'erself to git out o' bed, an' kept laying' just another minute and just another minute until it wer well after the time she ought to a-bin up an' about. When at last she did get down stairs, the hosskeeper were a-waiting for his breakfast, but o' course there were no fire in the big old kitchen grate. Afore she could get one lit, the farmer come a-storming into the kitchen demanding to know why the horsekeeper wern't gone to work. He upped and said as 'e wern't going to work on a morning like this, not for nobody, without 'is breakfast. That made the master more savage still, and 'e ordered the horsekeeper off to work, an' said 'e'd send Shady wi' the breakfast after him. So poor Shady 'ad to set to work to get the kettle boiling, but the farmer wou'n't let her stop to make the fire properly, only to light a few sticks an' boil the kettle on the pot 'ook over 'em. He told her where she'd find the horsekeeper—in a field about a mile an' a half away. As I'm said afore, it were a perishin' cold morning wi' snow on the ground, so when the kettle were nearly boiling, Shady left the kitchen to go upstairs to get a thicker frock and some proper shoes on, 'cos all she'd got on were 'er old cashmere house shoes. But her master 'eard her, and when she got to the bottom o' the stairs, she found him there with a horse whip in his hand. He wou'n't let her go upstairs, and said 'If you ain't out o' this 'ouse in five minutes with the can o' tea, I'll lay this round you.' So she made the tea and started out in the snow in her thin frock and shoes, wi' no coat, along the side o' the river in the bitter wind.

When she'd gone about a hundred yards, she were hid from the house by the stackyard. So she made sure she were out o' sight and then swacked the can and the tea and all the lot into the river, and turned and run towards the high road as fast as she could go. When she got nearly to the top o' the drove, she called at a cottage. An old woman as were a widow lived there, and it were a cottage belonging to the farm. Shady had bin in the habit o' going and spending her 'afternoon off' with this old woman, 'cos apart from exchanging her washing, there wern't nothing else to do. But when she 'eard that Shady were a-running away, she were frit to death o' taking 'er in, and wou'n't let her cross the threshold. So poor Shady di'n't get no 'elp nor comfort there, and had to go on. By the time she'd got to the high road the master had realised what had happened, and sent a boy after her on horseback to tell her she'd got to go back. When she see him coming she began to run. He kept shouting her to go back, and in the end she yelled over 'er shoulder 'I ain't never coming back no more' and run on. Two mile further on, exhausted and in a terrible state, she called at her aunt's house. Her aunt could see she cou'n't send her back, so she lent her one of her own child'en's coats and a pair o' shoes, and after a bit of a rest Shady set out again towards 'ome.

It were about seven mile altogether to where her mother and father lived, and she got there afore dinner time. Poor as they were, they cou'n't stand to see one o' their children treated like this, so about half-past-one Shady's mother and her set off to walk back again to Blackbushe. When they got there, they went upstairs and packed Shady's tin box, dragged it down the stairs and carried it atween them up the two mile long drove and along the high way to a public house that the carrier called at. They left it there for him to pick up, and then trudged home again. As she'd broke her service, Shady lost all her quarter's pay.

About this time, I had one o' my short spells in service. My mother worked sometimes at the big house nearby, and the family had a son as was a doctor. He had just been married, much to his parents' disgust, to a nurse, and I soon understood that he'd been forced to marry her quick. So his family had bought him a practice a little way away, and set him up in a house. There the baby were born, but the wife was a poor, ailing thing and cou'n't look after it, and they wanted a nursemaid. So mother offered me. I were quite glad to go, 'cos it seemed a real adventure to be going to live in a doctor's house! But little I knowed what I were going to. We were poor at home, but they were poorer. The house was falling to pieces and the furniture was terrible. The poor girl was paying dear for falling in love with a doctor. He ha'n't wanted to marry 'er, and 'e were cruel to her. She used to come to me in the kitchen an' cry her eyes out, day after day. There wern't no proper things for the baby, a poor, puny little thing, and I had to have it in a clothes basket on the kitchen table. One day I were preparing some beeswax and turpentine polish in an old saucer, to do the floors with, but it were so hard I cou'n't break it. So I popped it in the oven to soften. I'd forgot that the grate were so old and broke that this wern't a safe thing to do. A spark from the fire fell through the rusted side o' the stove and into the beeswax. There were a terrific explosion, and the grate blowed out into the kitchen, covering everything with soot and ashes. I clawed the clothes basket with the baby in it up and rushed outside. That finished me, so in less than a month I were back home again. I wern't at all sorry either, because although mother had only offered me as a nursemaid, the doctor had other ideas. Once he sent for me to clear up his study after he'd been operating on a dead cat, taking it to bits: and once he showed me a baby he'd took from some mother afore it were properly formed, as he kept in a jar on a shelf. I knowed my mother wou'n't let me stop long in a house where a man, even if he were a doctor, showed a young girl such things.

One more incident happened while I were there. My father had several brothers and sisters. He quarrelled with most on 'em most of the time, but very often they made it up again. However, one of his sisters had married and gone to live in the very village where the doctor lived. Her husband were something to do with the railway, and I don't suppose they were well off, though by our standards (and the doctor's) they were rich. I've heard it said that Aunt Anne's husband really was an earl, but he'd had to let the title go because he was too poor to keep it up. Anyway, father told me her name and where she lived, so one day I dressed myself up in all my best clothes and went to call on her. I knocked on the door and she opened it herself. 'Please' I said 'I'm Kate, and you are my aunty.' She had seen me about, I make no doubt, and knew I was only the doctor's nursemaid, and di'n't want to claim no relationship. So she looked me up and down, di'n't say a word, and carefully closed the door in my face. I'm never heard of her since.

That reminds me of another sad story of a servant girl. It was years after I was married, that this happened. I was at Peterborough one day with some friends, and when we went to the station to catch our train home, a girl sat on the platform crying her eyes out. So we asked her what was the matter. She said a woman from Peterborough had engaged her by letter as a maid. She had been living with her married sister, who di'n't want her, and she'd been glad to get the job. So her sister had give her her train fare to Peterborough, with sixpence over to pay for the cab from the station to the woman's house. When they reached the house, she gave the cabman the sixpence and he put the tin box on the doorstep. Then she rung the bell and the woman of the house come. She looked at the girl with her roughened hands and broken nails, and knees with corns on them from kneeling, and her poor darned clothes, and told her she wou'n't do for the position because she wasn't smart enough. Then she just shut the door and left the poor girl standing there, without a penny. She'd gone back to the station, and that's where we found her. We clubbed together and bought her a ticket back to her sister's, but I'm often wondered what happened when she got there.

To finish off this bit about service, though, I think I shall have to tell you one or two more o' Shady's tales. After she'd been at home a week or two, she got another job. This time it were in a bit bigger farm house, where they kept two maids. The farmer were a high and mighty man in his own eyes, and frightened everybody to death, very near. He had two boys, and he allus kept a cane actually laying on the table all through mealtimes. If anybody spoke, he picked it up and give 'em a cut with it, even his wife, who were frit to death of him. The older boy he hated, but the younger one cou'n't do no wrong. When the family went out in the trap, the young one rode, but the older one allus had to hang on to the back and run behind, though there were plenty of room for him. On Sundays the poor child were shut in a room by hisself all day, and Shady's told me she used to very often steal things out o' the larder, not for herself, but for this poor hungry boy whose only fault was that his father di'n't care for him, for some reason. Food were as scarce there for the maids as anywhere else, and the girl who were there with Shady were another as I had been to school with, and I knowed her well.

She wern't the sort o' gel to take things sitting down, specially being hungry. So when she went to look the eggs up, she used to hide four, and collect 'em later in the day. Then just afore they went to bed, they'd drop these eggs in the kettle what allus stood a-boiling on the hearth, so that if any o' the family come the eggs wou'n't be seen. When they were hard boiled they hid 'em in their clothes, usually above the tight band o' their knicker legs, till they went to bed. They were only allowed to keep their candle alight so many minutes, but the time would come when they could sit up in bed in the

pitch dark and eat their boiled eggs. A little while later the farmer and his wife had a new baby, and of course the maids had to have it in their bedroom so if it cried it di'n't disturb the master. One night the baby started to bawl, but the gel who were with Shady, and who were the nursemaid, were just eating her eggs. So she said 'Bawl, you little owlet, as 'ard as you like; I aint a-gitting out to yer till I'm made sure o' these 'ere eggs.' So it yelled and yelled till it woke its father. Then afore the poor girls could do anything, there he stood, in his shirt, in their bedroom, with a lamp in 'is 'and, to see why they wern't looking after the child. And there they set up in bed, both on 'em, eating hard boiled eggs. There were a to-do, and as they had been caught stealing,

they both had to go the next day. They stuck together, though, and the next job they took were in a doctor's house. It were a big house, and they were fairly well treated, except that the food was very poor and scarce. The doctor di'n't use all his house, and let the upstairs as another establishment. It were let to an old parson who had married a young wife. They were very poor, but the young wife had set her heart on a string o' real pearls, and the silly old parson was scrinching and saving to be able to buy them for her. The poor girl who were skivvy for them were like to be starved to death, and used to cry with hunger and cold. So Shady and her friend Annie used to keep scraps for her whenever they could, and after it got dark she used to hang a bit o' string down from the upstairs window to dangle in front o' their kitchen window, and they'd tie whatever they'd bin able to save for her to it, so she could pull it up.

The doctor and his wife were very fond of kidneys for breakfast, but there wern't nothing but bread and butter for Shady and Annie, who did the cooking. So Annie used to steal a little o' the kidney gravy every morning for them to dip their bread in.

One morning the mistress came out after breakfast to the kitchen, and accused the girl of stealing the kidney gravy. 'The master says there has always been plenty until now: if you wish to keep your place, you must see that there is enough in future.'

Annie was furious, but she di'n't want to lose a good place. She knowed how to deal with a situation like that, she said to Shady. She'd see as he had plenty o' kidney gravy the next morning. And she did. When the kidneys were all ready cooked in the pan, she took it off the stove and deliberately made water in it. It done her feelings a lot o' good, she said, and I don't suppose it hurt them. After all, what the eye don't see, the heart don't grieve over, and Shady and Annie both stopped on there till Annie left to get married. Then Shady come home, and it wern't long afore she married a man nearly old enough to be her father, and had such a hustle o' children that there were times when she wished she were back in service again.

I KEEP on coming back to thinking about the conditions people lived in, especially them as had such big families, like Shady. They made the most of it, of course, but it must a-bin a terrible hard life. I never had to put up with it, for my mother only had four children, and the first o' them died as soon as it were born. Then I only had three children myself.

Most o' the cottages only had two rooms, so when a couple 'ad as many as ten child'en, you can see how packed in they'd be, though of course there wern't likely to be a time when they were all at home together. As soon as the oldest girls got to eleven or twelve, they'd be packed off to service, and out of a family like that, there'd nearly allus be one or two drownded, or die o' diphtheria or something. Once there were a terrible epidemic o' some disease called 'black spotted fever' in the fen, and a family as I knowed called Emmington had five children all died of it in about a week. Still, there were plenty as did rear all their child'en, and they had to manage in two rooms somehow or other. They'd make a joke about it, if they could, like they would about anything else. You'd hear tales of how so-and-so used to pack their child'en into bed like sardines are packed into a tin, alternate head to foot. This was really done, as I know, many and many a time, and most mothers who had a lot o' little children 'ould make the bed sideways, to get more in, till they got too tall to go across the bed. Then they'd have to squeeze another bed into the room, somehow. The bedroom were allus so full o' beds that there were nothing else in it at all, only a tin box to put clothes in and set the candle on. The rest o' the clothes were kept in a chest o' drawers in the houseplace.

There were another joke about a couple as had so many child'en that they used to put 'em to bed one at a time, till they went to sleep. Then they'd take 'em out o' bed and stand 'em in a corner in a bundle. I suppose that must a-bin the same couple who used to give their child'en a ha'penny each to go to bed without their supper, and then make 'em pay the ha'penny back again next morning afore they'd let 'em have any breakfast. I remember going on an errand one day, when I were about sixteen, to the house of a small farmer (some relation o' my husband's, as I found out later) where the poor young wife, as 'ad 'ad a real gentle upbringing, had got so many child'en that she'd become nothing but a slut. I went to the door o' the farmhouse just after the father had gone back to work after breakfast. He'd had bacon, as usual, and when I looked in, there were this poor young woman, as 'ad been so smart and pretty ten year or so aforehand, in a pair o' pattens and a coarse sacking apron, with

her hair not done, but hanging all round her head. She were sitting on a low stool with the great black greasy frying pan in her lap, and all round her were dirty, uncared for, nearly naked children, with a bit o' bread in each of 'ems 'ands, dipping it into the fat in the pan. If a farmer's wife could get like that, it were no wonder a labourer's wife did, occasionally. But I never knowed many as di'n't keep their child'en, and their houses, clean and tidy, however poor they were, and however much hard work it took to do it. One family as lived near us in the fen had twelve children, but the mother were so houseproud that they wern't allowed to go into the house-place at all. That were kept like a new pin, with antimacassors on every chair, and so on. The family lived in a lean-to shed, outside, and the only time they went into the house-place were to tip-toe across it to get to the bedroom at night.

Ther's one thing that was pretty certain, and that was that they cou'n't put their child'en to sleep *under* the beds. That was where everything else was stored. Some beds 'ould have boxes and bags and father's tools and anything they wanted to hide for any reason. Others 'ould have the year's crop o' dried fruit and vegetables, apples and onions, and shallots, all set out carefully so as not to touch each other. They used to make the bedrooms smell queer, sometimes, specially late in the season when they begun to go rotten. Of course, you cou'n't see what was under the bed, because all beds in them days had bed valences round them, as come right down to the floor. It were fashionable, for one thing, and at its best, a very pretty fashion it was. But it did serve to cover up a lot o' what were underneath a bed, as well. The valences took a lot o' keeping clean and sweet, and though I had valences round my beds when I were first married, I were one o' the first to do away with them, when the fashion changed. I remember how disgusted my husband's sister Harriet was, when she first saw my bed without its valence. She said it looked naked, and made her feel ashamed, for she 'cou'n't a-bear to see even a cheer with its legs onkivered'. Fashions in what folks think to be right changed like all other fashions, and most folks in our young days were a bit more modest than what they are today, but I allus did think Harriet carried her particularness a bit too far. She used to make each of her nieces and nephews a 'Betsy' (a rag doll) when they were born, and dress it for them. And she allus took very good care to sew Betsy's knickers on good and tight afore she handed her over, so that however many times the child dressed and undressed her, the doll were never entirely naked.

Bed clothes caused the mother of a big family a good deal of trouble. Sheets were homemade, of unbleached calico for strength and wear. When this stuff was new, it was so thick with 'dress' as to be like thin cardboard. When you washed them, you just cou'n't get no lather on the water, however much soap you used, for the first few washes, and of course they were a mucky yellowish colour. We used to leave 'em out on the line all night in frosty weather as this tended to whiten 'em, and by the time they were wore out they'd be both soft and white. So would twill sheets, but them I hated and would never have 'em in my house. They were rough and coarse and so heavy to handle when they were wet. We never felt as if our washing were clean if it hadn't been hung outside to get hazelled, and to this day I can't get used to things dried inside or sent to the laundry. Bedclothes di'n't get washed in them days quite as often as they do now. I dare say a lot o' men just slept in the shirts they'd bin to work in, but particular women made their men wear nightshirts and nightcaps to keep the sheets and pillow cases clean. To boil a new, un-bleached calico or twill sheet in a oval boiler hanging on a pot hook over a turf fire were very nearly a day's work in itself. When it were dry, it still had to be smoothed, some way or other. Not many people had a mangle when I first remember. I used to have to take my mother's washing to an old woman named Alice Woodward, to be mangled. She used to mangle all her neigh-bours' washing for a penny a basketful. She'd take each article out o' the basket and fold it careful on to the board under the roller, and then load the top o' the mangle up with bricks. Then the old mangle 'ould rumble away as the roller turned over the clothes and the bricks fell down again.

There were all sorts of irons to smooth such clothes as 'ad to be ironed, like the men's best 'fronts'—collar and front com-bined. If you had flat irons, you were up to date, and they were really quite good in the fen because turf smoke don't black any-thing, so they got hot but kept clean. Most women used box-irons—a sort of iron where you got a bit of iron red hot in your fire and then put it into shaped box-irons. Women who had a 'polishing iron' for doing starched things with, made themselves a copper or two a week by doing things for their neighbours. They would wash and starch and iron and polish a collar and front for a ha'penny. I'm just been thinking that any woman as wern't real healthy and strong cou'n't deal with proper wash days then, so it were no wonder poor young women who were allus having child'en, or who had anything else serious the matter with 'em, got dilitory and took to 'slubbing a few things out for the child'en' instead o' setting up a proper wash. You had to be as strong as a man to lift the great wooden wash tubs, allus left full o' suds, to keep 'em binged, even without the weight o' the wet clothes; and then you had to lift the great iron pot, full of water, on and off the pot hook over a hot turf fire, and drag the wet washing in a clothes basket to the line down the garden, and put it in and out again, perhaps four or five times if it were a wet day. Then if your line broke, or one o' the black fen dust storms blowed up suddenly on a dry day, you could just resign yourself to starting all over again.

When we begun to have a proper brick copper to heat the water, it was easier, and there'd allus be a nice lot o' hot suds to scrub your doorway with when the washing was done. People took pride in their doorways, even when they were nothing more than a few bricks laid side-by-side in the earth. The women allus swilled their doorways down with their used soap suds, and on the first of March, every year, they would give the doorway an extra special good swilling, because this was 'foe-ing-out day' when you cleaned up after the winter and prepared for spring

They swilled their doorways, they said, to swill the winter fleas away. They brushed it well with a besom brush, which they afterwards stood on its handle beside the door to dry. But they'd be very careful not to leave it there, because everybody knowed what a broom standing outside a door meant, especially if the woman were a widow-woman, or one whose husband was away. It were a recognised signal that a man 'ould be welcome.

Most women, and a lot o' men, believed in signs and o'ems (omens), specially about death. There were all sorts of signs when anybody were a-going to die. Most people had their own pri ate signs, like hearing footsteps, or three separate knocks on the door when nobody were there, or finding a coffin-shaped crease in a sheet when you unfolded it, or dreaming of lice. Harriet had this one about dreaming she was lousy, or that she was dealing with someone else who was. If ever she dreamed this, she'd be worried to death herself, nearly, because she said she knowed she would lose a blood-relation within three days. And she very often did, so I used to dread her having this dream as well. My husband and my child'en were blood relation to her, of course. There were one occasion as she dreampt it as I shan't forget in a hurry. It were when my oldest girl had just had her first baby, and were terribly bad in hospital, so we had the baby to look after. Harriet used to come poddling round to our house every morning to hear what the news was. She'd be about seventy-five, then, but looked old for her years.

One morning when she come, we'd just had a very poor report from the hospital, and we were extra upset because the baby seemed to be ailing as well. Harriet shook her head over the news, and said 'Ah, well, you may depend upon't, if yer lose one, you'll lose both.' I said 'Lor, Harriet, you are a Job's comforter, an no mistake,' but she only looked more serious than ever, and away she went to report the tale to her neighbours. Next morning she arrived early, and in tears. Afore she got inside the door, a'most, she set down all of a heap, and said in a whisper 'I'm 'ad me dream.' There wern't one of us in our house whose blood di'n't run cold, I can tell you.

It were a terrible long day for us all, an the hours dragged on without any more news till about three in the afternoon. Then Harriet appeared round the end o' the house, out o' breath wi' speed and importance. As soon as ever she could make us hear she begun to call out 'It's all alright. De'yer 'ear, Will? It's all alright. It wern't THEM as it were meant fo'. I'm jest 'eard the news. Cousin Ally at Raveley died this morning.'

Some o'ems everybody believed, and if any o' these happened, they brought real terror with 'em. If a robin come into a house, it were a bad sign for a death somewhere in the family, but if an owl sit on the roof, or flew up against a window at night, that meant a death actually in the house. A ticking-spider was also a sure sign of a death, and a clock stopping suddenly for no reason sent everybody cold with terror; so did a dog howling. I used to be terrified of the word 'death' and I've never bin able to deal with things when anything did happen as brave as a lot o' women can. It wasn't that I'm exactly frightened, but there's such a eerie, creepy feeling about when there's a corpse about. Perhaps some o' my feeling about it is due to the customs I remember when I were a little girl, and all through my young life. It really were dreadful to be in one o' them tiny cottages with a corpse in it, because the dead body were so near. If there were a

Don't 'e look beautiful?

parlour, the dead person 'ould be laid out in there, and all the neighbours 'ould come in a hushed silence to view the corpse. If there wern't a spare room, it 'ould have to be either in the bedroom or the house-place, and the family 'ould have to manage as well as they could in an outhouse or lean-to until the funeral was over. At night a light 'ould be left with the corpse, and sometimes somebody 'ould set by it all night. When my brother Watson was about eight years old, he was taken by a neighbour to see the corpse of an old woman called Mrs Ginn. She were laid out on her own kitchen table, dressed in all her best clothes, with her outdoor bonnet on, and surrounded by six candles that just lit the little room enough for them to see her by, but made everything look ghostly and creepy. He come home in such terror that mother did have a job with him, and it made him nervous for years afterwards. There were a lot o' performance to go through about the laying out. Every village had (and still has) its layers-out, women who make a bit o' spare money by doing this horrible job. They get used to it, I dare say. But in my young day they expected that every household 'ould be properly prepared for a death at any moment. Somewhere in a drawer, there'd be a set o' laying out clothes all ready:

1 sheet for binding (to sew the body up in)
1 pair of long white stockings
1 clean shift or chemise
1 nightshirt or nightdress
1 white handkerchief (to bind up the jaw).

Sometimes there would even be some pads made of pennies to weight the eyes down.

While the layers-out were washing the dead body all over, and if it were a man, shaving him or clipping his whiskers, somebody o' the bereaved family 'ould be set to air the laying out clothes in front o' the fire. Then when the whole performance were finished, the family 'ould have to file in and take the first look afore the neighbours started coming to view the corpse. The women who had done the laying out would remain in charge between the death and the funeral, standing plates of salt about the room and under the bed or table, attending to the needs of the undertaker and his men, and finally preparing the funeral tea while the mourners had gone to the burying.

The interval between the death and the burial was often longer than was good, because the whole family 'ould have to be fitted up with their black. Most men had a black suit for best, so as they were generally alright, but it were a chance for women to get a new outfit, and they di'n't miss the chance. There'd be walking to Ramsey to buy the material, and visiting the dressmaker, and buying a hat and gloves, and then visiting the dressmaker to fetch the dress or coat two days later; and of course deciding on and ordering what you would have at the funeral tea. Most shopkeepers 'ould give credit for a funeral order, and they often kept dressmakers doing nothing else.

My sister-in-law, Harriet, went into a shop one day in Ramsey and talked to a young woman there who were buying her black. Harriet felt sorry for her, and asked her who she were burying. She said her young husband, what had just died, the night afore, o' diphtheria. It were a bit o' sympathy as cost Harriet, and all of us, dear. A fortnight later Harriet went down with it herself, and John, and then my mother-in-law who lived with them. While they were all in bed, my husband went to the bottom o' the stairs and called up to see how they were, and brought it home and we all had it. He had it so bad I thought he would die, and was delirious for three days.

When it came to the funeral, it were sometimes a bit difficult, especially in winter when the fen droves were up to your ankles in slud. For one person to walk it were difficult enough, 'cos the pad were usually down aside o' the dyke, which 'ould be full in the bad times o' the year, and though this were the highest and driest part o' the drove, it were so slippery and sliddery it were all you could do to stand upright. When the droves got as bad as this, it were well nigh impossible to get a horse and cart down them, so the corpse had to be carried up the drove to where it joined the high way. Two sets o' carriers 'ould be used, taking over from each other at points where it was easiest. And a terrible job it were, as well, even for the men who had done it many's the time, like my husband, to carry a fifteen stone corpse a mile and a half in such conditions. The undertakers di'n't reckon to supply the bearers, in them days. It were took for granted that folks 'ould be carried to the grave by their neighbours, who performed this last duty as a sign of respect. When my mother died, she were carried to her grave by six nephews, all brothers. Of course the bearers had to be strong men, and all of a size, so the task fell pretty heavy on the strong, tall and willing ones. Will 'En never could say no to anybody if he could do 'em a good turn, and he used to find this sad job come his way pretty often. He never grumbled, on'y when, as on one or two occasions, the corpse he carried were one as 'ad died in the union and put in a pauper's coffin, and kept too long. He lost a beautiful brand new suit that way, once, because he helped to carry a poor old woman, mother o' one of his old friends, and before they got her to the grave their shoulders were soaked through and through. It made Will 'En real bad for days, and though we done everything we could think of with his suit, he never did wear it again, not even for work.

When the bearers had got the coffin out o' the house, and more often than not through the window, the procession 'ould form up behind, two and two, and follow it up the drove. At the top o' the drove, there'd be a farm cart waiting, and the coffin 'ould be put in it, and the procession go on like that. If it were a very long way to the churchyard, sometimes they'd get a four-wheeled wagon instead of a cart. Then the coffin 'ould be put on the floor and the mourners would ride, sitting round the side o' the wagon. After the funeral were all over, they'd all go back to the house for the funeral tea, and the very next Sunday they'd all meet again in their full black at church or chapel, according to which the dead person had belonged to, for the funeral sermon. When it were at chapel, there'd be a real to-do if the local preacher had knowed the dead one well, and if he ha'n't knowed him at all, he'd still find a good deal to say. But there warn't quite so much personal about it at church.

If it were a child as were being buried, the coffin 'ould most likely be painted white, and be carried to the grave by a set o' young girls. They di'n't carry it on their shoulders, o' course, but had white linen towels passed through the coffin handles. I helped to carry a little girl as were drowned to her grave, when I were sixteen. (All men as had helped to carry anybody kept the black gloves they'd used at the funeral, as were found by the dead man's family, but that were all the pay they got when I first remember.) Afterwards, when the undertakers started doing bigger funerals with a hearse, and so on, they hired the bearers and paid 'em, though I can't remember how much. The folks as were a bit better off showed it when it come to a funeral. When

my husband's mother died, her family had to have the whole outfit with hearse and little 'mourning coaches' what held four, and
had black dolls on the top, like the hearse. By this time the ceme-
tery at Ramsey were in use, and had been a good many year.
Folks from the fen who could afford it took to asking to be
buried there, because it were high and dry and you di'n't have to
be lowered into water. But a lot were buried there just because it
were a bit more 'posh', not 'cos they cared about the watery
grave. My own father, who di'n't care much for my mother-in-
law (the bloody old wise-woman, he used to call her), allus had a
lot to say about folks being buried at Ramsey. So when Grandmother died, he said 'I 'sh' think you'll 'ev to tek her for a bloody
j'y ride, sharn't yer?' and of course we did. I often thought about
this, later still, because after buses started running down our road,
somebody 'ad the idea o' hiring a bus to take all the mourners in,
together. So instead o' the long queue of mourners, walking
sorrowfully after a farm cart, there'd be a hearse with four black
horses, all decorated with plumes and loaded with flowers, and
nothing following at all but a bright red bus, just crawling along.

My father died very soon after my mother-in-law. His brother
come to the funeral, in a black clawhammer coat and a black
shovel hat as had been his funeral outfit all his life. While we
were setting at the funeral tea, at my house, he suddenly raised
his voice over the other conversation and asked my husband if
he'd buy 'em.

'Why, uncle,' said Dad, took aback a bit by this sudden offer
as he certainly di'n't want. 'You'll be needin' 'em a good many
times yet, I reckon.'

'No, I shan't, Will 'En,' uncle said. 'Yer see, I'm made up me
mind to-day as I ain't never going mortaring arter bloody dead
folk no more.' He were a bit like another old man who lived in a
caravan with a poor old horse that pulled him and his wife about
from village to village, where he sold tapes and cottons and so
on, from door to door, for a living. He come to my door one
day, and I said 'Where a-yer bin Jim? I h'an't seen you for many
a long day.'

'Ah, gel,' he said 'I'm bin in trouble. I'm lost my poor wife.'
He were cast down, and I were sorry for him, and said so.

'Yes, gel,' he said 'that were a real blow to me, that were. I'd
nearly as soon a-lost me ol' hoss.'

But old Giles, who had lived right over in the fen with nobody
but his wife, looked after her all her life and to the very end.
He cared for her when she died, and on the day of her funeral
he put her coffin into their own little pony and trap, as they'd
travelled so many mile in together, and drove her up to the
churchyard hisself. There were nobody at the graveside but him
and the parson. Some folks thought that were terrible, but my
husband said it were just how it ought to be. He never could
a-bear a lot of ompologe at a funeral, and I dessay he wern't
far wrong.

10

B LOOD'S thicker than water, so they say. Whatever you
think and know about other folks and how they live, you
know more about your own. In a lot o' ways, we lived just like
everybody else did, but in a lot o' other ways, we were different.
As Dad 'ould a-said, that's 'cos everybody is different, like it
says in the bible 'We differ one from another like the stars in
glo-ry.' Dad (I mean Will 'En, my husband) could allus find
excuses for everybody, for the way they behaved, though he di'n't
approve of how they went on, nor yet like it any more than any
other man when it were him as they done down or done a dirty
trick to. He never could say no to anybody as wanted to borrow
money from him, and if he could a-done, I cou'n't, when they
come with a pleading tale. There were a difference atween us
though, I were allus willing to lend, but I expected to get it
back, and if the folks we'd lent it to di'n't make no attempt, I'd
go out o' my way to get it, an' I generally did, some way or other.
But Dad used to say 'Never lend nobody nothing unless you can
afford to give it to 'em.' Not that he kept to that, for we never
could afford to give anything much away, and he were continually lending folks money to get through with. 'There'll be enough
for me, Mam' he used to say 'but you must remember as you'll
live a long while arter I'm gone. If you're prepared to risk it, I
am.' In this way he allus managed to pass the decision on to me.
I used to call him soft when 'e wou'n't try to get it back, but 'e'd
find excuses for 'em, as I've said. When anybody were a real out-
an'-out bad character, he'd think an' talk a lot about him, an'
try to explain to me that we ought to be sorry for 'em a bit, the
same as if they'd got some other incurable disease as the rest of
us ha'n't got. I never could see eye to eye with him about this
though. 'Yer see, we're all *made* different' he'd say, 'and it
depends on what our parents an' gran'parents were like, as well
as 'ow we're bin brung up.'

253

He had plenty to put up with from my father, but he allus liked him an' stood by him to the very end. Since I'm got old myself, I often think about my own father, an' wish I'd a-bin a bit more understanding about him. But I cou'n't get over the way he treated my mother, and I loved her more than I could ever say, an' allus felt as I had to protect her and look after her. Father come of an Irish family what had come over from Ireland in the famine times, and they were a queer lot with uncertain tempers, though they were all good looking and as strong as

horses. My grandfather on this side were a dear old man, called 'Gramp', with soft, silky white hair and a long beard to match. They lived down Daintree Drove, and Gramp would walk to see us every now and again. Us children loved to see him come, an' never wanted him to go away again. He'd sing to us, sometimes —my favourite song was

> O what shall we make o' the red herring's head
> The finest oven that ever baked bread

through all the verses to

> O what shall we make o' the red herrin's tail
> The finest vessel that ever did sail.

Then we used to climb on his knee and brush and comb his hair and beard till his head was sore, and finally we'd braid 'em both into dozens o' little plaits sticking out all round him. When he had to go, he wou'n't disappoint us by taking 'em undone, but walk home with 'em still plaited like a stallion's mane. I dessay that's where we got the idea from, 'cos we allus loved to see a stallion being led down the road, with its tail and mane all plaited up and intertwined with coloured braid, prancing about and looking so strong and proud. My husband used to tell a tale

about some simple servant girl what were a-setting on the side o' the road on her half day off, because she ha'n't nothing else to do, when a strange man come down the road leading a stallion. When he got up to her, he passed the time o' day with her, as country folk usually do, and were prepared to pass on. But she had other ideas, an' pretended to be frightened.

'Oh!' she said 'You're a strange man, you are. Oh! Oh! Oh! what shall I do?'

The man were took back, and the horse started rearing an' curvetting about an' he had a job to hold it. 'What d'yer mean?' he said.

'Oh, you ain't gooin' to interfere wi' me, a' yer, man?' she said, pretending to cry.

'Don't be so soft, wench,' he said, very nearly being swung off his feet with the horse's capers, 'Can't yer see as I'm got this 'ere 'oss to see arter?'

'Well,' said the girl tearfully 'you could tie it to a gate.'

An' that's what Gramp did do wi' his next-door-neighbour's donkey, when it were took bad. The poor old man as owned it were in such a sweat, he went for Gramp, 'cos he'd heard that Irishmen knowed how to 'andle donkeys. So Gramp went, and the poor old donkey were already down. They carried it out to the side o' the road, and propped it up against the gate with its head tied up high, and lashed it there so as it cou'n't fall down. Then Gramp sent for a pint o' beer, an' they hotted it up, an' put some brandy in it, an' a lot o' ginger, an' poured it down the donkey's throat—and it died just the same. It *seems* to me as I can remember seeing the dead donkey tied to the gate, an' I know exactly where it happened, but it might be that I'm bin told about it so many times, I can imagine as I actually see it.

My other grandfather were called 'Pa' by everybody. He were a dapper, little man, very proud and careful about his appearance. He had ten child'en, and earned his living as a dealer. It appears he were a bit of a queer character, because he had a pet cockerel as was his constant companion. He'd walk o' nights down the village street wi' this cockerel on a little chain, an' when he got to the pub, 'e'd set it on the table an' it 'ould keep 'eving a sip out o' his pint mug.

When the very bad times come for all the farm people, his livelihood soon disappeared as well, because nobody could buy what they ha'n't got the money for, an' it were mostly among the poor people in the villages all round that he bought and sold. His wife an' big family soon used up what little bit he'd got put

away, an' the day come when they cou'n't go on no longer. So he decided he'd leave his own village an' go an' try to find work somewhere else. He packed 'em all into the cart he used for dealing, and locked up his little cottage, an' set off, saying that if they di'n't get no work after a week or two, he'd drive 'em all to the poor 'ouse. This happened when my mother were about four year old, so it 'ould a-bin about 1860. My gran'mother's sister Jane and her husband, William Marshall, lived nearly next door. They never had no child'en, and it were a great grief to 'em, though the reason were that Aunt Jane had a cancer in the womb. They were real well off, compared to most folks, and they made a rare fuss o' my mother. When Pa set off, the day in question, with all his family in the cart, Aunt Jane and Uncle Coggy, as he were allus called, went to see 'em off. The child'en were all a-crying 'cos they were cold an' hungry and frightened at what might happen to 'em, and when the cart begun to move, Uncle Coggy cou'n't bear it no longer. He begun to run to catch it up, an' when he did 'e snatched mother, who were four, out of it, and then stopped. Her mother an' father see what had happened of course, but they never stopped the cart, nor looked round. It were one less mouth to feed. When the Spring came round again, Pa and Grandmother and the rest o' the brood all come back home again and set up business as before. But my mother never went back home, but were brought up by Uncle Coggy and Aunt Jane. In this way she come to have a lot better time, in some ways, than all her brothers and sisters, but on the other hand, she used to be hurt and upset because they di'n't seem to want her. When she used to go home to see them, they'd say 'We don't want you 'ere, showin' us yer fine togs,' an' it grieved her to the end of her life that she'd growed away from them. The time come when she wanted some loving help and support from somebody near and dear, but she felt that they'd all got each other and she ha'n't got nobody.

Still, while she were a girl, she had a lot of adventures, one way or another, with Uncle Coggy and Aunt Jane. Their house were a little palace, compared wi' most o' the cottages, and Aunt Jane were a beautiful woman wi' money to keep herself dressed nice. She kept 'her Meery' nice as well. (Mother's name were Mary, an' her own family called her Polly, but Aunt Jane and Uncle Coggy pronounced her name 'Meery'.) I'm still got a picture, one o' the first photographs as ever come our way, I sh'd think, of mother when she were about twelve year old, with Uncle Coggy. She is wearing a little sealskin coat and hat and muff, and he is looking as proud as a peacock of her. Then Aunt Jane begun to be racked wi' pain in her body, as no doctor seemed to be able to ease. So she took to taking laudanum in bigger and bigger doses. It dulled the pain, but it made her dozy and stupid, and she got so she just set about all day and di'n't keep the house nice no more, or herself, or Meery. Poor old Uncle Coggy forbid her to take the laudanum, but then, he di'n't have the pain to bear. He used to forbid mother to fetch it for her, but when Aunt Jane's pain got bad, mother were on'y to glad to get her anything to ease her. Then Uncle Coggy 'ould lay in wait for mother, an' search her to see if she'd got laudanum for Jane on her. He'd feel in all her pockets an' all round her

258

but her never found where she'd be carrying it, in the pouched knees of her knickers, above the tight band.

The change in Aunt Jane soon worked a change in Uncle Coggy as well, and he begun to take to drink. One night, Aunt Jane and mother set up for him till after midnight, but Aunt Jane were in such pain she decided to go to bed without waiting for him to get his supper ready. So she cooked him a great pan of rump steak and thick brown gravy and left it on the grate. When he come in he were drunk, an' started to shout for her, but she'd took such a big dose o' laudanum she never heard him. Mother heard him an' went timidly down. When she told him Aunt had gone to bed he nearly went beside hisself with rage, and picked up the frying pan with all the steak and gravy in it an' went into the bedroom. Aunt Jane were in her beautiful four poster bed, with delicate blue silk curtains all round it. He just opened the blue curtains and swacked the contents o' the pan all over her an' them.

Things went from bad to worse, an' he took to gambling as well. He took mother once and went on a business journey with his white pony and trap. One night when she'd gone to bed in an inn, he started gambling with a party downstairs, and lost all the money he had with him, but he cou'n't and wou'n't stop, even then, till 'e'd gambled away his horse and cart as well. Then next morning he had to abandon his trip and him and mother had to walk back home. It took 'em best part of a week.

It were on the walk back home that mother found a little gold locket and chain in the road. She give it to her uncle, but somebody 'ad seen her pick it up, an' there were soon a hue and cry out for it. Aunt Jane and mother were anxious to give it back, but Uncle wou'n't hear of it. They knowed the police 'ould come, sooner or later, to make enquiries and search for it, so Uncle made Aunt Jane take her beautiful hair down. They were a great mass of thick, bright gold hair, rippling right down her back. He took a little strand of it, right at the back of her head, and tied the locket an' chain to it. Then he made her wind her hair all up again, an' there were no sign o' the locket to be seen. So they got away with it.

Not long after this, Aunt Jane died, and mother looked after

Uncle as long as she could. He'd lost all his money, all his business, an' all his self respect, and he soon cou'n't keep the home together at all. So he sold up, what he had left, when mother were about eighteen, and went to live in lodgings in Peterborough. Then poor mother ha'n't got nowhere to go, because they wouldn't have her at home. She did go home for a little while, though, very miserable and unhappy, and before long she met my father, and married him. She has often told me that she knowed all the way along what a terrible mistake she were making, but it seemed the only way out of an even worse plight she were in. She said that none of her family went to the wedding, and when she went inside the church door she stood still and prayed that the church 'ould fall on her afore she ever got outside again. She'd made her bargain, though, an' she stood by it. She had the most dreadful life o' hardship and poverty afore she, too, died wi' cancers all over her at sixty-two. Yet it seemed that the more she had to put up with, the more gentle and cheerful she got, and though there were times when even she cou'n't put up wi' my fathers tantrums, she stuck to him through thick and thin. After I were married, I used to beg her to leave him and come away, but she 'ould be real upset at my running him down, and say 'You don't know what your saying. Them as 'as mad bulls to deal with know best how to handle 'em.'

Or, very often, she'd say 'No cross, no crown. If your Dad's my cross, I shall wear a crown in glory for him one day.' She'd protect him like a mother protects her child, and though she often got upset, she'd soon be singing again in her sweet, clear voice. We were terribly afraid, when we were children, that something 'ould happen to her, or that she'd run away and leave us, and after we'd gone to bed at night, we used to call to her and say 'Sing mother, so we know you're there.' Then she'd sit an' sing till her voice give out, an' after that, if we still wern't asleep, she'd whistle to let us know we were safe.

Poor mother—where had she to run to? By the time she had got us three children, she'd got nobody at all to turn to. Uncle Coggy had pulled himself together and learnt a new trade. He took up as a corn cutter, and used to go round from pub to pub in the villages selling Sequaw's Oils and tending to people's feet.

'Hard corns, soft corns, warts or bunions, Sequaw's 'iles 'll cure the lot.' He kept a room at Peterborough still, an' whenever she could, mother went to see him to keep in touch with him. When he were took bad, he asked his landlady to get in touch with mother, and she were able to go and see him, so he kept writing to her till his end. I'm got the last letter he ever wrote to her. Here it is, just as he wrote it.

October 31st 1894.

O, Mary, i must die the doctor sayes i must diey i cannot liv much longer

cum on saturday just to take the last fairwell of me and when you cum call me dad they all think your my dorter

their is a woman sits up with me every nite god bless you all Amen

I recevd your kind leter on tusday and was plesed to here you was all well and i prays shall be in heven befor saturday i shant (live) many days but cum on saturday and dont bring me nothing to heat i have been in bed 13 dayes and cant get hup you mite bring me a litel bit of tea and sugar if i shoud live another day or too

25 kises for you for you and all if i should be gon to heven to liv with my wife and Jesus for ever no paine in heven and i do hope i shall meet you and your family and husbun in heven i do i do i do i do

o i hope the blessed Jesus will forgiv us and take us to heven god bles hus all

Amen

cum on saturday   William Couter Marshall.

In with this letter is his will, leaving what he had to my mother, ending with 'god love my Mary', and another scrap of paper that he must have treasured called

'a receit for the blanch hich'
1 peney of elebour
1 peney of black peper
2 peney of soft sope
2 peney of sulfer brimstone

2 peney of trupers ointment
put it in a bole and beat all up and rub yourself every nite and morning dry it in before the fire
take plenty of fisek brimstone and milk.

Mother kept these letters and things belonging to him, and they were in her diary when she died. She were took bad and had to stop in bed, so she had to be left days and days together, while my father was out at work. I used to go back'ards and for'ards to her as much as ever I could, but she were at her worst just when I were having my third child, and three days afore my second daughter were born, the doctor told me as my mother cou'n't possibly live three days; but in fact she hung on five whole years! While my baby were little, she had an operation, and after they brought her home from the hospital, she had to stop in bed. It were a bad winter, and the droves were so bad you cou'n't hardly

get along 'em at all. I used to set out with my baby in a light wicker push chair as 'ould let down far enough to lay the baby flat. When I got to a place in the drove where I really cou'n't get the push chair through, I left it and picked the baby out. Then I slipped an' slithered through the mud till I got to a bit higher place, and found a hump sticking out above the rest o' the wet drove. I laid the baby down on it, and went back for the push chair, so as we could get on again to the next bad place. I really cou'n't do this terrible journey many times a day, so I used to do my own work at home first, and leave going to mother till the afternoon. Then my two other child'en 'ould come there straight from school, and my husband when he'd finished work. I'd wait until my father come home, and get him his cooked tea, afore we all set off back to our own home across the mud, with my husband carrying the push chair with the baby in it, and me with a tired child hanging on to each hand. When we got home I were often too tired to set about cooking another tea, and Will 'En 'ould have to be satisfied with a cold meal. As for the baby, she were put to bed many's the time without being undressed, let alone bathed, because I really cou'n't do no more.

Mother kept a diary in her shaky handwriting, and took a interest in whatever were going on in the village, like births and marriages and deaths, and boys going to the army in the war, or coming home on leave. Now and again there'd be a detail or two about what work Dad was doing, or when 'Jack' (my father) 'set the speckled hen'. One entry reads 'Kate forgot to leave me a plate, so had my dinner in a soap dish' and another 'Sold our dear old pony. Put it in Mrs Edward's sale. Gone but not forgotten, by John and Mary Papworth.'

She made a note about where my father were working, and what he were doing. It were allus something a bit out o' the ordinary, for it were a part of his nature that he wou'n't do a ordinary job for a ordinary days pay. If anybody wanted a difficult job doing, or one as nobody else di'n't want to tackle, they knowed where to come. So instead o' being regular at work, either for hisself or for anybody else, he'd be helping to look for pheasants eggs in the fen, or stopping people going over a right-o'-way on the one day a year it were necessary, or hunting for some special herb or flower as somebody wanted a specimen of—anything rather than ordinary work. If he did take on a ordinary job, he'd spend most o' his time wisening how he could skimp it, or do the man he were working for down, for no other reason only because he enjoyed pitting his wits against other folks's. It were a sort o' game to him to get a living like this, but it were very often mother who suffered, because if she ha'n't been prepared to work, I don't know how they'd a-got through. She used to say that if she could but see ten shillings a week coming in regular, she'd feel like a millionaire.

If there were anything to laugh at, she'd laugh—and in this she were just like my husband. I sometimes used to wonder whatever they were laughing at 'cos I used to think that none of us 'ad got all that to be pleased about.

She did leave father, one time, when things got worse than usual. She took us with her, and we were gone two days. Then we went home again. My father were a-sitting by the hearth when we went in, looking so miserable we hardly knowed him. He never said a word, and we crept in like mice and mother hustled us off to bed, and then set about getting a meal. When it were ready, she went up to him, and at last he looked up at her and said 'If all the stars in heaven 'ad 'ave fell, I should never a-believed as you'd a-left me, Mary' and she said 'An' if they do, I never will again.' Once, years afterwards, she got so wore down with his going's on we persuaded her to go an' have a holiday with one of her sisters at Manchester. She consented, and we 'ad to smuggle her out o' the house, because he never would have agreed to her going. So my sister and me took her as far as Huntingdon, where we were going to put her on a train. We'd got our heads together in the carriage, talking, when we looked up and see we were at Huntingdon station, and the train had just started moving again. So we clawed the door open and tumbled out on to the platform. When the train had gone, we realised we'd got out at Huntingdon East, and the train had gone on without us to Huntingdon North, where Mother were going to get her connection to Manchester. A porter told us that if we hurried we could walk to the other station in time. We set out, lugging mother's case between us, half running, with her panting along behind, 'cos at this time she weighed about 17 stone. When we got to the middle of Huntingdon, mother said 'Stop running, do, and try an' look more respectable. They'll think you're Crippen and I'm le Neve!'

We got her to the station in time, and bundled her on to the train, but it were a lot of trouble wasted. She on'y stopped a day or two, because she cou'n't settle for thinking what my father were doing without her to look after him, and he pleased her by actually telling her he were pleased to see her back. Ah, he were a queer character, there's no mistake, were my father, but he wern't all bad, no more than anybody else; it were as though 'e loved to wear the bad side outside, just to be different.

11

WHEN young folks ask me sometimes nowadays about getting married, I have a job to advise 'em. It does seem a pity, to me, for young girls to tie theirselves down when they're only about twenty, specially in these days when they can earn good money and do as they like for a few years between leaving school and getting married. In my day, it were very different, an' if a gel got a good chance of a nice steady man what 'ould provide her with a home and a roof over her head, she took it. I were more 'n' lucky, though I were only twenty-one, because it wern't many girls o' my sort as had the chance o' going into a house all bought and paid for, (even if it were above a mile down a fen drove). But I suffered in my first year or two o' married life all the same. I'd had a taste o' different sort o' life since I were eighteen or so, and I di'n't reckon much to going back down the fen again, for one thing. Then I soon had two small children, only eighteen months apart, and they kept me tied down. When Dad were married and had got the children, he never seemed to want nothing else, only a book forever in his hand. I dessay he used to get tired. He were allus up afore five, and away to his mother's farm to bait the horses. He worked as hard as he could all day, and then when he got home, there were all our own pigs to feed and our bit o' land to be done. Besides that, he had the mill to look after, and all winter he'd have to be there till late at night. O' course, in flood time, he'd be there night and day, and in 1912 he spent fourty-four days and nights there at a stretch, only coming home to have a wash and a meal once a day, after it were dark, and after his helper had got there to keep the mill going while he come home. So I had a lot o' time by myself, except for the children. When I knowed he'd got to be away all night, I made preparations for going to mother's, or getting a girl in to sleep with me, for I were allus terrified out o' my life to be by myself once it got dark. It were a fear as I never am been able to conquer, and I'm nearly as bad now as I were when I were a youngster. Once the lamp were alight and the curtains drawed, I darn't a-went outside the room, whatever had happened. Dad knowed how frightened I were, but he cou'n't understand it, and I very often thought he ought to a-come home sooner. I were young and silly, I suppose, and di'n't stop to think as we cou'n't have had all the extra comforts and things as we did have if he ha'n't worked all them extra hours. Everything 'ould be so still an' quiet in the house, and every time a shuft o' wind rattled the door or the window, I frez nearly stiff with terror. I used to try and keep the child'en awake by playing with 'em, but they'd drop off to sleep and I darn't move to undress 'em. So I'd sit in the rocking chair with both of 'em on my lap, and the fire 'ould go out for want o' making up. Then about nine o'clock the lights o' other cottages all over the fen 'ould begin to go out one by one, and very often it 'ould be nearly midnight afore Dad come in, black as a sweep with oil from the mill, and his eyes all red with tiredness. And there he'd find me sitting, cold and miserable and cramped, and no fire or hot water for him till he'd made one again and boiled the kettle. Sometimes I'd force myself to move and do things, but the sweat 'ould pour off me with fright. I will say for Dad as he never grumbled at me, though I often grumbled at him in my relief when he did come at last.

I only ever spent one night all by myself, as I remember, an' then it were by accident and misunderstanding. I'd bin to see my sister at St Ives, and left the two child'en, as I often did, with mother. The bargain were that Dad should go round that way when he come home from work, and have his tea there, and that I'd go on my way home an' call for 'em so's we could all go home together.

When I got to the station on the way back, it were cold and raining, and after I'd walked a mile I got to the top of our drove wet through. To go on round by mother's made very nearly a mile extra o' walking, so instead o' doing what I'd agreed to do, I turned down the drove and went home. I thought Dad and my mother 'ould guess what had happened, an' that he'd be home with the child'en as soon as I was. It did'n't work out that way, though. When I di'n't come, they all took it for granted that I'd decided to stop the night wi' my sister, and 'cos it were so rough and cold, mother persuaded Will 'En to let her put the child'en to bed, and to make a bed up for him as well. He'd never done such a thing afore, and he certainly never done it again afterwards. Well, I got in and made a fire to get myself dry, and then set down and waited for the others to come. I waited and waited, and it got pitch dark, and they still di'n't come. By this time I realised what had happened, I darn't a-set out to go across the fen to mother's if anybody 'ould a-give me a thousand pound to do it. I were in a taking—for I darn't stop by myself neither. When it got about ten o'clock, I realised as I'd got to, and made up my mind to go to bed. Then I were in another difficulty. I were a-wearing my latest new frock, as done up all the way down the back with dozens of hooks and eyes. They were sewed on one one way, the next another, so as they shou'n't spring undone. The frock fitted me tight everywhere, because that were the fashion then. In fact, it fitted me extra tight everywhere, because although I di'n't know it at the time, I were about three months gone with my third child. Well, there I were in it, Dad had hooked me up in the morning, and I cou'n't and never did, get it off that night. I got a few o' the hooks undone, and sweated and strained to reach the others, as well as sweating with terror, but the rest I cou'n't reach, so in the end I fell into bed still in my frock. Then begun the worst night I'm ever spent in my life. I laid in a cold sweat o' fear, nor daring to move even to cover myself up. Every board as creaked, or window as rattled, sent me into such a thrill of terror as I thought I should die. All I could think about were a little man called Tommy-dod as 'ad 'ung 'isself a little while afore, and every time I half-drifted off to sleep, I could see him a-hanging at the foot o' the bed. I must a-slipped into a doze when it got towards the morning, and about half-past five

268

o'clock Dad come home on his way to work. I di'n't half set for him, but he never said a word, because he were so sorry to think as he'd let me down. I don't believe he ever did forgive hisself for it.

In summer, the child'en, as soon as ever they were old enough, 'ould be with him over at the mill every hour they could. Then they'd all come in as black as your hat and have to be bathed afore they could be put to bed. One afternoon I remember 'em both coming in blacker than usual, and like he allus did, Gerald wanted me to cut him 'fourteen slices o' bread and jam' straight away. They wou'n't be washed, 'cos they were so hungry, and followed me into the big pantry while I cut 'em the food. Then I see through the pantry window, a man from Peterborough coming to the door. He were a chap as kept a big draper's shop, and he come taking orders and selling things round the fen about once in a month. He were a very over-bearing chap as talked posh, and Dad used to laugh at him for all the while using such long words. He allus called him 'Candidly' because he begun half his sentences like that. I di'n't want anything from him, this particular day, so thought as I could get rid of him quick. I di'n't want him to see my two looking like they did, so I pushed the bread and jam in front of 'em and told 'em to eat it in the pantry and not to come out, nor make no noise, whatever they did, till he'd gone. He come in without being asked, and started using his long words to try and make me buy something. It di'n't seem very long to me, but it did to the children, and suddenly, the pantry door opened and two black faces appeared round it, and Gerald said in a loud whisper 'Ain't 'e ever a-going Mammy, so's we can come out?' I did feel ashamed on
'em, more than ever then! I wern't very much of a hand at being strict wi' my children, ever, and neither me nor their Dad could punish 'em very well. Once, when they were about eight and seven year old, I sent 'em off to school as usual, but they stopped

watching a threshing tackle. Then somebody told 'em it were too late to go, so they turned round and come home again. I di'n't want 'em to start playing such games as that, and I felt as I must punish 'em straight away. So I said how cross I was, and told them they could either go to bed or be smacked. Gerald said, straight away 'I'll be smacked' but Lois said 'I'll go to bed.' So I told Gerald to sit down and wait till I'd put Lois to bed. I took her upstairs and put her in bed, and she started to cry. I went out and pulled the door half-to behind me, and then watched her through the crack. She started to pretend to have a fit, and screamed and squealed and threshed about, and then laid stiff, until I cou'n't stand it no longer and rushed in and picked her up again. She's told me since she's been growed up that she knowed very well as I were there a-watching her, 'cos she could see me, and what effect she were having on me.

So I took her downstairs and quietened her; but I still had to deal with Gerald. He set on the sofa where I'd left him, and kept saying 'When are you going to smack me, Mammy? Smack me now and let me go to play.' He were rocking hisself back'ards and for'ards and looking so miserable, I cou'n't a-smacked him if I could have had a thousand pound for doing it. So I give him a tap or two on his legs as wou'n't a-brushed a fly off, and out they went to play. They used to get up to some tricks, an' all, but then so does all children.

Anyhow, I were pleased for more than one reason when the time come for us to move from the house in the fen. For one thing, it aggravated me more than I could stand to see Will 'En lugging his insides out at work and taking all the responsibility o' the farm, for only eighteen shillings a week, when other men were getting as much as a guinea for doing an ordinary week's work. I kept on at him to ask his mother for a rise, but he were allus afraid of her, and wou'n't. One day I lost my temper, and told him if he didn't ask her I should. In the end, we went together. She were a hard, mean old woman. She di'n't think I were good enough for her son, and I hated her. When we told her what we'd come for she said 'I can't and wou'n't pay a penny more than eighteen shillings' and I could see Will 'En were going to accept it. So I said 'I'm married your son to keep me an' my children, an' I'll see to it as he does. If you won't pay him fair wages, somebody else soon will.'

She were took a-back, for nobody in her own family had ever dared to stand up to her, and I think it must a-come over her all of a sudden that if Will 'En did leave her, she cou'n't carry on. But she wern't a woman who could take back anything she'd once said, so she simply said 'You'd better take the farm over yourselves' and it were settled there and then.

I think she liked me better for standing up to her than she ever

| Grandmother Edwards | Mam |

had done afore, and I learnt a lot from it, as well. Once, after we'd been in the farmhouse for a little while, we had another similar set-to. She lived next door with Harriet and John, and very miserable and unhappy she were, most o' the time. I'd ordered some new stair carpet, and when it were delivered, they ha'n't sent the one I'd ordered at all, but another at the same price. I were disappointed, specially as the one they'd sent were such poor quality stuff. I took it round to Harriet and Grandmother to show 'em. 'Look at this stuff' I said, 'That ain't what I ordered. I wou'n't have it if they'd give it to me. It's so thin you could riddle oats through it!'

Instead of answering me, Grandmother looked at me and said 'You get yer rent paid, an' then if you've got anything left you can think about new stair carpet.' I were so savage that I di'n't know how to stop to gather the carpet up, for it were nowhere near rent time anyway, and we knowed her too well to expect a ha'porth of help in any way from her, though she were well off. She had lent Will 'En some money to set hisself up with, but this were a proper business deal and I di'n't see how it put us under any special obligation to her. So I looked her straight in the eye and said 'When I ask you for any money, you can tell me how to spend it. Until then, mind your own business and keep your advice for them who ask for it,' and I stalked out.

She were mean and masterful to the hour of her death, and on her deathbed insisted on doing just as she liked. All her family were there, and tried to keep her in bed, when she wanted to get out. She said 'I'm bin master all my life, and I will be to the end.' So she got out, and set down on a chair, and died sitting there. She were eighty-three.

I soon found out that being a farmer's wife weren't all sunshine, by a long chalk, neither. Things went fairly well for us for a little while, but there were allus things going wrong that caused worry at the time, and Will 'En weren't a bad hand at what we called 'maunch-gut'—keeping on and on about it and making it a lot worse than it were, or so it seemed to me. There'd be things like swine fever, when you'd go out one morning and see a beautiful sow as you'd expected to pig in the next few days just laying there, not getting up for grub. You'd sent for the vet, but you knowed very well there warn't much hope, and afore night you'd know that it warn't just that sow, but every other pig as you'd got on the premises, that you'd lost. 'Never put your trust in

nothing what's got a life to lose,' Dad 'ould say—and it very often seemed as if he were right.

If it were nothing else, it 'ould be a horse in the dyke. This were a common enough thing, but it were serious, all the same. Horses were the most valuable things of all on a small farm like ours. We had three generally. You see all fen fields are bounded by dykes, some wide and fairly deep, others not so bad. If anything startled a horse as were standing still, or being loaded up with sheaves in a harvest field, it 'ould quite likely bolt, and in its fright make straight for the dyke. But this wern't the only chance. Fen land's too valuable to leave much untilled, so it were necessary to get as near to the dyke side as possible, with whatever sort o' implement were being used. Then sometimes the whole side o' the dyke 'ould cave in, and the horse and plough or whatever 'ould be in afore you could think. From one field to another, the on'y way across a dyke or a main drain were usually by a bridge made o' railway sleepers. These bridges 'ould only just be wide enough to get a cart or a roll across, and it took a experienced man to make sure his horses started to cross it just right, else the roll got more and more over to one side till it overbalanced and pulled the horses in after it. Then it were really dangerous, because the roll and the top horse held the underneath one down, and of course they'd both be frightened and plunge and kick and hurt each other as well as theirselves. Whatever were done had to be done quick, and it were more than any one man could tackle by hisself, though o' course he'd have to do the best he could. But this were one case where the flat land helped, 'cos you could see for miles across the fen, and knowed wheer everybody else were working an' what they were doing. If a horse did run away, or get in the dyke, somebody else 'ould see

it from half a mile away, and put his fingers in his mouth an' whistle a ear-splitting noise as 'ould make everybody else stop and look. Then they'd come from all directions, running as hard as ever they could, jumping dykes and drains to get there in the shortest time. They'd be careful to bring any tool as they'd got with 'em, specially fork or shovel, and they'd very soon be a properly organised team. They'd cut the horse free if they possibly could, and keep it from plunging about and hurting itself. Others 'ould start and dig the side o' the dyke away to make a shallow slope to get it up, an' as soon as ever they could they'd encourage the horse to try and get out of its own accord. If it cou'n't, then they'd tie a cart rope round it and all pull till they got it out. But it were allus a worrying thing to have happen.

We had one horse as must have had something wrong with it, because every now and then it 'ould suddenly fall down as if it had been shot. This were dangerous when it had got a cart with a load behind it. It had broke the shafts off more 'n one cart, and once it fell down and managed to get the shaft of a loaded cart right across its chest. Poor thing, I could hear it groaning for breath two fields away. It were the same one that suddenly backed, with a cartload o' gravel, till it got on the slope down to the side o' the main drain. Then the weight o' the gravel were too much for it, so it had to keep backing until the cart went into the dyke, still with its load, and lifted the front with the horse right up, clear o' the ground. That time the poor thing were in danger o' being strangled instead o' drownded.

O' course the bottoms o' the dykes were soft as butter with slimy, oozy mud, and if you once got in you sunk down in it, and the more you struggled, the farther in you got.

But there were things as I loved about it all, apart from being a bit better off, in general. I tried my hand at keeping poultry, and though I were never much of a one to keep to any rule about anything, an' often got into difficulties, I had some good luck as well. We had a pond in the farm yard, and that meant as I could keep ducks and geese, as well as hens. I were never very fond o' the hens, though the eggs were profitable. But the ducks and geese I loved for their own sake. When they were hatched out first, all yellow and fluffy, and whistling in their queer little voices, I used to think they were the prettiest babies I had ever seen. They'd get so used to me that after they'd growed into dazzling white Aylesbury ducks and dignified geese and ganders, they'd come to meet me whenever I set foot in the yard. The geese 'ould stretch out their long necks and whirr across the ground, and the ducks 'ould waddle up in a long line one behind the other, like they allus do walk. Very often the geese 'ould take 'old o' my frock and walk along wi' me, and the ducks and ducklings 'ould follow on behind, still in a line, wherever I went. Once or twice I had bad luck with the geese, usually when I lost whole broods by drowning. It may seem queer to some folks that geese and ducks can get drownded, but they can. When they are little, they'll follow an old duck or goose down to a pond and fall over a steep side into the water, and start swimming straight away. But where the old ones can climb or flap their way out, the little 'uns can't, and they'll swim and swim till they're exhausted or die o' cold. I lost one beautiful lot o' fifteen half-growed goslings at one go like this, only it were the horse trough they'd got into.

Then there were the butter making, and that I loved. I had a real up to date butter making outfit, and took a real joy in making my butter. Sometimes in summer it 'ould be a bit difficult because it got too soft with the heat, but in a hot spell I used to get up at 5 o'clock in the morning and churn, afore the heat o' the day. Occasionally it 'ould 'go dumb', or 'get pins and needles', when it 'ould either refuse to turn into butter at all, or else come in tiny little seeds o' butter no bigger than a pin's head, and try as you might, you cou'n't knock it into a lump. Mostly, though, it 'ould be straightforward enough. My churn were the end-over-end sort, and it had a little glass peep-hole at the lid end as 'ould come clear as soon as the butter turned, though you di'n't really need that, to know. When you first put the cream in, the noise it made were a thick, liquid sound, but as soon as the butter come you felt the difference in the feel o' the churn as the weight o' the lump o' butter shifted from end to end, and it hit each end in turn with a soft thud as the thin buttermilk squelched all round it. When you'd washed it once or twice, you took the lid off and lifted the butter out, as gold and smooth and shiny as the petal of a yellow rose. And into yellow roses I often made it, when I'd knocked up all the bulk of it into pounds for our use or whatever surplus we had for market. I'd bin trained to do dairy work well when I were young, and I could do a'most anything with butter. I used to strain it through a bit o' muslin and make 'grass butter' or wind it into a birds nest to put my little butter balls in for the supper table, or make a basket o' grass butter to fill with flowers modelled out o' butter, roses, primroses, daffodils, lent-lilies and irises. Best of all I liked making roses. We had a real rose bush in the garden that 'ould be smothered with tiny half-open buds just the colour o' my butter. Then I'd gather some o' these buds and some sprays o' beautiful leaves, and arrange them on a glass or a silver dish with butter roses laying atween 'em, specially if we'd got company coming. You really cou'n't tell the difference unless you looked close, and many's the time I've seen a visitor from a town staring as one o' my family picked a yellow rosebud out o' the flower bowl in the middle o' the table and took it on his plate to eat.

Any eggs, butter or poultry as I had to spare went to market, and I had the money as they made 'extra', though most of it went back into the housekeeping, or on the children. As time went on and we got better off, I used to take it to market myself, because I had a beautiful little high-stepping pony and a smart little trap. During the years, I had a lot o' different ponies, but the one I loved best were a chubby, gentle little thing called Peggy. I know Dad were allus a bit worried about me being out on the roads by myself, specially after cars and lorries begun to be about, on account o' my being so deaf. But I were never nervous, and used to love to sit up there with my hat tied on with a veil, and my big brown leather gauntlets that were soft enough still to let you feel the reins through. Like any other driver, I had some anxious moments, but they never put me off driving enough to make me give it up, till the time come when there really were too much traffic to be safe with a horse and cart. By that time the buses had begun to run regular, and I di'n't miss it so much as I should a-done earlier on.

We used St Ives market mostly for our farm stuff, whether

dairy produce or animals. It were about twelve mile away, and took a fairish time to get there and back. If you took a load o' pigs, or a calf, in the cart, you had to sit over the top on 'em for the whole twelve mile, and every now and then they'd get under the seat and heave it up with their backs till you were very nearly pitched for'ard out o' the cart. O' course they had a net over 'em to keep 'em from getting out, but it di'n't prevent 'em from

Mam

moving about. If it were a cow or a horse to be bought or sold, Dad had to walk the whole twelve mile with it. I used to love my days at St Ives market, and sometimes in the summer we 'ould end the day with a punt on the river, though there wern't many o' our sort as 'ould a-done anything as frivolous as that. I used to try to get some o' the other farmer's wives to go with me, just for the sake o' the day out, sometimes, but unless they had something special to go for, they never would.

There were one farmer and his wife as we were very friendly with. The woman were the man's second wife, and she'd brought up quite a big family of his children, but she allus seemed a bit scared of him. Still, they were a family as were more like us than

277

most others in the fen because they did love a bit o' fun. One o' the girls, especially, were a real tomboy, and so full o' life and spirits she were a treat to have about. Her name, I believe, was Ethel, but she were never called nothing but 'Ett', and a lovely girl she was, as well, with a mass of shining gold-auburn hair and a pair o' the merriest grey eyes as you ever did see.

One Monday we decided to take our stuff to market together, and because there were three of us to go, as well as all our butter and eggs and stuff, my trap wern't big enough, so we took the other farmer's old buggy and pony. There were Ett, and her step-mother, and me, and the floor o' the buggy loaded down with basket's o' produce. Ett drove, and we'd no sooner got a good start than it begun to tipple down with rain. My old friend were all for turning back, but me and Ett wou'n't hear of it. We'd got raincoats, and we'd got a great gig umbrella, made specially for the purpose, to keep us dry in the buggy. So we put the old gig up, and spread the rugs over our knees, and on we jogged in the pouring rain. It wern't long afore Ett and me begun to remember things and swop tales until we started to laugh. And we laughed until we cou'n't get our breath, and wiped our eyes, and tried to stop, and then looked at each other and away we went again. And all the while the poor wet old pony splodged on through the teaming rain, and the rain streamed off the umbrella like waterfalls all round us. Now Ett's mother ha'n't got the same sort o' funny-bone as we had, and for the life of her she cou'n't see what we had to laugh about. She kept looking from one o' us to the other, and saying 'Well, of all the ninnies!' and giving a little snigger herself—and of course that made us laugh more. We'd done about eight out o' the twelve mile when Ett told me some particular funny tale about one of our neighbours and we were rocking to and fro and screaming with laughter, when Ett's mother joined in again. She screamed, as well, and we heard her, but we di'n't take any more notice than we had done afore. 'Stop' she was saying 'Stop, you fools, STOP!' In desperation she clutched the reins out of Ett's hands, and that made us take notice. 'STOP you silly fools' she said again 'THE WHEEL'S A-COMING OFF!'

We stopped, just in time. Behind us, down the road for as far as we could see, laid the spokes o' one o' the wheels, and the rim were all broke and the iron rim bending under the weight. In another minute we should a-bin in the road as well, and all our eggs and butter with us. My poor friend were in such a state o' worry and anxiety about what her husband 'ould say that she cou'n't see the funny side of it, but we could, and did.

Luckily for us, we were in front o' the carrier from the next village, so we pulled the buggy on to the side o' the road and got the pony out from between the shafts. When the carrier come along, we hoped he would pick us all up and our stuff, and tie the old pony behind his van. But he were an awkward old customer, and though he agreed to take me and Ett's mother and the stuff, he wou'n't have no truck with anything else. So Ett folded the rugs across the pony's back and put the gig umbrella up. She had one parting shot at me as we drove off in the carrier's old van, leaving her to get home with the pony.

'You get on, Mis' Edwards,' she said. 'And pretend you're Jesus riding into Jerusalem!'

Now Ett is the only one of her family left, and she's been a grandmother and a widow for more years than I like to remember. A lot o' things has happened since that buggy ride in the rain, most on 'em things as I don't particularly want to remember. It wern't long after that that farming took such a down-hill slide, and we soon di'n't know where to lay our hands on the next penny. Will 'En and me were both took bad, him with the gout as he never got over, and me with the artheritis as finally landed me in this wheel chair. Then the second war come, and finished everything, and drove us out from the old fen for ever, though Will 'En's gone back there now to the graveyard where we used to play when we were child'en, without a headstone or anything else to mark his grave, like he allus asked us to let it be. It's over sixty-five year now since I met him that Easter Sunday outside the church, and seventy-eight year since he watched me being christened inside it. Sometimes it only seems like yesterday, and sometimes it seems as if the years lay

strewed behind me as far as ever I can see, getting smaller and smaller away in the distance, just like the spokes o' the old buggy wheel that day when Ett and me were so merry in spite o' the rain.